Pope
New contexts

Pope
New contexts

EDITED BY
David Fairer

HARVESTER
WHEATSHEAF

New York London Toronto Sydney Tokyo Singapore

First published 1990 by
Harvester Wheatsheaf
66 Wood Lane End, Hemel Hempstead
Hertfordshire HP2 4RG
A division of
Simon & Schuster International Group

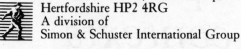

Typeset in 10½/12pt Erhardt
by Witwell Ltd, Southport

Printed and bound in Great Britain by
BPCC Wheatons Ltd, Exeter

British Library Cataloguing in Publication Data

Pope: new contexts.
  1. Poetry in English. Pope, Alexander, 1688–1744 –
  Critical studies
  I. Fairer, David
  821.5
  ISBN 0–7450–0791–0

---

1 2 3 4 5   94 93 92 91 90

Contents

Contents

vi

Acknowledgements

Twelve of the essays have developed from papers originally delivered at the Alexander Pope Tercentenary Conference, held at Newbold College, Binfield, Berkshire, 4–7 September 1988. I should like to thank the staff of the college for making the conference possible, and especially to record my gratitude to Andrea Luxton for her thoughtfulness and energy. As editor I am grateful to all the contributors for being so co-operative throughout, to Nicholas Roe and Jane Stabler for helping to prepare the index, to John Whale and Shirley Chew of the School of English, University of Leeds, for much stimulating discussion, to Lila V. Graves of the University of Alabama at Birmingham for various helpful suggestions, to Nigel Wood, Julian Lethbridge and John Goodridge who have also been an important part of this enterprise, and finally to Jackie Jones of Harvester Wheatsheaf for her invaluable help and encouragement.

Carolyn Williams and Thomas Woodman both acknowledge the assistance of the Reading University Research Board.

Abbreviations

BJECS   British Journal for Eighteenth-century Studies
Dryden, *Poems*   *The Poems of John Dryden*, edited by James Kinsley,
   4 vols (Oxford, 1958)
EC   *Essays in Criticism*
E-CS   *Eighteenth-century Studies*
Enduring Legacy   *The Enduring Legacy: Alexander Pope Tercen-
   tenary Essays*, edited by G. S. Rousseau and Pat Rogers
   (Cambridge, 1988)
JEGP   *Journal of English and Germanic Philology*
MLR   *Modern Language Review*
MP   *Modern Philology*
The New Eighteenth Century   *The New Eighteenth Century: Theory,
   Politics, English Literature*, edited by Felicity Nussbaum and Laura
   Brown (New York and London, 1987)
POAS   *Poems on Affairs of State: Augustan Satirical Verse, 1660–
   1714*, edited by G. de F. Lord *et al.*, 7 vols (New Haven 1963–74)
PQ   *Philological Quarterly*
SEL   *Studies in English Literature 1500–1900*
Sherburn   *The Correspondence of Alexander Pope*, edited by George
   Sherburn, 5 vols (Oxford, 1956)
SP   *Studies in Philology*
Swift, *Prose*   *The Prose Works of Jonathan Swift*, edited by Herbert
   Davis *et al.*, 14 vols (Oxford, 1939–68)
TE   *The Twickenham Edition of the Poems of Alexander Pope*, edited
   by John Butt *et al.*, 11 vols (London and New Haven, 1939–69)

Note: All quotations from Milton are taken from *The Poems of John Milton*, eds John Carey and Alastair Fowler (London, 1968). Unless otherwise stated, all references to Pope's *Dunciad* are to the four-book version of 1743.

Introduction

David Fairer

In the past few years the study of eighteenth-century English
literature has become the location for lively methodological debate,
exemplified by two impressive collections of essays: the tercentenary
of Pope's birth was marked by G. S. Rousseau and Pat Rogers's *An
Enduring Legacy*, and the previous year (1987) saw the publication of
The New Eighteenth Century edited by Felicity Nussbaum and Laura
Brown. The contrast between them is a conceptual one. It is clear that
the notion of an 'enduring legacy' is as polemical as a 'new eighteenth
century'. The first implies the sustaining of a sure line of inheritance
just as clearly as the second implies a break with the pre-owned.
Where Rousseau and Rogers preface their collection by locating its
origins in a sociable walk around the gardens at Stourhead,
Nussbaum and Brown argue for a criticism which decentres and
destabilises. One volume aspires to permanent value, the second aims
to initiate debate. The contrasting discourses of these texts – continuity and revolution, authority and revisionism – are striking and
each on its own terms fulfils its aims.

By breaking down barriers between so-called major and peripheral
texts, those which express the dominant culture and those which find
a voice outside it, *The New Eighteenth Century* offers a challenge to
the kind of criticism whose ultimate concern is in the editors' words,
'the preservation and elucidation of canonical masterpieces of cultural
stability'. Inevitably, to present a collection of essays on Alexander
Pope seems to declare a resistant 'old' eighteenth century with Pope
still enshrined at the centre of his age. One of the aims of *Pope: New
Contexts*, however, is to challenge both the cultural stability of the
eighteenth century and Pope's centrality or representativeness within
it, and to do so by locating the power of his work in its resistance to

1

discourses of coherence and stability. The present volume recognises that there is a wide range of methodologies available and that acts of recovery through history need not be embarrassed by engaging with newer critical practices, indeed that they can co-operate in the same enterprise.

In a recent article, 'English in crisis?', Ian Small and Josephine Guy argue that the current, well-documented 'crisis' in literary studies is one in which irreconcilable epistemologies are struggling for mastery. This present collection obviously contributes to such a crisis, and confidently so. The volume has in Small and Guy's terms no 'common epistemology', nor does it attempt some kind of 'resolution' in the way they suggest:

> For a theory to rebut or refute contending theories there has to be a common epistemology, or at least the conditions for an agreement about epistemology . . ./. . . either English as a discipline will exist in a state of continuing crisis, *or* a dominant epistemology and therefore a dominant intellectual authority will begin to re-emerge. But for this to occur, an initial debate about epistemology has to take place: *these* are the grounds for an intellectual debate, and perhaps for its resolution.[1]

The medical connotation implied here (crisis as the condition of a patient on the threshold of what may be either death or recovery) is unfortunate. The patient's condition is not 'critical' in quite this sense: indeed, the present debate should indicate a state of health. Perhaps the last thing criticism needs is an authorised epistemology which establishes agreed principles of meaning and truth, allows the emergence of a new consensus to refute aberrant theories, and sends the critical project virtuously on its way. We should recall that both crisis and criticism are rooted in the Greek *krinein*, to distinguish, decide, judge, and the 'critical' task has traditionally flourished in such a context of choice and dispute.

An epistemological consensus was certainly not something that the eighteenth century offered Pope. The historical moment in which he wrote was a time of fierce epistemological debate: contending theories of knowledge set idealist and materialist ideologies against each other, Shaftesbury and Hutcheson against Hobbes and Mandeville; in philosophy, Bishop Berkeley was taking issue with Locke's notions of abstraction, matter and human perception; in religion the clash between deism and revelation remained controversial; in literary studies the 'affective' criticism of Addison and Dennis challenged the Aristotelian inheritance; aesthetics, sublimity, 'sympathy',

2

'enthusiasm', 'taste' offered a new terminology and with it new criteria, and the 'grounds of criticism' like the grounds of philosophy, religion and social theory, were being urgently fought over. From our present-day perspective it is possible to see these disputes as aspects of a sustained and wide-ranging epistemological debate contending for the location of truth, meaning and value.

After his death, Pope himself became the locus for competing ideologies. But the well-known Byron–Bowles controversy of the early nineteenth century was merely the culmination of decades of argument about the principles not just of literary judgement but of truth, meaning and value. The debate on Pope was inaugurated by the *Essay on the Writings and Genius of Pope* (1756) by Joseph Warton, who grounded his judgement on the central role of imagination and inspiration in poetry, and therefore consigned Pope to the 'second rank' of poets (the 'moral and ethical'). Dr Johnson's championing of Pope's *Homer* as the peak of poetical achievement was part of his wider project to declare 1660–1744 the great age of English poetry, and this involved the demotion of the work of the early Milton, whose rediscovery had encouraged the shift in poetic taste during the 1740s of which Warton had been a part. In response, Joseph's brother Thomas Warton produced his 1785 edition of Milton's early verse to confront Johnson's 'specious' judgement and explicitly elevate the 'school of Milton' above the 'school of Pope'. William Lisle Bowles, a pupil of the Wartons, continued the debate in overtly anti-Popeian terms, questioning whether Pope should be regarded as a poet at all. Byron's championing of Pope, like his aversion to Keats, was correspondingly a function of his distaste for the Warton–Bowles poetry of sensibility which had established itself in the mid-eighteenth century. These are just a few related contributions to what was not merely a debate about Pope, but a prolonged disagreement over standards of literary judgement and their consequences for the canonising and demoting of specific texts. It was fundamentally a clash of epistemologies, of underlying principle regarding the subjective, affective elements of poetic meaning, the status and function of imagination, the issue of art's allegiance to an empirically-perceived 'reality', the location of meaning in relation to the interplay between author, text and reader – and it could never be resolved because there was no common ground.

Much of our contemporary critical debate finds itself echoing the canonical and epistemological issues underlying eighteenth-century controversy. To author, text and reader we would now wish to add history and society as constituents of an intricate force-field within which meaning can be located, and although the forces are more complex and the terminology vastly expanded, the critical struggle, the crisis, goes on.

In adding history and society, I am conscious that the relationship between text and context is a lively issue in the current debate, and that the hitherto serene placing of text *within* context is now in question. Which is the text and which the context? Can the text 'write' the author, in the sense that the 'author' is no longer originary, but contingent? Is the complex freight that words carry (contextualisation via usage, etymology, association, etc.) in any sense under control, and if so by whom or what? Few poets have been so insistently contextualised as Pope, and the relation of his 'poetry of allusion' to current debate about text/context is a fascinating one. With its title of 'New Contexts' this volume partly draws on the traditional notion by placing Pope's poetry in less familiar settings and regarding it from unexpected angles. But etymology can usefully remind us that *text* as well as *context* is a 'weaving', a texture, and that *context*, rather than seen as detachable, was considered to represent the full weaving-together of meaning. When Milton in 1642 speaks of 'that book, within whose sacred context all wisdom is infolded,'[2] he is asserting the completion, entirety – even plenitude – of meaning-as-truth within the Bible: the truth is in the seamless weaving-together of each part. In such terms the context could be the whole structure, the connection and coherence of any text: it was not something within which a text resided or was placed, but implied a kind of totalised reading. Criticism can probably never return to its old confidence in an available totality, yet our currently more comprehensive ideas of text allow us to examine discourse as overriding the traditional text/context distinction, expressing meanings which are totalised not in the sense of 'universal' but as signifying a complex system of culture, individual and society, and speaking concurrently for, in and through its language.

The traditional notion of Pope's context is, of course, 'Augustanism', a category still used to shape university literature courses on both sides of the Atlantic (and often to ensure that the eighteenth century remains persistently unpopular); the term seems to make sense of a contradictory period and can be useful in preparing the way for a glorious romanticism. Like any 'movement' romanticism needs a 'structure' to overturn, and Augustanism (which has never been graced with the title of 'movement') has always offered itself up as structure (Blake found this useful); but the need for the term tells us

4

more about ourselves as readers and critics than about the literature of the eighteenth century.

Concepts of 'Augustan satire', an 'Augustan reader', or one of the many variants on 'Augustan ideology' (a compound of stability, balance, correctness, reason, classicism, sociability, etc.) are endemic and useful fictions. The 'attitudes and values of Augustan England' (to quote one recent blurb writer) provide the bulwarks for a set of critical, social and moral values which an 'Augustan' Pope can articulate for us. Wallace Jackson is right to note how Pope's admirers during the last forty years have tended 'to fortify a diminished position, to build it upon the solid foundation of a poetry of allusion, and to hold strenuously the middle ground of high poetic competence'.[3] But an 'Augustan' Pope can also be invoked when some revisionary enterprise is under way, and it is less than ironic that these discourses are being given a new lease of life in some literary theory. In prefacing Laura Brown's *Alexander Pope* (1985), for example, Terry Eagleton finds it useful to evoke 'the age of Pope, with its good sense and fine taste, its appeal to universal Reason, its passion for symmetry and stability' (p. vi). In a subversive critical project, no less than a rearguard defensive one, Pope is useful as a cultural spokesman for his dominant 'Augustan' group; hence Eagleton's need to see Pope 'at the very centre' (p. vii) and Brown's declaration that, 'Pope has been the centre of the canon in traditional eighteenth-century literary history for good reason, it seems. This study keeps him there.' (p. 5)[4]

Brown's critique works powerfully from her epistemological premises, but in splitting off in a paradoxical way Pope's conscious and intentional *text* (as exemplary, symptomatic, documentary of his age) from her own subversive reading of the poems ('remorselessly questioning' the age's ideological structures) she likewise projects a separable *context* in which ideology resides at the conscious level of Pope's text yet can be undermined through criticism's scrutiny of its supposedly 'suppressed' elements. Her procedure therefore makes little play with incompatibilities between the age's competing ideologies or with the rich complexities of contextualised poetic meaning. The latter is in danger of separating out into the intentional-official and the suppressed-subversive, with the result that the poet himself ends up being taken hostage for one cause against another ('This study keeps him . . . as a lever against the whole canon of eighteenth-century studies' (p. 5)), yet at the same time being remade and redeemed by the critic as a subversive voice.

To raise the issue of Pope's context and to find spaces for him

5

Introduction

outside the stockade of Augustanism, is therefore perhaps timely. The essays in this volume are often less than confident about Pope's representativeness or centrality. J. A. Downie and Christine Gerrard in different ways expose the problematic nature of Pope's relationship to the political alignments of his day, and Thomas Woodman suggests that when Pope does have a role in mind he exposes the inherent contradictions within it. Stephen Copley and I argue for a strategic contradictoriness in *An Essay on Man* as being a direct intellectual challenge to the sociable Addisonian 'polite' essay, and my own contribution attempts to read Pope within an 'oppositional' mode of thought offered by Heraclitus and Blake. In fact, rather than use Romanticism as a simple counterpart to a Popeian Augustanism, or on the other hand to posit a 'Romantic Pope', several essays propose ways of engaging his work in more complex ways with a traditionally Romantic discourse. Nicholas Roe reads *The Rape of the Lock* from the standpoint of Wordsworth in the late 1790s, concluding that Pope's 'inward register of crisis' offered him a precedent for the fusing of political and personal experience at a crucial moment in his poetic career. John Whale, discussing the virulent attacks which some Romantic writers made on Pope, concludes that they saw in his 'ruinous self-contradiction' (De Quincey) a betrayal of man's humanity, enough even to make Pope a threat to social stability.

In this volume Pope's relationship to stable categories of any kind is shown to be an uneasy or contradictory one. Brean Hammond reveals how during Pope's writing life social spaces were being fought over, and cultural lines of demarcation precariously held, in a context where 'cultural seepage' and 'imaginative energy' were subtly linked. But sometimes the categories themselves are less stable than we think. Carolyn Williams isolates a feminine seam in epic, focusing on incidents which place a strain on gender demarcations to show that Homer's text in particular could offer a 'nexus of indecorum, immorality and effeminacy' for Pope's satire to exploit.

The problematic nature of Pope's relationship with the feminine links several of the essays. Susan Matthews shows how women novelists found themselves having to negotiate with Popeian images of women, displacing and transposing them into their own work in sometimes unsettling, and far from liberating, ways. Sexual tensions are at issue in Steve Clark's interrogation of the 'feminine Pope' of critical tradition, and he suggests that this topos is a response to the poet's antagonism towards the desiring body with its projectiveness and autonomy. Indeed, Rebecca Ferguson's anatomising of the metaphor of Pope's text–body reveals a whole series of subversions,

6

rebellions, defilements, deviations and mutilations, within which authorial control over category and identity would seem impossible. Appropriately it is the mutilated body of Abelard which provides the starting-point for Stephen Bygrave's enquiry into Pope's 'rhetoric of incorporation', the energy that drives a text to 'recuperate or appropriate' another – an ambition which he locates in the best Pope criticism, but also within the poet's own texts, for which a metaphor of spectacle (implying scenic arrangement and a spectator) is preferable to one of voice (implying a more elusive self-expression).

To various degrees all the essays tackle the issue of appropriation, the awkward question of *'whose* Pope?' which is as audible now as ever, and they confront some of the ways in which 'Pope' has been appropriated for culture, politics, personal myth – not in order to strip these away so as to reveal an essential text beneath, but to read Pope with a consciousness of what can be claimed for and through him. In this way, to read back to the eighteenth century from the standpoint of modern theories[5] is no more an 'appropriation' now than those Pope's texts were subjected to in earlier ages, including his own (and the historical Pope was a master of the same technique). If at this point we were to use Berkeley's powerful argument against Lockeian abstraction,[6] we could declare that there is in fact no essential, residual 'Pope' concealed beneath layers of appropriation which it is criticism's task to strip away. On the contrary, we would say that Pope's text lives through its appropriations, finds its meanings there.

Certainly criticism should avoid being, in Steve Clark's words, 'a perpetual speaking for', and this applies most pointedly to introductions: the essays in this volume speak for themselves and they engage with one another's arguments and assumptions in more ways than an editorial introduction can suggest. If they have common ground, it is the conviction that Pope deserves to be more than a representative spokesman for any set of ideas. Within his work a fascinating and fruitful crisis is evident, and the full Popeian context is one of tension, contradiction and engagement. The centre (whether seen in organic or structural terms) was not the place for Pope.

Notes

1. Ian Small and Josephine Guy, 'English in crisis?', *EC*, 39 (1989), 185–95 (p. 194).
2. Preface to *The Reason of Church-Government, Complete Prose Works of John Milton*, 8 vols (New Haven and London, 1953–82), i, 747.

3. Wallace Jackson, 'The genius of Pope's genius: criticism and the text(s)', in *The Enduring Legacy*, pp. 171–84 (p. 171).
4. Colin Nicholson, in prefacing one of the tercentenary volumes, speaks of 'Pope's evident centrality during his life of writing. His axial significance in a varied convergence of discourses – from poetics to politics, from economics to ethics, from form to fashion – makes him at once characteristic of his age and almost correspondingly alien to our own.' (*Alexander Pope: Essays for the Tercentenary* (Aberdeen, 1988), p. ix.)
5. Paul Alkon ('Recent studies in the Restoration and eighteenth century', *SEL*, 29 (1989), 579–614) proposes a classification of critical studies 'according to whether they primarily attempt to see the eighteenth century as it saw itself, discussing it so far as possible in its own terms, or whether they look back to view eighteenth-century literature from the perspective of later developments, discussing it mainly in *our* terms.' (p. 583).
6. George Berkeley, *The Principles of Human Knowledge* (1710), introduction, paras. 7–13; i, 102.

1

1688
Pope and the rhetoric of Jacobitism

J. A. Downie

Everybody knows that Alexander Pope was born in 1688, and that he died in 1744, but for Pope and his poetry the dates have additional significance. 1688 was the year that James II fled to France, abandoning the three kingdoms – but *not* his claim to the crown – to his son-in-law, William of Orange. Pope died before the Stuart cause was finally and irredeemably laid to rest at Culloden moor in the aftermath of the Forty-Five rebellion. Thus Brean Hammond, beginning his recent 'New Reading' of Pope by listing the 'four things we need to know about [his] life', concludes by stating that Pope 'was a Tory, an opponent of Sir Robert Walpole's twenty-year-long Whig administration, and probably a Jacobite' – an adherent, in other words, of James II after his 'abdication', or of his descendants, or of the Stuarts.[1]

The last of Dr Hammond's indispensable biographical facts is particularly pertinent to my purposes, but I would choose to put it rather differently. In that Pope was born in 1688 and died in 1744, his lifetime in effect spanned the years during which Jacobitism was perceived as a genuine threat to the political stability of the British Isles. Whether the Jacobite menace was real or imagined makes little difference to the interpretation of Pope's work. In much the same way that the human race post-1945 finds itself conditioned by the possibility of nuclear war, so Pope, for the whole of his life, lived, breathed and worked within a political context conditioned by the events of 1688.

The circumstance has not, of course, passed unnoticed by critics. John M. Aden begins his book on satire and politics in Pope's early career by pointing out that:

> Pope's work falls between, and gives answer to, the hopes and fears, the trust and distrust, of three royal houses: the Stuart, the Williamite, and the Hanoverian. It begins in the first minutes after noon of Stuart decline, falls quickly under the shadow of a militant Protestant regnancy, enjoys a brief if uncertain respite in the chequered sunshine of Anne, and falls again under a Hanoverian winter of discontent.[2]

Metaphor is made to do an inordinate amount in order to sustain Aden's thesis about Pope's early poetry: indeed there is a lot of 'must have' about his approach in general, according to which Pope 'almost certainly would have seen' this, and 'could scarcely have been unacquainted' with that.[3] Vincent Carretta, Chester Chapin and others have expressed misgivings,[4] but Aden is not alone in discerning underlying political meaning in Pope's early poetry. Howard Erskine-Hill has also asserted that the 'earlier poems are more political than used to be thought'. Going beyond the more obviously crucial 'And Peace and Plenty tell, a STUART reigns' of *Windsor-Forest* (to which I shall return later), Erskine-Hill has drawn attention to the 'flexibility in handling Jacobite issues [to be] found in *The Rape of the Lock*, whose political dimension becomes apparent against the background of controversy over the Revolution'.[5]

Until recently, I had always assumed that the title of Pope's heroi-comical poem introduced the master trope, a yoking of the serious and the trivial to which the repeated zeugmas draw attention:

> Here Thou, Great *Anna!* whom three Realms obey,
> Dost sometimes Counsel take – and sometimes *Tea*.
>
> (iii, 7–8)

But no; although the image of rape is not exclusively Jacobitical (indeed, writers used the topos of James-as-rapist to justify the Revolution) it is now being suggested that *The Rape of the Lock* refers to the rape of the kingdom in 1688, and that Belinda is the antitype of Queen Anne.[6] Pope undoubtedly uses language which might be judged to have political overtones. But is he actually implying that Belinda/Anne has Jacobite sympathies when she asks for her ravished lock of hair to be returned?

> *Restore the Lock!* she cries; and all around
> *Restore the Lock!* the vaulted Roofs rebound.
>
> (v, 103–4)

10

True, the verb Pope chooses is a vibrant one – 'restore the lock' rather than simply 'return the lock' or 'give back the lock' – but is it the 'rhetoric of Jacobitism', evidence of Pope's adherence to the exiled descendants of the deposed James II? I remain unconvinced. Somehow Pope's playful hyperbole fails to carry the emotional ring of Jacobitism.

Because that is what we are talking about: *emotional* Jacobitism. While Howard Erskine-Hill suspects that *The Rape of the Lock* 'is also, by allusion, an heroi-comical reworking of 1688',[7] Douglas Brooks-Davies, believing that 'Pope's Jacobitism has now been firmly established by Howard Erskine-Hill', and having decided that Jacobitism is 'an ultimate clue to' the meaning of another major poem, has published *Pope's Dunciad and the Queen of Night: A Study in Emotional Jacobitism*.[8] This seems very close to Aden's position. Commenting on Dennis's suggestion, in his *Reflections*, that, 'he who Libels our Confederates, must be by Politicks a *Jacobite*', Aden writes: 'What must have made this all the more painful for Pope is the fact that there is, for all the overreading, just enough truth in the accusation to be politically awkward', because 'the truth is that Pope probably was Jacobitical in sentiment, if only wistfully so.' In Aden's hands, hunches become hard facts: 'The *truth* is that Pope *probably* was Jacobitical in sentiment, *if only* wistfully so'[9] (my italics). We could scarcely ask for his Jacobitism to be more emotional than that.

What principally concerns me about the tendency to detect a 'rhetoric of Jacobitism' in Pope's poetry is the way in which such an interpretation requires us to reject the *apparent* meaning of his poems in favour of a hidden meaning lurking beneath the surface of the text. It could be there, even in *The Rape of the Lock*. The *Key* could indeed be part of an elaborate game of double bluff on Pope's part: 'You want a political meaning, I'll give you a political meaning', he seems to be saying, demonstrating at the same time how ludicrous the whole idea is, while what he is really doing is drawing attention away from the Jacobite rhetoric with which he has deviously (and dangerously) imbued his flight of poetical fancy. But such interpretations appear to raise massive methodological problems.

In his 'New Reading' of Pope, Brean Hammond turns back on 'post-structuralist' or 'deconstructive' criticism in favour of an approach which seeks to bring about 'a greater awareness of the relationship between literary texts and ideology'.[10] Yet the searcher after ideologies – Pierre Macherey in particular – often works along similar lines to the deconstructionist. He looks for a loose end, a thread which, when pulled, will unravel to lay bare the ideology underneath. This seems to me to be much like the way in which critics 'deconstruct' texts. Assuming that the author intends one thing, the would-be deconstructionist demonstrates how the author's own words subvert this intention. If we apply this to the 'rhetoric of Jacobitism' in Pope's poetry, warning lights begin to flash. Pope's words may appear to be saying one thing, but they can always be 'deconstructed' by an ingenious critic so that they mean something very different.

Douglas Brooks-Davies readily acknowledges that: 'to write about Pope's emotional Jacobitism is . . . to write about a metaphor, and it may be that what I have done is to produce a book that is not so much about Pope's political feelings as about his imaginative mythology, the pantheon of his subconscious.'[11] But how are we to gain access to Pope's subconscious? How are we to deal with alleged hidden meanings? How can we be confident that they are there in the text, and not merely in the mind of the critic? Pierre Macherey is also interested in the text's unconscious as he looks for those unspoken assumptions underpinning the writer's words. But ideologies, like texts, are after all primarily *affairs* of words. As a book called *Freudianism*, published under the name of V. S. Voloshinov but probably the work of Mikhail Bakhtin, points out:

> [The] motifs of the unconscious revealed during psychoanalytic sessions by means of the method of 'free association' are *verbal reactions* of the patient, as are all the other habitual motifs of consciousness. They are different . . . not by any generic distinction of their being, but only by their content, that is *ideologically*.[12]

Following Voloshinov (or Mikhail Bakhtin – whichever it happens to be) I shall take *ideology* to mean 'the set of reflections and refractions of social and natural reality that is held by the human brain and which the brain expresses and fixes through words, drawings, lines, or whatever signifying form'.[13] Rather than concentrating on silences, gaps and inconsistencies, however telling they may appear to be, surely one of the most fruitful methods of interrogation is to examine the language in which an ideology is actually couched. As Geoffrey Holmes pointed out in his classic study *British Politics in the Age of Anne*, by studying 'the vocabulary which contemporaries used to describe the political attitudes and questions of their own age', we can move towards an understanding of their 'political world'.[14] That political world, that *Weltanschauung*, is in a sense a cumulative

12

picture of reality, the sum of individual contemporary attitudes interacting with each other as part of a never-ending dialogue, because 'no utterance in general can be attributed to the speaker exclusively'. As Voloshinov/Bakhtin points out, 'it is the *product of the interaction of the interlocutors*, and, broadly speaking, the product of the whole complex *social situation* in which it has occurred'.[15]

But if an utterance is the product of a complex social situation, then presumably a writer's utterances serve both to reflect *and to form* those 'political attitudes and questions' which together characterise the political world in which he lives. Even if we start from different directions, such as those suggested by Heidegger or Wittgenstein or Derrida and his American disciples, it seems to me that, despite the various objections of cognitive atheists of all creeds, we end up pretty much in the same place. If our language determines our view of reality, rather than reflecting a reality that is 'objective' in any real sense, then the study of the way in which, say, Pope's ideas are controlled by language leads, if not in the same, then certainly in a very similar direction: following Geoffrey Holmes's advice, we end up examining the 'world' as described in the language used by Pope.

Brean Hammond writes that Pope 'was a Tory, an opponent of Sir Robert Walpole's twenty-year-long Whig administration, and probably a Jacobite'.[16] This casual linking of Toryism, opposition to Walpole, and Jacobitism (and Dr Hammond is by no means alone in hinting that they are somehow tautological) seems very close to suggesting a causal link. It was not necessary to be either a Tory or a Jacobite to oppose Walpole. Nor, *pace* Lord Hervey,[17] Horace Walpole[18] and Eveline Cruickshanks,[19] was it necessary for a Tory to be a Jacobite. Wondering why 'it should have become fashionable of late to ignore' the terminology used by contemporaries to describe their own political realities, Geoffrey Holmes suggests that 'an instinctive distrust of the obvious is one of the occupational hazards involved in applying new methods of enquiry to any period'.[20] If we wish to put forward the interrogation of ideology as a valid critical approach to Pope's poetry, then we must pay attention to his diction. And if we examine his diction we find, first of all, that Pope persistently described himself as a Whig, or at least as 'half a Whig', and *not* as a Tory.

This strikes me as an interesting but virtually unexplored aspect of his life and work. If we are to interrogate an ideology, we should at the outset consider the ways in which Pope chose to describe himself. Why did he write that on account of his prologue to *Cato* he had been 'clapped into a stanch Whig sore against his will'?[21] Why, the

13

following year, did he first admit to being 'half a Whig'[22] before writing playfully 'I am a Whig'[23] shortly after asking Gay if *he* were 'a *Whig*, as [he] rather hope[d]', given that Gay's principles (like Pope's and Swift's) 'had ever a byas to the Side of Liberty'[24] – a key term in Pope's 'imaginative mythology'? Why, in 1716, did Swift have to enquire about Pope's 'principles in the common form, "Is he a Whig or a Tory?" '[25] – a question those critics who simply assume that Pope was a Tory have never bothered to ask. Why, as late as 1730, did Pope choose to commend Samuel Wesley's commentary on Job to Swift in this way: 'Lord Bolingbroke is a favourer of it, and allows you to do your best to serve an old Tory, and a sufferer for the Church of England, tho' you are a Whig, as I am'?[26]

Given all these references to Pope's Whiggery, it is curious that scholars still tend to take it as axiomatic that his politics were Tory. I do not know why this should be so. Psephologists often use a questionnaire on key issues – nuclear deterrence, for instance, or capital punishment – to determine political inclinations. As the key issues of Pope's day can be readily identified, the same approach is perfectly feasible for the early eighteenth century. The extent to which Pope's known views coincide not with Tory, but with Whig perspectives is illuminating. Writing of the period from about 1680 to 1714, for instance, H. T. Dickinson explains that:

> The Whigs were certainly not as conservative as the Tories, but only a minority of them were committed to political principles which might be regarded as genuinely liberal. Most Whigs were certainly opposed to absolute monarchy and were ready to support the right of subjects to resist an arbitrary tyrant, but in many other respects they were deeply conservative. It is essential to remember that the Whigs shared many of the prejudices, assumptions and ultimate objectives of their Tory opponents.[27]

Literary critics tend to overlook this 'essential' point. For instance, commenting on how Pope describes himself in *The First Satire of the Second Book of Horace Imitated*:

> In Moderation placing all my Glory,
> While Tories call me Whig, and Whigs a Tory
> > (67–8)

Howard Erskine-Hill recognises that, 'attractive as these lines are, with their repudiation of political labels and apparent affirmation of the middle way, they do raise certain problems'. He then asks how, 'if this poem is . . . carefully aimed at the government of Walpole and the court of George II', Pope can 'make such light play with "Whig" and "Tory?" '[28] But this is to create a difficulty where none exists. Pope's description of his own politics makes perfect sense *unless we are taking it as read that opposition to George II and his ministers is by definition Tory.* The set of political ideas, the ideology, that Pope is trying to fix through words in *Satire II i*, as well as in his other poetry, appears to be perfectly congruent with what we know of the range of Whig political principles.

After all, Pope had written to much the same effect twenty years earlier, during Anne's reign:

> I have . . . encountered much malignity on the score of religion, some calling me Papist and a Tory, the latter because the heads of that party have been distinguishingly favorable to me. . . . Others have styled me a Whig, because I have been honoured with Mr Addison's good word, and Mr Jervas's good deeds, and of late with my Lord Halifax's patronage.[29]

Throughout his life, Pope was found guilty by association of all sorts of things, and twentieth-century critics often follow suit. Howard Erskine-Hill notes that 'something like two to one of Pope's closer friends . . . turn out to be Jacobite at one time or another'.[30] His list is no more impressive than the list in the copy of the *Pastorals* extant in Pope's own hand, which says that it 'past thro ye hands of Mr Walsh, Mr Congreve, Mr Mainwaring, Dr. Garth, Mr Granville, Mr Southern, Sr H. Sheers, Sr W. Trumbull, Ld Halifax, Ld Wharton, Marq. of Dorchest^r, D. of Bucks, &c'.[31] (Presumably Pope's *et cetera* refers to others, like Somers, Wycherley and Henry Cromwell, who undoubtedly also saw the *Pastorals* in manuscript.) Granville and Buckingham were indeed Tories with Jacobite inclinations, but Addison, Walsh, Congreve, Maynwaring, Garth, Halifax, Wharton, Dorchester and Somers were members of the ultra-Whig Kit-Kat Club. Despite Pope's repeatedly-alleged 'Jacobite background', if association is anything to go by, something like two to one of Pope's early advisors turn out at one time or another to be Whigs.

Given that the manuscript of the *Pastorals* passed through so many staunch Whig hands prior to being published by another Kit-Kat Whig, Jacob Tonson, is Howard Erskine-Hill right to suggest that they, too, contain 'nicely managed' Tory signals?[32] 'Spring' is dedicated to Sir William Trumbull, Secretary of State under William III ('An honest Courtier, yet a Patriot too,/Just to his Prince, yet to his Country true'; as Pope later put it in his *Epitaph. On Sir William*

15

Trumbull, 5–6), 'Summer' to Samuel Garth, and 'Autumn' to William Wycherley. What we appear to be seeing here is Pope, apparently oblivious of *political* leanings, interested only in *poetical* issues. If we look at the friendships Pope maintained throughout his life, it is hard to contradict his own insistence on 'that strict neutrality as to publick parties, which I have constantly observed'.[33]

But if the *Pastorals* were addressed to Whigs, *Windsor-Forest* was dedicated to the Tory Lansdowne who later threw in his lot with the Jacobites. Everybody knows how Pope's idyllic portrait of Britain concludes:

> Rich Industry sits smiling on the Plains,
> And Peace and Plenty tell, a STUART reigns.
>
> (41–2)

Not 'great Anna' this time, as later on in the poem (and in *The Rape of the Lock*), although the metre would permit it. In one sense, Pope's statement is perforce Jacobite, as he is indicating adherence to the House of Stuart, but of course during Anne's reign the mass of Whigs also gave their wholehearted support to a Stuart monarch. None the less, here, if anywhere in the early poems, Pope seems quite deliberately to be making a political point. Given the unequivocal reference to Queen Anne as 'a STUART', the temptation is to assume that he wishes to draw attention to the Jacobite cause.

Indeed, in the 1712 manuscript, as opposed to the published version of the poem, Pope went further still. Immediately following his paean on 'Peace and Plenty' he reminds his readers that:

> Not thus the land appear'd in Ages past,
> A dreary Desart and a gloomy Waste,
> To Savage Beasts and Savage Laws a Prey,
> And Kings more furious and severe than they
>
> (43–6)

before launching into an attack on William Rufus. Critics, from John Robert Moore onwards,[34] have stressed that Pope is drawing parallels between two foreign kings, and that in the figure of William Rufus he is also criticising William of Orange, and by implication the Revolution of 1688. Yet on its own, dislike for William III, either before or after his death, is no evidence of Toryism, much less of Jacobitism. It was perfectly acceptable for both Tories and Whigs to express a preference for Anne over William because, unlike 'great Anna', William was never popular. The most notorious satire on the Dutch king was written by a man whose Revolution principles were impeccable, John Tutchin. His poem *The Foreigners* elicited Defoe's *The True-Born Englishman* as a response.[35] That is why, on her accession, so much was made of a queen whose heart was 'entirely English'. Anne was not a foreigner.

None the less, in the 1712 version of *Windsor-Forest* Pope concluded his criticism of William with the heartfelt cry:

> Oh may no more a foreign master's rage
> With wrongs yet legal, curse a future age!
> Still spread, fair Liberty! thy heav'nly wings,
> Breath plenty on the fields, and fragrance on the springs.[36]

Given the entailing of the British throne in the House of Hanover, the first couplet is highly topical, insinuating perhaps that Pope would have preferred Queen Anne to have had a different successor. But, curiously conflicting political signals are apparent in the second couplet: the invocation of 'fair Liberty' was more likely to have appealed to Whigs with revolution principles than to Jacobites. As we are trying to determine how, through words, Pope is trying to fix a set of ideas, we should note the way in which he chose to revise the lines. In the printed version, Pope not only removed the loaded reference to 'a foreign master's rage' (thus weakening a signal which was at least potentially Jacobite), but by accentuating his praise of 'fair Liberty' he replaced it with the rhetoric not of Jacobitism, but of Whiggery:

> Fair *Liberty, Britannia*'s Goddess, rears
> Her chearful Head, and leads the golden Years.
>
> (91–2)

In the form in which the poem was first published, 'And Peace and Plenty tell, a STUART reigns' is the interpretative crux of *Windsor-Forest*. But another important political signal must not be overlooked: *Windsor-Forest* bears the same relationship to Pope's *Pastorals* as Virgil's *Georgics* to his *Eclogues*. Pope quite conspicuously followed Virgil in making the final line of *Windsor-Forest* echo the opening line of the *Pastorals*. In the *Georgics*, a poem which 'asserts moral principles, supports political attitudes, and implies philosophical and religious views',[37] Virgil praises Augustus Caesar as *princeps*, just as in *Windsor-Forest* Pope praises Queen Anne. Pope also chooses to follow Virgil in emphasising the combination of 'Peace and Plenty'. Virgil refers to the widespread warfare of his age, but hopes to see a

17

time when hostilities are forgotten. Augustus Caesar is portrayed as the saviour of a world much like the Europe described by Pope in 1711 in the satirical couplet, *The Balance of Europe*:

> Now *Europe*'s balanc'd, neither Side prevails,
> For nothing's left in either of the Scales.[38]

Just as Virgil envisages the *pax Augustus*, so Pope looks forward to the martial arts of William III giving way to the peaceful arts of Queen Anne.

While Virgil's is a prayer for peace, in Pope's poem peace has already been won, and *Windsor-Forest* is a poem of national reconciliation as well as national celebration. Pat Rogers and others have observed that Pope's theme is peace, 'rather than patriotism pure and simple',[39] albeit that the peace Pope envisages, like Virgil's, has an imperialistic air about it:

> There Kings shall sue, and suppliant States be seen
> Once more to bend before a *British* QUEEN.
>
> (383–4)

The last time kings bowed before a British monarch was during the reign of Elizabeth, but, strictly speaking, Elizabeth was queen not of Britain but of England. Anne is the first Queen of Britain because, once again, Britain is a post-revolution phenomenon. Perhaps more significantly, in drawing comparisons between Elizabeth and Anne, Pope has succeeded in passing over the line of previous Stuart monarchs (including William and Mary, who were also Stuarts).

Apart from 'great Anna', indeed, there is little evidence that Pope admired the Stuarts. Spence records him saying that James I's reign was 'absolutely the worst reign we ever had – except perhaps that of James the Second',[40] and, despite Douglas Brooks-Davies's insistence that Jacobitism is the 'ultimate clue' to *The Dunciad*, James I's pedantry is openly mocked in book IV.[41] Charles I is usually cited with respect by Pope as 'the Martyr', but even that phrase is open to ironical interpretation in the *Epistle to Augustus*.[42] Pope was at one with his contemporaries in criticising Charles II. We know what he thought of 'mighty WILLIAM's thundring Arm'.[43] If Jacobitism is to be defined as adherence to James II after his deposition or to the Stuarts, Pope shows remarkably little sign of it. But, as I have mentioned, the *Georgics* express moral principles, political attitudes, philosophical and religious views – in other words, an *ideology*. Pope's version of

18

the *Georgics*, *Windsor-Forest*, does the same. The signals are paternalistic, certainly, as Pope looks to the *princeps* as a *pater patriae*. The ideology being expressed is conservative, sure enough, but not specifically Tory.

What I think Pope is doing is expressing a rhetoric not so much of Jacobitism but of order, hierarchy and stability.[44] Using key words which recur time and time again in his poetry, he sets up a series of binary oppositions that serve to fix his ideology – order versus chaos, liberty versus slavery, and so on – much as he does in, say, the *Epistle to Burlington*. In urging Burlington to proceed

> Till Kings call forth th' Idea's of your mind,
> Proud to accomplish what such hands design'd
>
> (195–6)

Pope is expressing a similar vision of the national role. The sustained irony of the *Epistle to Augustus* serves the same purpose. The crucial difference is that in *Windsor-Forest* Pope, like Virgil, anticipated the dawn of a new Golden Age, with '*Britannia*'s Goddess', 'Fair *Liberty*', leading 'the golden Years' to come under Queen Anne. By the time he was writing the *Epistle to Burlington* and the *Epistle to Augustus* such hopes had been cruelly dashed. The Hanoverian kings had not called forth the ideas of the minds of men like Burlington. The version of Virgil's *pax Augustus* proclaimed in *Windsor-Forest* had not materialised, as far as Pope was concerned; instead he recognised 'Th' Augustus born to bring Saturnian times', and feared that Dulness, not Liberty, was Britannia's new goddess.[45]

Less than five years after the Revolution, Charlwood Lawton had pointed out that, although the Prince of Orange had been invited 'to get or give us all the laws we wanted; to have made the elections of parliament secure and frequent, trials impartial, the militia our standing force, and the navy our strength',[46] something had gone horribly wrong. By the 1730s, contemporaries were claiming, apparently in all sincerity, that 'the power of the crown' was 'infinitely greater' than it had been after the revolution.[47] It is against this backcloth that Pope's progressive disillusionment with the Hanoverian dynasty has to be seen. Charlwood Lawton was one of those Whigs who, according to John Oldmixon, 'out of Disgust join'd with the *Tories*'[48] before finally finding their way into the Jacobite camp, looking to a Stuart restoration as the only way of stemming what they saw as the rising tide of absolutism. But Pope shows as little indication of 'Whig Jacobitism' as he does of Toryism. In *One*

Thousand Seven Hundred and Forty – a poem which is light years away from the optimism of *Windsor-Forest* – Pope begins by asking:

> O wretched B[ritain], jealous now of all,
> What God, what mortal, shall prevent thy fall?
>
> (1–2)

yet ends up focusing not on James Stuart as a possible saviour, but on Frederick, Prince of Wales, the Hanoverian heir-apparent.

That Pope was unhappy with the Hanoverian régime is a truism – one of the things we need to know about his life – and he seems to have been tireless in satirising the state of the nation under George II. What I am less confident of detecting, for all his criticism of the reigning monarch and his ministers, is a rhetoric of Jacobitism. It has been assumed, wrongly I believe, that Pope and his circle blamed the Revolution itself for the situation which obtained under the Hanoverians. The bitter disappointment which Pope undoubtedly felt over what he perceived as a missed opportunity to hatch the new Golden Age envisaged in *Windsor-Forest* is confused with support for the Pretender. It is then a short step to regarding Pope, Swift and Gay as Jacobite sympathisers, or at least emotional Jacobites.

Swift responded to St John's anxiety over the growth of the monied interest, arguing that: 'We have seen a great part of the Nation's Money got into the Hands of those, who by their Birth, Education and Merit, could pretend no higher than to wear our Liveries'.[49] Years later, the passing of the old ways was still being lamented by paternalists like Goldsmith:

> As duty, love and honour fail to sway,
> Fictitious bonds, the bonds of wealth and law,
> Still gather strength and force unwilling awe.[50]

Such developments were felt to have taken place largely since the Revolution. As early as 1701, Charles Davenant's *True Picture of a Modern Whig*, Tom Double, offered to 'name . . . fifty of our Friends who have got . . . Fortunes since the Revolution, and from . . . poor Beginnings'.[51] This galled Pope's friends. They felt threatened, their traditional position in society undermined. That Walpole seemed happy to appear the type of the modern, self-seeking, unscrupulous Whig did not help.

In this respect, their *Weltanschauung* has much in common with Tillyard's Elizabethan world picture. The *Epistle to Burlington* presents a providential view of the universe not far removed from

20

that of *To Penshurst*, an ideology of order in which everything recognises and accepts its allotted place in the scheme of things, so that even rivers can 'roll obedient . . . thro' the land'. Timon behaves abominably, abusing his divinely-ordained position of trust, and yet the providential plan is fulfilled because

> What his hard Heart denies,
> His charitable Vanity supplies.
>
> (171–2)

Although Tillyard's description of the Elizabethan world picture has been largely discredited, critics such as Stephen Greenblatt and Jonathan Dollimore have been interrogating ideology to suggest that the stress on order in the literature of the period was in fact a reaction to the threat posed to the social structure by emergent, insubordinate tendencies.[52] In other words, the reason that Elizabethan and Jacobean literature is so concerned with reasserting the existence of a providential universe in which everyone knows his place is that traditional social bonds were beginning to loosen.

Similar points are made throughout the writings of Pope and his friends. By interrogating *this* ideology, as Brean Hammond has done, much-needed attention can be drawn to what he calls 'the unconscious ideology of class' in Pope's poetry.[53] What remains to be recognised is that most Whigs and Tories were in fact members of the *same* élite. As H. T. Dickinson reminds us, they shared many prejudices, assumptions and ultimate objectives: 'Most active Whigs were also men of substance who wanted political power to be exercised by responsible men of their own type, and who wanted a stable, orderly, even hierarchical society which would protect the privileges and property of the wealthy and influential.'[54] Ultimately, what most Whigs and Tories were arguing about was simply the best method of protecting their privileged position in society.

In searching for a 'rhetoric of Jacobitism' in Pope's poetry, it seems to me that critics have been going about things in the wrong way. Assuming, because of his background, that Pope *had* Jacobite sympathies which he was either unable or unwilling to express clearly in his writings, critics have found ways of bringing his alleged Jacobitism to light. Surely it is more sensible to examine what he says, and then decide whether or not evidence of Pope's Jacobite leanings exists. I know of nothing in the gamut of Pope's writings to suggest that he disapproved of the revolution (as opposed to developments which took place *after* 1688), or that he supported either

21

James II or the Old Pretender. I would be glad to be informed of such statements. Instead, there are numerous affirmations of Pope's Whiggery – yet we persist in calling him 'a Tory . . . and probably a Jacobite'.[55] Ideologies are fixed in various ways, but in the case of a writer born three hundred years ago, what we are left with, above all, are his words. Although those words indicate one thing, we seem determined to make them signify something else. I wonder whether this is fair?

Notes

1. Brean S. Hammond, *Pope* (Brighton, 1986), p. 9. The *OED* defines the term *Jacobite* as: 'An adherent of James II of England after his abdication, or of his son the Pretender; a partisan or supporter of the Stuarts after the Revolution of 1688.'
2. John M. Aden, *Pope's Once and Future Kings: Satire and Politics in the Early Career* (Knoxville, 1978), p. viii.
3. Aden, p. 39.
4. See Vincent Carretta, *The Snarling Muse: Verbal and Visual Political Satire from Pope to Churchill* (Philadelphia, 1983), pp. 173–4; Chester Chapin, 'Pope and the Jacobites', *Eighteenth-century Life*, 10 (1986), 59–73.
5. Howard Erskine-Hill, 'Literature and the Jacobite cause: was there a rhetoric of Jacobitism?', in *Ideology and Conspiracy: Aspects of Jacobitism, 1689–1759*, edited by Eveline Cruickshanks (Edinburgh, 1982), p. 53.
6. Erskine-Hill, pp. 53–4; Douglas Brooks-Davies, *The Mercurian Monarch: Magical Politics from Spenser to Pope* (Manchester, 1983), p. 181.
7. Erskine-Hill, p. 54.
8. Brooks-Davies, *Mercurian Monarch*, p. 195; Douglas Brooks-Davies, *Pope's Dunciad and the Queen of Night: A Study in Emotional Jacobitism* (Manchester, 1985), p. vii.
9. Aden, pp. 30–1.
10. Hammond, p. 7.
11. Brooks-Davies, *Pope's Dunciad*, p. viii.
12. Quoted in Tzvetan Todorov, *Mikhail Bakhtin: The Dialogical Principle*, translated by Wlad Godzich (Manchester, 1984), p. 31.
13. Todorov, p. 18.
14. Geoffrey Holmes, *British Politics in the Age of Anne* (London, 1967), p. 13.
15. Todorov, p. 30.
16. Hammond, p. 9.
17. In 1737 Hervey said that, 'the majority of the Tories are certainly Jacobites'. Quoted in Howard Erskine-Hill, 'Alexander Pope: the political poet in his time', in *Modern Essays on Eighteenth-century Literature*, edited by Leopold Damrosch, Jr (Oxford, 1988), pp. 123–40 (p. 125).
18. 'In truth,' said Horace Walpole, 'all sensible Tories I ever knew were

either Jacobites or became Whigs.' Quoted in John Brewer, *Party Ideology and Popular Politics at the Accession of George III* (Cambridge, 1976), p. 41.
19. Eveline Cruickshanks, *Political Untouchables: The Tories and the '45* (London, 1979), *passim*.
20. Holmes, p. 13.
21. Pope–Caryll, 30 April 1713 (Sherburn, i, 175).
22. Pope–Swift, 18 June 1714 (Sherburn, i, 231)
23. Pope–Ford, 2 October [1714] (Sherburn, i, 259).
24. Pope–Gay, 23 September 1714 (Sherburn, i, 254).
25. Swift–Pope, 30 August 1716 (Sherburn, i, 358).
26. Pope–Swift, 14 April 1730 (Sherburn, iii, 95).
27. H. T. Dickinson, *Liberty and Property: Political Ideology in Eighteenth-century Britain* (London, 1979), p. 57.
28. Howard Erskine-Hill, *The Augustan Idea in English Literature* (London, 1983), p. 298.
29. Pope–Caryll, 1 May 1714 (Sherburn, i, 220).
30. Erskine-Hill, 'Alexander Pope: the political poet in his time', p. 127.
31. Maynard Mack, 'Pope's *Pastorals*', *The Scriblerian*, 12 (1980), 85–161 (p. 86).
32. Erskine-Hill, 'Alexander Pope: the political poet in his time', p. 127.
33. Pope–Swift, 6 January 1734 (Sherburn, iii, 401).
34. J. R. Moore, '*Windsor Forest* and William III', in *Essential Articles for the Study of Alexander Pope*, edited by Maynard Mack (revised edn, Hamden, 1968), pp. 242–6. The most recent essay on these lines is by Douglas Brooks-Davies. See *The Yearbook of English Studies*, 18 (1988), 125–42.
35. For Tutchin, his relations with Defoe, and annotated texts of the two poems, see *POAS*, vi, 224–47, 259–309.
36. See *TE*, i, 159.
37. Virgil, *The Georgics*, translation with introduction and notes by L. P. Wilkinson (Harmondsworth, 1982), p. 11.
38. *The Balance of Europe*, 1–2.
39. Pat Rogers, '*Windsor-Forest, Britannia* and River Poetry', *SP*, 77 (1980), 283–99.
40. Spence, p. 583.
41. Brooks-Davies, *Pope's Dunciad and the Queen of Night*, p. viii; *Dunciad*, iv, 175–88.
42. *Epistle to Augustus*, 386–7.
43. *Second Epistle of the Second Book of Horace Imitated*, 63.
44. It has been suggested (F. P. Lock, *Swift's Tory Politics* (London, 1983), p. vii) that these 'fundamental political values (order, hierarchy, and stability) . . . were those of a "natural" tory', but see Dickinson, p. 57.
45. *Dunciad Variorum*, iii, 318.
46. *Cobbett's Parliamentary History* (London, 1806–20), v, appendix, pp. xcix-civ.
47. Quoted in Paul Langford, *The Excise Crisis: Society and Politics in the Age of Walpole* (Oxford, 1975), p. 18.
48. John Oldmixon, *The History of England* (London, 1735), p. 89.
49. Swift, *Prose*, iii, 12.

50. *The Traveller, or a Prospect of Society*, 350-2 (*The Poems of Gray, Collins and Goldsmith*, edited by Roger Lonsdale (London, 1969), p. 651).
51. *The True Picture of a Modern Whig* (London, 1701), p. 32.
52. See *Political Shakespeare: New Essays in Cultural Materialism*, edited by Jonathan Dollimore and Alan Sinfield (Manchester, 1985), p. 5.
53. Hammond, p. 5.
54. Dickinson, p. 57.
55. Hammond, p. 9.

2

Pope and the Patriots

Christine Gerrard

In the grounds of Stowe School in Buckinghamshire, former seat of the Temple family, stands a half-hidden monument to Pope – an inscribed bust of the poet, enclosed in a niche at the end of a winged arcade housing fifteen other 'British Worthies'. The Temple of the British Worthies, designed and built by William Kent in 1735, was one of the many buildings which Richard Temple, Viscount Cobham from 1697 to 1749, added to the gardens of Stowe after his abrupt dismissal from Walpole's ministry in 1733.[1] Like most of Stowe's post-1733 monuments, the Temple of the British Worthies was strongly political in theme, to the extent that it might equally have been called the Temple of the Whig Worthies. The first eight busts included William III, a British worthy by adoption; John Hampden, the local Aylesbury parliamentarian; John Milton, the republican poet; Locke, Bacon and Newton. They personified revolution principles, and testified to a theme that was anti-Stuart and anti-clerical.[2] In the later 1730s Cobham filled the remaining niches with more busts: the heroes of the dissident Whig or Patriot opposition to Walpole, such as King Alfred, guardian of Saxon liberties; Edward the Black Prince; and the anti-Spanish naval heroes Drake and Raleigh. What is the Catholic Alexander Pope, fervent admirer of the Stuart Queen Anne, critic of William III and supposed crypto-Jacobite, doing in such a Protestant Whig enclave? Was Cobham simply paying a graceful tribute to his personal friend and fellow opponent of Walpole, or did Pope really belong in a more meaningful sense to the dissident Whig Patriot opposition which was being shaped, trained and supported by Cobham in the 1730s?

Despite a lengthy involvement with Cobham and his political circle between 1735 and 1742, Pope could never have been dubbed 'Laureate of the Patriots'.[3] This soubriquet has been more aptly

Christine Gerrard

bestowed on James Thomson, whose literary output of the 1730s and early 1740s in the service of the Patriot cause far outweighed (in terms of length, if not of merit) his Seasons.[4] Pope's attitude was altogether more ambiguous: political idealism alternating with political scepticism. Pope certainly had the highest personal esteem for both Cobham and his nephew George Lyttelton, leader of the Patriots in parliament, and towards Bolingbroke – author of the refashioned Country Party ideology which lay behind the Patriot programme of the 1730s – his admiration bordered on hero worship. Bolingbroke's Idea of a Patriot King (1738), with its visionary hope of an England restored to peace and prosperity under a quasi-Divine paternalistic monarch, must have touched a latent chord of idealism in the former poet of Windsor-Forest. So, too, did the sheer youthful promise of the Patriots themselves, many of whom, like Lyttelton, the Pitt brothers, George and Richard Grenville and Hugh Polwarth, were in 1735 well under the age of thirty. Pope, whose letters of the 1730s reveal a painful sense of isolation following the death of old Scriblerian friends such as John Gay and John Arbuthnot, often alluded to them as his 'new' or 'young' friends, Britain's best hope for the future.[5] Pope's self-esteem and confidence as a public spokesman were undoubtedly raised by finding himself courted by the Patriots as potentially their most valuable public asset – more valuable than Bolingbroke, with his Jacobite-tainted political history – if only he would act as poet and personal advisor to their royal figurehead, Frederick, Prince of Wales.

For all his protestations of personal esteem, Pope was, however, reluctant to commit himself openly to the Patriot cause. He shared the Tories' suspicion that out-of-office Whigs were adopting Country Party or Patriot rhetoric primarily in order to court Tory votes and broaden the basis of their support, to oust Walpole from power and then to replace him with themselves. Since 1714 the Tories had been proscribed by the Hanoverians: only a change of dynasty, rather than a mere change of ministry, would have offered them the chance of office. Pope may secretly have cherished the hope that if certain things came to pass, Bolingbroke's anonymous Patriot King might ultimately be a Stuart Charles rather than a Hanoverian Frederick. Despite editing and attending the Patriot plays that stormed the London stage in the late 1730s, Pope never produced a Patriot work of his own. The half-worked-out plans for Brutus were the nearest he came to Lyttelton's request for an uplifting epic portraying a patriotic prince as the deliverer of Britain. Like the half-cynical, half-despairing poem One Thousand Seven Hundred and Forty,

26

the *Brutus* project remained a fragment in manuscript, not discovered until years after Pope's death.

Pope first alluded to the Patriots in a letter to Swift of March 1736: 'Here are a race sprung up of young Patriots, who would animate you'.[6] But the seeds of his involvement with them, however, are rooted in the 1720s and in his personal friendship with Cobham. Pope's summer rambles frequently took him to Stowe – singular evidence of the non-partisan nature of his friendships, since Cobham was a staunch Whig of the old school, a hero of Marlborough's campaigns and a stalwart supporter of Walpole and the Hanoverians. Cobham's abrupt dismissal from office, and the removal of his colonelcy in June 1733 as punishment for his outspoken criticism of Walpole's Excise Bill and the ministerial cover-up of South Sea Company corruption raised him in Pope's esteem. This indeed looked like the principled response of a man not known hitherto for his political activism. In the final lines of the *Epistle to Cobham* (1733), Pope complimented his friend with the imagined dying words – ' "Oh, save my Country, Heav'n!" ' (265).

There is some irony in the fact that this replicates the death-bed plea which Pope had only a few months earlier assigned to the epitaph on the exiled Bishop Atterbury, undoubtedly a Jacobite.[7] It is a telling sign of Pope's new-found preoccupation with a man of Whig Hanoverian sympathies, a hero for a cause other than that of the Stuarts. Cobham's reputation as a British patriot depended in large measure on his heroic leadership at the capture of Vigo from the Spanish in 1719 during the war of the Quadruple Alliance – a war designed in large part to put a stop to Spanish-supported Jacobite forays on British soil. Cobham had been promoted to the colonelcy of the 'king's own' horse in 1721, and George II's removal of that honour in 1733 (the post was subsequently given to Walpole's son-in-law Cholmondeley, a man who had never seen active service) was widely viewed as an outrage.[8] In response, Cobham turned to cultivating both his estates at Stowe and his extensive network of young male relatives as testaments to the incorruptible Whig opposition to Walpole. Now behind the scenes, he played a more active role in politics than he had hitherto, using his vast wealth to ensure that all his young nephews, by birth or marriage, entered parliament as opposition MPs. By 1735 Richard Grenville, Thomas Pitt, William Pitt and George Lyttelton all had seats, and George Grenville came in, with his uncle's assistance, after the general election of 1741.[9] Cobham's shy and scholarly nephew Gilbert West contributed support of a more literary kind.[10]

The close family organisation of Cobham's Cubs, as they were soon called, has been used to support a Namierite interpretation of eighteenth-century politics well before the 1760s.[11] Cobham may have been determined to take his revenge on Walpole, but the establishment of a political dynasty was probably not uppermost in his mind. His young nephews were motivated in part by a desire to vindicate the family name from dishonour, and in part by their political principles. To enter parliament as an opposition MP under Walpole's oligarchy was not the most promising career for a young man in 1735 – indeed, George Lyttelton went against his father, Sir Thomas, who remained a staunch court Whig.[12] Shortly after Bolingbroke had, in *The Craftsman* (1730–1), appropriated for opposition purposes the 'Old Whig' platform of Britain's ancient Gothic liberties under threat, Gilbert West paid tribute to those ideals in his description of Stowe's tutelary Saxon deities:

> Gods, of a Nation, valiant, wise and free,
> Who conquer'd to establish *Liberty*!
> To whose auspicious Care *Britannia* owes
> Those Laws, on which she stands, by which she rose.
> Still may your Sons that noble Plan pursue,
> Of equal Government prescrib'd by you.
> Nor e'er indignant may you blush to see,
> The Shame of your corrupted Progeny![13]

Walpole could not ignore this new and active force in opposition, who now joined ranks with older opposition Whigs such as Pulteney, Carteret and Chesterfield. Walpole apparently tried to bribe Thomas Pitt, who controlled several seats in the Commons, to keep out his younger brother William and his brother-in-law Lyttelton;[14] and in April 1736 he managed to deprive William Pitt of his cornetcy of horse for his provocative mock-congratulatory speech to George II and Walpole upon Prince Frederick's marriage – a long-overdue event which neither of them had done anything to promote.[15] The 'Boys' were distinguished by their youth, eloquent political oratory and their support of Prince Frederick. The first of these Walpole could dismiss as inexperience, the second as mere 'Patriot cant'. On the third score – support of Frederick – he had some reason to be alarmed. Lyttelton had been a favourite with the Prince since 1733, finally replacing Dodington as his private secretary in 1737, and the Patriots exploited Frederick's poor relations with his parents George II and Caroline in order to win him over to their side. Despite earlier failures, such as the attempt to force through parliament an increase in the Prince's allowance, by September 1737 Frederick had finally been dismissed from his parents' presence – for carrying away his wife to give birth to their first-born in London, rather than at Hampton Court where the king and queen were currently residing, an act of defiance which also set up suspicions of a 'warming-pan' birth. Frederick subsequently established his alternative court at Norfolk House, and the Patriots had him in their hands. It was this factor above all others which revived opposition hopes in the mid-1730s. In the unsettled atmosphere following Caroline's death in late 1737 Chesterfield was buoyant: a revival of the allowance issue, with Walpole and the Prince of Wales as adversaries, could tilt votes towards the future monarch, Frederick. Walpole, Caroline's former protégé, might no longer enjoy the king's confidence.[16]

In broader terms, the Patriots hoped that Prince Frederick would unite under his banner an opposition which had always been dogged by failure because of its very disunity. Bolingbroke's Patriot programme of the 1730s, designed to bury old party distinctions of Whig and Tory, had now found a 'head.'[17] Bolingbroke's *Patriot King*, with its synthesis of Whig constitutionalism and the Tory romance of kingship was not, however, a programme for practical political success, except in so far as it offered inspiration. The opposition's acquisition of Frederick, legitimate Hanoverian heir to the throne, made it harder for the government to discredit them with accusations 'of Jacobitism. But Bolingbroke and Chesterfield were well aware that the Tories, divided from the opposition Whigs by serious ideological and doctrinal differences, by a mistrust of Whigs in general, and by their suspicion that Frederick would turn out to be just as proscriptive of the Tories as his father and grandfather had been, would be reluctant to give the Patriots the support they needed to oust Walpole from power.[18]

The Patriots, nevertheless, used every opportunity to exploit Frederick's undeniable popularity on behalf of their cause. One asset was his well-publicised marriage to Augusta – domestic felicity in contrast to Queen Caroline's much satirised domination of George II, who sought solace in the arms of unpopular German mistresses such as Madame Walmoden. Another was his close identification with merchant interests as the pressure for a trade war against Spain mounted. Frederick's royal 'progresses' through Bristol, Bath and down the Thames had their effect, as did his sympathetic audience with London's Aldermen after his ejection from St James's.[19] Furthermore, Frederick, unlike his father, was not devoid of artistic tastes and interests. George Lyttelton, genuinely seen by some as a new

29

Maecenas to the prince (but also satirised by ministerial writers as 'Mr Little-Done,' propaganda agent *extraordinaire*), found no shortage of writers willing to lend their talents to Frederick's cause.[20] James Thomson, Gilbert West and David Mallet received pensions; others such as William Somerville, Richard Powney, Richard Glover, Aaron Hill, William Paterson and Henry Brooke all produced Patriot poems and plays in the late 1730s. These works are easier to describe than to define. The constitutional Whig bias of Thomson's *Liberty* (1735–6) or the political Gothicism of Patriot plays such as Henry Brooke's *Gustavus Vasa* (1739) and William Paterson's *Arminius* (1740) were not necessarily representative. Richard Powney's *Stag Chace in Windsor Forest* (1739), in which Prince Frederick appears as an idealised, semi-mythical hunter-king, is clearly based on Denham's and Pope's earlier allegories of Stuart monarchy. With its allusions to royal oaks, James, Duke of Ormonde, and Charles, Earl of Arran (portrayed as a wounded stag), it is the most overtly Jacobite poem of its time, yet Powney attempts to make Frederick, rather than Charles, the heir to the lost Stuart cause.[21] For all their stylistic disparity, however, these works share certain features. They are all governed by historic or heroic themes. A nation threatened by domestic corruption or foreign oppression is saved by a 'deliverer of his country' – Frederick by name or by implication. Their language is elevated, their ethos romantically patriotic; and their concluding vision, like that of Bolingbroke's *Patriot King*, optimistically pictures the conquest of faction and corruption and a new golden age of peace and national prosperity through trade and foreign commerce.[22] No Patriot work, except by a loose historical parallelism, adopts the satiric mode.

During the late 1730s Lyttelton made persistent efforts to cajole Pope into writing a Patriot piece of his own, and into acting as companion and advisor to Prince Frederick. His *Epistle to Mr. Pope from a Young Gentleman at Rome* (1730) urges Pope to renounce satire and to produce a 'lasting Column to thy Country's Praise,' thereby anticipating the Patriots' literary programme of the 1730s which condemned satire as a negative form of political writing.[23] The nation needed inspiring, lofty verse to stir it into action – a programme not as unrealistic as it seems, since even Edmund Burke conceded that the Patriot writing of the late 1730s was a significant factor in influencing public opinion to force the government to declare war on Spain.[24] Aaron Hill kept a close check on Pope's poetic output while offering for his scrutiny an interminable succession of manuscript drafts of his potential Patriot plays such as *Caesar: or an Enquiry into the Merits of*

Assassination. Like Lyttelton, Hill criticised Pope for squandering his talents on satire: his *The Progress of Wit* (1730) warned Pope of his imminent descent into the vortex of Dulness. Even Henry Brooke, author of *Gustavus Vasa,* heartily wished all the profits of Pope's translations of Homer in the sea, if only Pope could produce an epic of his own: 'Is it yet too late?' he asked.[25] The most provocative barb of this kind came in Lyttelton's extravagant puff in *Common Sense* for the city merchant Richard Glover's epic *Leonidas* (1737), whose popularity reached even the ears of Swift in Ireland – less by virtue of its poetic merit than by its topical political message. Lyttelton hinted that Pope had exhausted his epic energies in the monumental task of translating Homer, thereby clearing the thorny slopes of Parnassus so that Mr Glover could ascend more easily. 'Nothing, I am sure, can be of such Advantage to a rising Genius as *the Praise of Mr. Pope.*'[26]

How did Pope respond to all this? His early tentative allusions of 1736 to the Patriots became more frequent and assured, and by 1738 Lyttelton was the dominant figure in his correspondence. Lyttelton seems to have fulfilled Pope's need for political friendship left by the departure to France in 1735 of Bolingbroke, the guiding spirit behind his opposition writings of the early 1730s. Even if Pope's outspoken support for Bolingbroke, then in liaison with the Jacobites, might have reflected a hidden sympathy in that direction, Pope's subsequent letters to Lyttelton suggest that he found little difficulty in embracing the broader aims of the dissident Whig Patriots. Walpole's ministry liked to accuse the Patriots of harbouring dangerous 'democratic' tendencies, but in fact their political works are scarcely radical:[27] Lyttelton's *Persian Letters* (1735) reflect a middle-of-the-road opposition policy, rehearsing standard complaints about septennial parliaments, standing armies, Spanish depredations on English ships and a defence of the balanced constitution. If Pope objected to the anti-Stuart pro-Revolution Settlement bias of the *Persian Letters*, his objections took the form of a passive resistance to the part Lyttelton asked him to play, rather than an overt criticism of his writings.[28]

Dialogue Two of *The Epilogue to the Satires* (1738), which praises Pulteney, Chesterfield, Cobham and Lyttelton by name, in addition to other opposition luminaries, suggests Pope's readiness to identify himself with the Patriot cause. But this was still a satire – not quite what Lyttelton had in mind. The year 1738 also witnessed Pope's most intense involvement with the Patriot plays of Thomson, Mallet, Glover and Hill: he edited, acted as go-between with Bolingbroke (now back in England and under Pope's roof), and even made rare appearances on their opening nights.[29] But Pope was unwilling to glamorise Prince Frederick in a piece of his own. In October 1738 Lyttelton urged him to spend more time with the Prince: Pope is the age's 'Greatest Dispenser of Fame,' and if the Prince 'wou'd Immortalize himself, the only way he can take, is to deserve a place by his conduct in *some writings*, where he will never be admitted only for his Rank'.[30] As late as 1741 Lyttelton was still dropping heavy hints to Pope to produce a historical piece expressly for Frederick's benefit, 'a new Edifice, that wou'd be fitt to Enshrine the Greatest of our English Kings, and Last to Eternity'.[31] Pope, however, had no intention of 'immortalising' Frederick: his contempt for Sir Richard Blackmore, 'whose indefatigable Muse produced no less than six Epic poems', two of them thinly-disguised propaganda pieces for William III, suggests that he was inherently suspicious of political myth-making or requests for panegyric on a royal figurehead.[32] By this stage, even the Aeneid had become for Pope a mere 'party piece'.[33] Like Swift's, all Pope's recent exercises in panegyric had been satirical, playing on the gap between an ideal fiction and the all too unheroic reality. For the Hanoverians, praise undeserved was scandal in disguise. There could be no more *Windsor-Forests*.

For all the Patriots' attempts to transform Frederick into the king that his father was not, he was still a Hanoverian. Pope was just as chary of supplying the role of Renaissance-style counsellor to the prince as he was of contributing to his poetic glorification. He was never, as Johnson sneered, a mere 'follower of the Prince of Wales'.[34] As Pope himself exclaimed in 1738: 'And if yet higher the proud List should end,/Still let me say! No Follower, but a Friend!'[35] He was a reluctant friend at that. Pope's long letter to Lyttelton of 1 November 1738, despite its protestations of regard for Frederick, alludes to the letter which he had intended to give Bathurst on how to treat Prince Frederick – advice to an advisor at one remove.[36] Pope must have been flattered by Frederick's 'unexpected Visit of 4 or 5 hours' in 1735, but could he have erased from memory his earlier squib on the Prince's affair with Harriet Vane and his sexual intrigues with Caroline's ladies-in-waiting?[37] Due respect, on Pope's part, must have been lacking. Lyttelton did not find it easy to drag Pope from Twickenham into the Prince's company: 'I was almost forced to compell You to go and dine at Kue the last time you was there. And yet there never was a morning better spent by you, no, not in conversing with Lord Bolingbroke.'[38] An invitation to Frederick's elaborate wedding festivities in May of 1736 forced Pope to rearrange a private dinner with his friend Fortescue. As if by way of asserting his own simple values, Pope adds as a postscript: 'I have put pickled pork and pease in readiness for dinner'.[39] More telling still is his curt refusal of Nash's request for an inscription to the monument in Bath honouring the Prince's freedom of the city (although he later relented): 'I am the worst person you could have pitched upon for this purpose, who have received so few favours from the great myself, that I am utterly unacquainted with what kind of thanks they like best'.[40] Pope's gift to Frederick of one of his beloved Bounce's pups, and the subsequent *Bounce to Fop: an Heroic Epistle* (1736), is the closest he came to a genuine tribute. Bounce's wish to see two of her pups accompanying Frederick –

> Attending each with stately Pace,
> *Iülus'* Side, as erst *Evander's*,
> To keep off Flatt'rers, Spies, and Panders,
> . . .
>
> Then might a Royal Youth, and true,
> Enjoy at least a Friend – or two:
> A Treasure, which, of Royal kind,
> Few but Himself deserve to find.
>
> (72–80)

– must surely have been written by Pope rather than Swift. The benign association of Iülus with the simple 'country' values of Evander contrasts sharply with Swift's earlier satire on the heir to the throne: 'Our eldest hope, divine Iülus,/(Late, very late, O, may he rule us.)'[41] Swift, in Ireland, had no finger on the pulse of opposition activity. It was only in 1739 that he realised who Lyttelton was, and that Frederick could no longer be tarred with the same satirical brush as the rest of the Hanoverians.[42]

Pope's letter to Lyttelton of 1 November 1738 ends with what has often been interpreted as his unequivocal commitment to the idea of Frederick as the Patriot King:

> Pray assure your Master of my Duty & Service: They tell me he has every body's Love already. I wish him Popular, but not Familiar, and the Glory of being beloved, not the Vanity of endeavouring it too much. I wish him at the Head of the Only Good Party in the Kingdome, that of Honest Men; I wish him Head of no other Party.[43]

But how much is Pope really saying here? The reference to 'the Only Good Party in the Kingdome, that of Honest Men' seems telling in the context of a letter which rehearses Wyndham's suspicion that the Patriot party is riddled with dishonesty in the shape of power-seeking fifth columnists such as Carteret and Pulteney. His 'R.H.' must attract support away from them by exerting 'his Whole Influence' and making himself the charismatic head of his party. But Pope admits that the prince is 'a little short-sighted' and is wholly dependent on others for advice and motivation. The prospects scarcely look hopeful. By December 1739 Chesterfield's letters had become increasingly gloomy, and in early 1740 he wrote to Marchmont that 'The Opposition is, in truth, become no Opposition at all . . . . The views of the individuals are too different for them to draw together'.[44] Wyndham's death on 17 June 1740 and the opposition's failure to gain any ground in parliament threw Pope into a profound depression. To Marchmont (by 1740, Pope's one real remaining hope for a revival of the spirit of patriotism) he complained that Britain is now left with 'those Scourges, which a mercenary People deserve, tho' the Partiality of a few Virtuous or Brave men (who happen to be among them) would save them . . . . We are not to imagine the most dirty, rascally Race on Earth are the Favorite People of God.' For Pope, 'Patriot' has begun to be a term of opprobrium: 'our Great Men & Patriots . . . hate Honour openly, & pray devoutly for the Removal of all Virtue.'[45]

This is the mood in which *One Thousand Seven Hundred and Forty* was written. John Butt has claimed it as Pope's third projected Horatian dialogue, a belated response to Lyttelton's promptings for a Patriot king poem for Frederick.[46] But is it? Pope clearly admired Bolingbroke's *Idea of a Patriot King*, even to the extent of privately printing 1500 copies of a revised manuscript for later publication ('The proofs are ready, and the world *will* see them'[47]). Its final lines, with their Virgilian banishing of the Vices under an Augustan monarch, and their vision of British ships voyaging 'as far as waters roll and as winds can waft them,' contain more than an echo of *Windsor-Forest*, with its praise of the Stuart *deus-ex-machina*, Queen Anne.[48] As Simon Varey has argued, the *Patriot King*, a panegyric without a named prince, was vague enough in its wording to admit the possibility of a candidate other than Prince Frederick for that title – Charles Edward Stuart – should circumstances change, a not altogether hopeless possibility given the opposition's covert but recurrent negotiations with the Pretender during the 1730s and the increasing likelihood of war.[49] Pope's *One Thousand Seven Hundred and Forty* ends with these lines:

34

> Alas! on one alone our all relies,
> Let him be honest, and he must be wise,
> Let him no trifler from his [father's] school,
> Nor like his [father's father] still a [fool]
> Be but a man! unministered, alone,
> And free at once the Senate and the Throne;
> Esteem the public love his best supply,
> A —'s true glory his integrity;
> Rich *with* his [Britain] *in* his [Britain] strong,
> Affect no conquest, but endure no wrong.
> Whatever his religion or his blood,
> His public virtue makes his title good.
> Europe's just balance and our own may stand,
> And one man's honesty redeem the land.
>
> (85–98)

The absence of any hint of a name at this crucial point in a poem which is nothing but a catalogue of names (suggested by initials and blank spaces) seems significant. Pope's nineteenth-century editors J. W. Croker and F. H. Bowles, whose inspired guesswork filled in the poem's lacunae, were probably closer to the mark than John Butt in assuming that Pope was gesturing as much in the direction of Charles as Frederick.[50] Why otherwise the allusion to 'his religion or his blood' – surely not an issue as far as the Protestant Hanoverian Frederick was concerned? Pope could be playing a double game here: either hinting to the supporters of Charles Stuart that it does not matter who your king is – even a Hanoverian Frederick – provided he has Britain's interests at heart; or suggesting to loyal Hanoverians that even a Catholic Stuart – provided he has the right kingly qualities – ought to be acceptable to Britain in her present state. But Pope's opening lines ('O wretched B[ritain], jealous now of all,/What God, what mortal, shall prevent thy fall?') are less than optimistic: it will take more than one man's honesty to redeem the land. Pope openly condemns Carteret, and Pulteney who 'foams a Patriot to subside a Peer' (10), but goes much further in his criticisms by roundly condemning the faint-heartedness and self-preserving instincts of opposition supporters, who will never pull together when the need arises. The Tory backbenchers are semi-illiterate, easily manipulated country squires, who travel up to town to vote only when land-tax is the issue. Even Chesterfield, praised in Dialogue Two of *The Epilogue to the Satires* for his '*Attic* Wit' now finds Britain merely the 'butt to crack his joke on' (29). Cobham, Bathurst and Gower, those stalwart opposition peers, will certainly pay Britain their due regards 'Unless the ladies bid them mind their cards' (24): displays of patriotism are all well and good, so long as they do not interfere with one's future prospects of ministerial office.

This is a flat piece: even Walpole, elevated in the *Imitations of Horace* and later in *The New Dunciad* to the status of arch-tempter and diabolic corrupter of Britain, is here presented as first minister *faute de mieux*: 'Rise, rise, great W[alpole] fated to appear,/Spite of thyself a glorious minister!' (43–4). Pope's implicit comparison (47–8) of Britain with Molly Skerett, Walpole's former mistress and second wife ('Espouse the nation, you [debauched before]') at least implies an honesty of some sort. Pope's 'compliments' are often back-handed, smug in their poetical powers to damn or praise, but like his earlier allusion to Walpole's 'happier hour/Of Social Pleasure, ill-exchang'd for Pow'r', this might just have been a genuine, if grudging testament to Walpole's resilience.[51] The tone of *One Thousand Seven Hundred and Forty* is in fact strikingly similar to Fielding's *The Opposition: A Vision* of December 1741, a work signifying Fielding's total disillusion with the opposition and his recognition of Walpole's tenacity and political ability.[52] Fielding allegorises the opposition as a heavy wagon stuck in the mud, going nowhere because its several drivers (the opposition's competing leaders) all want to go in different directions. Pope adopts the same image in *One Thousand Seven Hundred and Forty*, in the poem's only extended metaphor:

> Can the light packhorse, or the heavy steer,
> The sowzing Prelate, or the sweating Peer,
> Drag out with all its dirt and all its weight,
> The lumb'ring carriage of thy broken State?
> Alas! the people curse, the carman swears,
> The drivers quarrel, and the master stares.
>
> (69–74)

One Thousand Seven Hundred and Forty must have been written in the second half of that year, following Wyndham's death in June. But its mood strikingly anticipates the opposition gloom and ministerial triumph of six months later, following Sandys' disastrously divisive motion of 13 February 1741 to remove Walpole from the king's presence and councils for ever. Fielding's *The Opposition: A Vision* was based in part on the series of pro-ministerial prints entitled *The Motion*, which portrayed various configurations of Sandys, Argyll and Carteret spurring on a stage coach with Cobham and Chesterfield hanging on behind exclaiming 'Lost it', 'O! my Pl—e' and 'Z—ns its Over.'[53] Opposition success at this stage looked further away than ever. As one print commented: 'They are All undone, There is no more Fun, At Bull-Ing-Brook Fair'.[54] Pope never published *One Thousand Seven Hundred and Forty*. By 1738, as Paul Whitehead's arraignment for *Manners* suggests, satire may have become as unsafe as it was ineffectual. Perhaps, as Dr Wilson of Dublin (the librarian who discovered the manuscript) argued, Pope 'left many blanks for fear of the Argus Eye of those who, if they cannot find, can fabricate treason; yet, spite of his precaution, it fell into the hands of his enemies.'[55] Yet *One Thousand Seven Hundred and Forty* looks less like a treasonable piece of anti-government satire than a private expression of Pope's fears and doubts about the opposition. However disillusioned about dissension within the party, or suspicious of the motives of its leaders, Pope would not have aided the ministry by publicly unveiling those sensitive areas.

One Thousand Seven Hundred and Forty came in the middle of those years of silence, 1739-41, which may also have witnessed the manuscript plans for Pope's projected epic *Brutus*.[56] These plans abound, as Donald Torchiana has remarked, with all the common-places of Patriot literature: the benevolent prince with his scorn of factions, the heroic 'deliverer of his country'; the machinations of evil ministers; the struggle against tyranny and corruption to establish an enlightened government.[57] Even the druidic prophecy that Britain's long decline would ultimately be redeemed by Brutus' descendant, Julius Caesar, embodies the Patriots' longer-term optimism regarding the historical cycle and the possibility of regeneration following decay. The epic form would certainly have accorded with Lyttelton's request for a structure 'fitt to Enshrine the Greatest of our English Kings, and Last to Eternity'. Yet the extant plans for *Brutus* place little emphasis on the myth-making potential of the Brutus/Troy-novant legend, and they are singularly devoid of patriotic sentiment. Even had *Brutus* been completed, it would evidently have been a philosophical work, part of Pope's larger, ethical *Opus Magnum*.[58] By 1740 Pope had become increasingly disillusioned about the future of the Patriot cause. Shortly before Walpole's fall in 1742 he commented to Lady Marlborough:

Madam, – I said nothing to your Grace of Patriots, & God forbid I should. If I did, I must do as they do, & Lye: for I have seen none of 'em, not even their Great Leader [Pulteney], nor once congratulated any one Friend or Foe, upon his Promotion, or New Reveal'd Religion . . . call it which you will; or by the more distinct & intelligible Name, his new Place or Pension. I'm so sick of London, in her present State . . .[59]

Christine Gerrard

The existing fragment of Brutus, in which Pope wishes to be:

> with Britains Glory fir'd,
> Me, far from meaner Care or meaner Song,
> Snatch to thy Holy Hill of Spotless Bay,
> My Countrys poet, to record her Fame.

(5-8)

oddly echoes Lyttelton's plea to Pope of 1730:

> 'No more let meaner Satire taint thy Bays,
> 'And stain the Glory of thy nobler Lays;
> . . .
>
> 'Of Thee more worthy were the Task to raise
> 'A lasting Column to thy Country's Praise.[60]

But by the 1740s, Pope would clearly have thought himself worthy of the title 'My Countrys poet' in his own right – not on the Patriots' terms, but his own.

Notes

1. For a general account of Stowe's third major phase of development under Cobham, Kent and Gibbs, see Christopher Hussey, *English Gardens and Landscapes, 1700–1750* (London, 1967), pp. 100–6. George Clarke has offered the fullest reading of the political significance of Stowe's post-1733 Elysian Fields: see 'The history of Stowe. X: Moral gardening', *The Stoic* (July 1970), 113–21; 'Grecian taste and Gothic virtue: Lord Cobham's gardening programme and its iconography', *Apollo*, 97 (1973), 566–71.
2. The busts of Elizabeth I, Bacon, Shakespeare, Hampden, William III, Locke, Newton and Milton had previously been housed in a building by Gibbs erected some time prior to 1732. These 'British Worthies' were moved from their old site on the far side of Home Park to Kent's new temple in 1735 and a further eight busts were gradually added. Originally court Whig in intention, after 1733 they became opposition Whig properties.
3. Isabel Rivers, *The Poetry of Conservatism* (Cambridge, 1973), p. 73.
4. Thomson's deepening involvement in Patriot politics is also mirrored in his post-1730 revisions of *The Seasons* (see, for example, the panegyric to Lyttelton and Hagley House (*Spring*, 904–64); the panegyric to Cobham and Stowe (*Autumn*, 1037–81); the extended paean to public-spirited heroes and the panegyrics to Chesterfield and James Hammond (an opposition poet and protégé of Frederick) in *Winter* (424–540, 656–90, 555–71); and the catalogue of Whig worthies in *Summer* (1478–1579),

eleven of whom also appear in Stowe's Temple of British Worthies.

5. Pope complained to Orrery (10 May 1736) that, 'I may outlive every Man & every thing I love or esteem. . . . I begin almost to wish for *Young* Friends' (Sherburn, iv, 15). See subsequently Pope–Swift, 30 December 1736 (Sherburn, iv, 50–1); Pope–Swift, 23 March 1737 (Sherburn, iv, 63); Pope–Swift, 12 October 1738 (Sherburn, iv, 134).

6. Pope–Swift, 25 March 1736 (Sherburn, iv, 6). This sentence is omitted from Pope's authorised text of the 1741 London quarto, perhaps a sign of his readiness to dissociate himself from his earlier displays of enthusiasm about the Patriot cause.

7. Norman Ault, *New Light on Pope* (London, 1949), pp. 281–5, suggests that Pope duplicated the line out of sheer forgetfulness, and was forced to cancel the Atterbury epitaph from volume II of his *Poems* (1735) at the eleventh hour to avoid embarrassment. This seems both improbable and politically naive, as Howard Erskine-Hill has recently pointed out ('Life into letters, death into art: Pope's epitaph on Francis Atterbury', *Yearbook of English Studies* 18 (1988), 200–20). In 1735 Pope may have been warned of the political imprudence of publishing an epitaph to the Jacobite Atterbury, which is why he cancelled it from the printed copies of volume II. But Erskine-Hill's explanation as to why Pope chose to end the Cobham epistle with the same patriotic sentiment as the Atterbury epitaph seems confusing. He attributes it to Pope's desire to associate Cobham, newly gone over to the opposition, with the Jacobite Atterbury's concern for his sinking country, 'an imprudent gesture, perhaps, but concealed in time' (p. 220). Surely Pope would not think (at this stage at least) of associating Cobham, whose family had always been militantly anti-Jacobite, with the Pretender's cause? His father Richard (1634–97), known as the 'Stoe Monster', was an exclusion Whig and, like his son, a firm supporter of William III and 1688.

8. HMC: *Diary of Viscount Percival afterwards first Earl of Egmont*, ii, 34.

9. Richard Grenville was elected for Buckingham in the general election of 1734. In 1735 Old Sarum returned William Pitt and at a by-election in March of that year George Lyttelton was returned for the Pitt family borough, Okehampton in Devon, joining Thomas Pitt in representing the town. George Grenville was brought into Parliament for Buckingham by Lord Cobham in 1741.

10. The strongly oppositional character of West's poetry has completely escaped critical notice. His anonymously published *Canto of the Fairy Queen* (1739), later reprinted as *The Abuse of Travelling*, is a scathing political allegory with satirical portraits of Walpole, George II, Hervey and Caroline. The latter may have influenced Pope's presentation of the court of Queen Dulness in *The New Dunciad*. West's *Institution of the Order of the Garter* (1742), an extraordinary and unperformable masque (later adapted for the stage by David Garrick), contains Pindaric odes, bards, druids, Arthurian knights and many other properties associated with the mid-century poets Gray, Collins and the Wartons. Yet its concluding paean to a miraculous Patriot King is only one of the many debts it owes to Bolingbroke's work of that title: West's *Order of the Garter* is the last and most imaginative expression of the Patriot ideology of the 1730s.

11. The most extreme of these is Lewis M. Wiggin, *The Faction of Cousins: A Political Account of the Grenvilles, 1733–1763* (New Haven, 1958). Thomas Cleary, *Henry Fielding, Political Writer* (Waterloo, Ontario, 1984) resurrects Wiggin's Namierite analysis to try to make sense of Fielding's tortuous political career.

12. Wiggin (p. 8) argues the reverse – that George Lyttelton attached himself deliberately 'to the seemingly more prosperous branch of the family'. Although Walpole's position may have looked tenuous immediately after his defeat over the Excise Bill (1733), he survived the parliamentary elections of 1734 with only a slightly smaller majority and his authority seemed, to adversaries and allies alike, as great as ever. In 1735 neither George Lyttelton nor William Pitt could have acted in expectation of political office.

13. Gilbert West, *Stowe, The Gardens of the Right Honourable Richard Lord Viscount Cobham* (1732), pp. 17–18. These statues of the Saxon gods later found a home outside Stowe's Temple of Liberty (Gibbs, c. 1740), the most striking expression of the Patriots' idealisation of 'Gothic' political institutions. Their presence in Stowe's grounds before 1730, when *The Craftsman* began to publish Bolingbroke's 'Remarks on the History of England' (nos 218–55: 5 September 1730–22 May 1731), suggests the Temple family's long-standing allegiance to the political tradition of Saxon liberty. See Clarke, 'Grecian taste and Gothic virtue', pp. 570–1, and S. J. Kliger, *The Goths in England* (Cambridge, Mass., 1952). For Bolingbroke's use of the Gothic argument, see Isaac Kramnick, 'Augustan politics and English historiography', *History and Theory*, 6 (1967), 33–65; Quentin Skinner, 'The principles and practice of opposition; the case of Bolingbroke versus Walpole', in *Historical Perspectives: Studies in English Thought and Society in Honour of J. H. Plumb*, edited by Neil Mackendrick (1974), pp. 93–128; R. J. Smith, *The Gothic Bequest: Medieval Institutions in British Thought 1688–1863* (Cambridge, 1987), pp. 57–70.

14. Lord Rosebery, *Chatham* (London, 1910), p. 147.

15. Hervey, p. 553.

16. Chesterfield–Lyttelton, 15 November 1737, *Letters of Lord Chesterfield*, edited by Bonamy Dobrée (London, 1932), ii, 311–3.

17. See Bolingbroke–Wyndham, 3 February 1738, William Coxe, *Memoirs of the Life and Administration of Sir Robert Walpole, Earl of Orford* (1798), iii, 506.

18. The structure and cohesiveness of the opposition is clearly a matter of continuing debate amongst historians. Although W. B. Speck and H. T. Dickinson have continued to argue the case for a 'Country Opposition' with shared ideological values cutting across, and thereby minimising Whig and Tory differences (see most recently H. T. Dickinson, 'The politics of Pope', in *Alexander Pope: Essays for the Tercentenary*, edited by Colin Nicholson (Aberdeen, 1988), pp. 1–19), others, most notably J. C. D. Clark, have challenged this view. See Clark, *Revolution and Rebellion* (Cambridge, 1986), pp. 136–44; 'The politics of the excluded: Tories, Jacobites and Whig Patriots 1715–1760', *Parliamentary History*, 2 (1983), 209–23. The case for arguing that opposition Whig Patriots and Tories had almost nothing in common is supported by

contemporary documentation and the hard evidence that the Tories refused to vote with opposition Whigs on any issue which smacked of 'forcing the king's hand'. In 1737, when Pulteney pressed for an increase in the Prince of Wales's allowance, the government was saved from defeat by the abstention of 45 Tories. The mass exodus of Tories from the House on 13 February 1741 in disapproval of Sandys' motion for an address to the king to remove Walpole from his presence and councils for ever was an even more striking example. The Tories' sudden co-operation with the opposition Whigs in the new parliament of December 1741 stemmed from the fact that they had been instructed to do so by James III's circular letter of 16/27 September 1741 (Romney Sedgwick, *The House of Commons, 1715-1754*, 2 vols (London, 1970), i, 70-1), Clark's argument for the fundamentally opposing dynastic loyalties of Tories and opposition Whigs (i.e. hopes for a Stuart restoration were both serious and widespread among the Tories) is illustrated by both Hervey's remarks to Caroline in 1737 (Hervey, 680-1) and Bolingbroke himself in 1739: 'The whigs have always looked on the protestant succession, and the torys on a restoration of the Stewarts, as a sure means to throw the whole power of the government into the hands of one or the other of them, and to keep it there' (Coxe, iii, 524).

19. See *Gentleman's Magazine*, 8 (1738), 555, 602-3; Sir Robert Phillimore, *Memoirs and Correspondence of George Lyttelton, from 1734 to 1773* (1845), i, 84.
20. See *Daily Gazetteer*, 14 April 1737. Modern critical accounts of the Patriot poets and their writings have scarcely been more flattering, e.g. M. H. Cable, 'The idea of a Patriot king in the propaganda of the opposition to Walpole, 1735-39', *PQ* 18 (1939), 119-30. Bertrand Goldgar's *Walpole and the Wits* (Lincoln, Nebraska, 1976), pp. 134-62, offers a succinct but limited account of some of the distinctive features of Patriot poetry and its political impact.
21. Richard Powney was the brother of Peniston Powney, an important Tory MP (and Verderer of Windsor forest from 1736-57) whose family seat in Maidenhead was close to Frederick's country residence at Cliveden. In the 1740s Richard acted as an agent for the prince: he and his brother had strong Oxford connections which helped give Frederick channels of communication to the Tories. *The Stag Chace* seems to have been his only published poem.
22. Many Patriot works of the 1730s and early 1740s contain pronounced echoes of the Augustan vision of Dryden's *Annus Mirabilis* and Pope's *Windsor-Forest*. See, for example, Powney's *Stag Chace*, p. 16; Thomson and Mallet's *Alfred: A Masque* (1740), p. 43; Thomson's *Liberty* (1735-6), v, 565-716.
23. George Lyttelton, *An Epistle to Mr. Pope, from a Young Gentleman at Rome* (1730), p. 5.
24. Edmund Burke, *Two Letters . . . on the Proposals for Peace with the Regicide Directory of France* (London, 1796), pp. 71-2.
25. Brooke-Pope, November 1739 (Sherburn, iv, 199).
26. *Common Sense*, 9 April 1737.
27. See, for example, *London Journal*, 29 September 1739; *Daily Gazetteer*, 20 June, 1737.

28. George Lyttelton, *Letters from a Persian in England to his Friend at Ispahan* (1735), nos 63–5, pp. 191–201.
29. See Malcolm Goldstein, *Pope and the Augustan Stage* (Stanford, 1958), pp. 46–64. I disagree with his casual dismissal of Pope's hectic involvement with these plays as mere 'fun – an intellectual parlor game which [Pope and Bolingbroke] could play in the pleasant summer air' (p. 61).
30. Lyttelton–Pope, 25 October 1738 (Sherburn, iv, 139).
31. Lyttelton–Pope, 13 June 1741 (Sherburn, iv, 349). Lyttelton's last eloquent attempt to rekindle Pope's public-spirited muse came on 7 November 1741 (Sherburn, iv, 368–70).
32. *Dunciad Variorum*, ii, 256n.
33. Joseph Spence, *Observations, Anecdotes, and Characters of Books and Men*, edited by J. M. Osborn, 2 vols (Oxford, 1966), i, 229.
34. Samuel Johnson, *Lives of the Poets*, edited by G. B. Hill, 3 vols (Oxford, 1905), iii, 179.
35. *Epilogue to the Satires*, ii, 93.
36. Sherburn, iv, 142.
37. Pope–Bathurst, 8 October 1735 (Sherburn, iii, 500). For an account of 'The Six Maidens', Pope's squib on Frederick, see Ault, pp. 276–80.
38. Lyttelton–Pope, 25 October 1738 (Sherburn, iv, 139).
39. Pope–Fortescue, [5?] May 1736 (Sherburn, iv, 15).
40. Pope–Nash, [? April 1739] (Sherburn, iv, 170).
41. 'On Poetry: a Rhapsody', 483–4. *Jonathan Swift: The Complete Poems*, edited by Pat Rogers (Harmondsworth, 1983), p. 534.
42. See Swift–Pope, 10 May 1739 (Sherburn, iv, 175).
43. Sherburn, iv, 143–4.
44. Chesterfield–Stair, May 1740: Chesterfield, *Letters*, ii, 404.
45. Pope–Marchmont, 22 June 1740 (Sherburn, iv, 249–50).
46. See *TE*, iv, xl–xli.
47. Spence, i, 124.
48. See Frederick M. Keener, *An Essay on Pope* (New York, 1974), p. 153, n. 2.
49. Simon Varey, 'Hanover, Stuart and the Patriot King', *BJECS*, 6 (1983), 163–72. Howard Erskine-Hill had made the same point more briefly in 'Alexander Pope: the political poet in his time', *E-CS* 15, (1981–2), 123–41, p. 139.
50. See *The Works of Alexander Pope*, edited by W. Elwin and J. W. Courthope, 10 vols (1871–89), iii, 500–1.
51. *Epilogue to the Satires*, i, 29–30.
52. Interpretations of Fielding's motives and political loyalties in this allegory differ widely. Pat Rogers (*Henry Fielding: A Biography* (London, 1979), pp. 112–13) argues that Fielding 'changes sides' less on account of ideology than financial expedience. But Thomas Cleary, *Henry Fielding: Political Writer*, pp. 152–67, offers a complex (and not altogether convincing) argument to prove that *The Opposition* demonstrates Fielding's continued allegiance to the Cobham/Lyttelton circle.
53. For a description of prints in the 'Motion' series, see F. G. Stephens, *Catalogue of Prints and Drawings in the British Museum, Division I: Political and Personal Satires*, 3, i, nos 2478–92.
54. 'The Political Libertines, or Motion upon Motion', Stephens, no. 2490.

55. *TE*, iv, 330.
56. There is some doubt about the date of the *Brutus* plans. The Twickenham editors ascribe them to 1739, but see Miriam Leranbaum, *Alexander Pope's 'Opus Magnum' 1729–1744* (Oxford, 1977), pp. 155–62.
57. Donald T. Torchiana, 'Brutus: Pope's last hero', *JEGP*, 61 (1962), 853–67 (p. 858).
58. See Leranbaum, pp. 165–174.
59. Pope–Sarah, Duchess of Marlborough, 19 January 1742 (Sherburn, iv, 382).
60. Lyttelton, *Epistle to Mr. Pope*, p. 5.

3

'Wanting nothing but the Laurel'
Pope and the idea of the laureate poet

Thomas Woodman

Various of the contributors to this collection compellingly describe the forward-looking aspects of Pope's work. Leopold Damrosch in *The Imaginative World of Alexander Pope* has gone so far as to call Pope 'the first modern poet'.[1] I find myself wanting to reassert that despite these insights Pope is still essentially a conservative or traditionalist poet. His is, to be sure, a conservatism comprehensive, flexible and complex enough to contain many impulses, both conscious and unconscious and, indeed, a degree of contradiction. He certainly confronts what is new in his society with great boldness and power, but he does so largely in the hope of channelling new developments in traditional directions. It is the *tension* between the old and the new that is at the heart of Pope's work, and it is a specifically ideological tension.

For Pope's whole enterprise is ideological, and that in a much more specific way than in the sense that all literature is ideological. The central image of the role and status of the poet to which he adheres is one of the clearest examples of a tradition that is, in Bakhtin's terms, 'ideologically saturated', 'unitary': one in which the poet speaks or purports to speak with a stable voice of authority.[2] It is in fact an important key to Pope's whole career to understand that he is the last major poet in England to aspire to the great Renaissance ideal of the laureate poet.

This tradition took Horace and Virgil, Ariosto and Ronsard as its representatives, and was to some degree followed in this country by Spenser, Ben Jonson and Dryden. In such a mode the poet has the enormous ideological responsibility of acting as a celebrant of and moral adviser to the monarch, court and aristocracy.[3] In educating and guiding them he is at the same time, on this essentially tradition-alist, hierarchical model, improving the moral health of the whole nation. As Davenant, a good theorist if poor practitioner of the mode, explains in a well-known passage,

> Princes, and Nobles being reform'd and made Angelicall by the Heroick, will be predomanant lights, which the People cannot chuse but use for direction; as Glowormes take in, and keep the Sunns beames till they shine, and make day to themselves.[4]

It is in recognition of this important role in the state that such a poet is to receive financial patronage. Ben Jonson writes in another famous passage, 'Learning needs rest: Soveraignty gives it. Soveraignty needs counsell: Learning affords it', and he has the 'learning' of the poet very much in mind.[5]

Clearly this was a role model of inestimable importance for poets, enabling them to claim status and patronage and to write with a sense of ideological assurance and centrality. Pope himself frequently expresses his interest in this tradition. He even repeats its supposed genealogy, commenting on Homer that, 'In ancient times Princes entertain'd in their families certain learned and wise men, who were both Poets and Philosophers, and not only made it their business to amuse and delight, but to promote wisdom and morality.' In another significant early statement he makes clear his belief that the court is the proper source of patronage, for:

> when Shakespeare's performances had merited the protection of his prince, and when the encouragement of the court had succeeded to that of the town, the works of his riper years are manifestly raised above those of the former.[6]

The responsibility Pope undertakes is to adapt and apply such traditions to the new age, or, more precisely perhaps, to assert their ideological authority over it. In the course of his career, however, the task becomes increasingly problematic and even paradoxical.

We need to understand, though, that the role had always been more of an ideal than a reality. In a sense, the logic of Pope's development merely acts out and reveals the contradictions that had always been inherent in the laureate ideology. What we actually hear, as the title of Richard Helgerson's excellent book *Self-crowned Laureates* intimates, is the ardent self-promotion of poets eager to persuade patrons of their worth, rather than an unequivocal tribute to that worth from the patrons themselves. Such poets also have the problem of distinguish-

46

ing themselves from mere 'prince-pleasers': 'the poet of laureate ambition inevitably found himself caught up in a system of courtly patronage of which flattery was an integral and inalienable part'.[7]

These problems of dependency and integrity are concentrated in the official court post of 'king's poet' or poet laureate. This institutionalised the true laureate ideal, but certainly cannot be identified with it completely. Not all true 'laureate' poets held such a position (Spenser, for example, did not). Nor, of course, could all those who did hold the official post be considered worthy of it: unworthy laureates became the rule rather than the exception in the eighteenth century, and Thomas Gray indignantly refused the post. The official position had by then come to represent the complete debasement of the ideal that it was once meant to embody.[8]

Davenant, in the passage quoted above, simply assumes that celebration and praise of the court will in itself bring about reform where it is needed. Indeed it is precisely thus, according to Renaissance theory, that panegyric is to be distinguished from flattery and propaganda. Spenser, for example, presents a beautifully imagined mirror of the court's idealised norms, and in so doing combines classical ethics, Protestant nationalism, court ceremonial and new royalist ideologies that anticipate the Stuarts. The fact that the reality is somewhat different is suggested by the small element of direct criticism that is also present in *The Faerie Queene* and, of course, Spenser later grew deeply disillusioned with the court he praised. But the idea is the same as that in Sidney's *Apology*. The portrayal of the ideal is to be so attractive that it will itself persuade to virtue by drawing men's passions in that direction. All the same, there is at least a potential gap between the poet's roles as corrector and enhancer.

Ben Jonson's fiercely independent spirit chafed at the restrictions that patronage imposed while at the same time complaining that there was not enough of it. On one occasion he invokes a new muse to lead him to full poverty and thus at least grant him the freedom to write 'Things manly, and not smelling parasite'. Yet this is followed by a famous afterthought, the wry and disingenuous but also serious defence of his own panegyric:

> But I repent me: Stay. Who e're is rais'd,
> For worth he has not, He is tax'd, not prais'd.[9]

Increasingly, however, he finds the satiric function becoming primary. He attacks, for example, those

> Who with their ofish customes, and forc'd garbes,

47

Would bring the name of courtier in contempt,
Did it not live unblemish't in some few.

The last line indicates that Jonson is still traditional enough to suggest that his authority to criticise the court comes from the ideal standards of that very court, which thus in a sense licenses him to correct it. But the 'better race in court,/That have the true nobilitie, call'd vertue' clearly constitute now for Jonson no more than a tiny faithful remnant.[10] He was later to lose influence and leave court because of illness and a quarrel with Inigo Jones.[11]

Enormous changes in the political system in the seventeenth century made the role of the true laureate not just problematic, but in the end impossible. The rise of puritanism was a major factor in displacing much of the moral authority of the court. What amounted to an organised opposition developed, and this led into the growth of political parties. It is a measure of the depth of the crisis that John Milton writes *Paradise Lost*, in one sense the greatest of all the Renaissance laureate poems, in 'isolation from the institutions of power'.[12]

Dryden is nevertheless able to continue some genuine aspects of the role, though with a degree of blatant cynicism. He announces of the court that, ' 'Tis necessary for the polishing of Manners to have breath'd that Air', though he adds wryly, 'but 'tis infectious even to the best Morals to live always in it'.[13] There is the clear sense that he is more self-consciously aware of being a political propagandist than were his predecessors. In *Absalom and Achitophel* he is arguing a tactical and highly political case. So to some degree is Spenser in book v of *The Faerie Queene*, but Dryden is much more deliberately conscious of putting his argument forward in the face of an actual opposition and in the context of an immediate political crisis. After Dryden's later enforced retirement from the court, the split between the Renaissance ideal and the official post becomes total, and the latter turns into a party political appointment and then no more than a sinecure.

Whatever his own and others' sense of his responsibilities, Pope as a Catholic could never have been appointed to the official court post of laureate, at least under the Hanoverians. Nor, after the success of the Homer translations, did he need to worry about the financial implications of laureateship, the aspect that characteristically strikes Gay:

Had *Virgil* ne'er at Court improv'd his Strains,
He still had sung of Flocks and homely Swains;

And had not *Horace* sweet Preferment found,
The *Roman* Lyre had never learnt to sound.[14]

Pope is as keen as anyone to attack the debased modern version of the
tradition, the flattering 'birthday songs' that so disgust Swift, but the
decline of the ideal still leaves a gap. As a poet of enormous ambition
and idealism Pope cannot afford to give up completely the original
aspiration that the laureate's role once represented.

Windsor-Forest is itself a genuine laureate poem, though it appears
so strikingly early in Pope's career that the poet's very youth makes
it necessary to conceal its vast ambitions. The close makes a
conventionally modest pastoral gesture:

> Here cease thy Flight, nor with unhallow'd Lays
> Touch the fair Fame of *Albion*'s Golden Days.
> The Thoughts of Gods let *Granville*'s Verse recite,
> And bring the Scenes of opening Fate to Light.
> My humble Muse, in unambitious Strains,
> Paints the green Forests and the flow'ry Plains,
> Where Peace descending bids her Olives spring,
> And scatters Blessings from her Dove-like Wing.
> Ev'n I more sweetly pass my careless Days,
> Pleas'd in the silent Shade with empty Praise;
> Enough for me, that to the listning Swains
> First in these Fields I sung the Sylvan Strains.
>
> (423–34)

But it is Pope himself, of course, who has written the final vision of
England's triumphant commerce and has associated it with the reign
of Anne. Pope is the happy man 'whom this bright Court approves,/
His Sov'reign favours, and his Country loves' at the same time as he
is the next happy one 'who to these Shades retires,/Whom Nature
charms, and whom the Muse inspires' (235–8). The attribution of the
laureate role to Granville rather than himself seems to come more
from the youthful poet's need for a conventional disclaimer than from
a radical ambivalence about the role of public celebrant; and the
rhetorical strategy is fairly transparent.

Even after the fall of the Tories in 1714 it is a long time before
Pope's stance becomes simply adversarial like Swift's. Instead he tries
as far as possible to control and direct the new developments. His
self-presentation remains that of enlightened traditionalism, of a
greater flexibility and comprehensiveness: 'Nor yet the *last* to lay the
Old aside', though by no means either 'the *first* by whom the *New* are
try'd' (*Essay on Criticism*, 335–6). He continues throughout his career

49

to make a claim to the true laureate's elevation and responsibility, signalling thereby a greater degree of ambition and optimism than Swift.

Yet his growing political disaffection leads naturally enough to a more pronounced disgust with the corrupt poetics of a sycophantic court. As obsessively as Swift, he comes to attack the terrible trivialisation that the office of court laureate now embodies. Among *The Dunciad*'s prefaces, for example, is a Scriblerian parody of the origins of the institution of the laureateship in the coronation of Camillo Querno under Leo x. This brilliant piece, originally written in 1730 before it was known who was to succeed Eusden as laureate, canvasses the merits of several candidates: Theobald, Stephen Duck the thresher poet, John Dennis and Colley Cibber – the actual successor to the post.[15] Pope misses no opportunity for personal digs at each of these, as well as the laureateship, writing, for example, that the laureate must be crowned with vine leaves, cabbage and ivy, the latter 'Not only as it anciently belonged to poets in general; but as it is emblematical of the three virtues of a court poet in particular; it is *creeping, dirty* and *dangling*' (*TE*, v, 415).

In one or two places, though, a more serious and even positive note is apparent. Pope makes the point that Querno was ruined after the fall of his master, and so modern monarchs have made the laureateship for life, 'And it hath been the practice of our Princes, never to remove from the station of Poet Laureate any man who hath once been chosen, tho' never so much greater Genius's' might arise in his time. A noble instance, how much the *charity* of our monarchs hath exceeded their *love of fame*' (*TE*, v, 415). Without being so simplistic as to suggest that the 'much greater Genius's' are meant to include Pope himself, it is clear that he cannot resist mentioning true poetic genius and the original idea of giving fame to the great – even though his satire on the debased version of the role purports to cover the whole institution.

Swift's attack on court verse and birthday songs goes together with his rejection of an elevated public role for the poet at all in so corrupt a society.[16] Pope condemns the absurd modern laureates just as fiercely; but as 'My Countrys Poet, to record her Fame' ('Brutus, A Fragment') he finds that he cannot completely do without the ideological authority of the true laureate role himself.

In *The First Satire of the Second Book of Horace Imitated*, for example, he clearly identifies himself with the laureate tradition, though at the same time he tries radically to redefine it, so as to make his independence of patronage a strength rather than a weakness:

50

Could pension'd *Boileau* lash in honest Strain
Flatt'rers and Bigots ev'n in *Louis'* Reign?
Could Laureate *Dryden* Pimp and Fry'r engage,
Yet neither *Charles* nor *James* be in a Rage?
And I not strip the Gilding off a Knave,
Un-plac'd, un-pension'd, no Man's Heir, or Slave?
I will, or perish in the gen'rous Cause.

(111-17)

While Pope is performing the true laureate's role, he is at the same time totally independent, the spokesman for a greater truth and justice, now no longer associated in any way with the court.

Pope frequently thus declares his hatred of courts and courtiers, his distance from dependency and the establishment. A certain ambivalence about the relationship with power had always been present in the laureate tradition, despite the fact that such a relationship was its whole *raison d'être*. Pope's own temperament and his growing disgust with the present order combine to make independence a crucial value for him. It is not then to say that Pope is insincere to suggest that his protestations cannot be taken at face value. There is a sense in which 'independence' was forced upon him by circumstances, and he never ceases to yearn not so much for patronage as for the cultural authority which the old model seemed to confer.

The full difficulty and paradox of Pope's position has, in other words, not always been appreciated. It is revealing on this score to see how Swift, on the occasion of the vacancy, cannot help juxtaposing, in some bewilderment, thoughts of his friend's reputation and greatness, his actual position of retirement and the laureate's office:

> The Doctor [Arbuthnot] hath ill informed me, who says that Mr Pope is at present the cheif poeticall favorite; yet Mr Pope himself talks like a Philosopher and one wholly retired. But the vogue of our few honest folks here is that Duck is absolutely to Succeed Eusden in the Lawrell, the contention being between Concannen or Theobald, or some other Hero of the Dunciad.[17]

In a letter to Arbuthnot as late as 1734 there seems to be an element of complaint, even of regret, along with the disingenuous self-justification when Pope says that:

> much freer Satyrists than I have enjoy'd the encouragement and protection of the Princes under whom they lived. Augustus and Mecœnas [sic] made Horace their companion, tho' he had been in arms on the side of Brutus . . .[18]

The responsibilities Pope seeks to fulfil, the seriousness with which he regards himself, require a model in some way analogous to the old one, and his work continues to be haunted by its absence. As Ian Jack puts it, Pope always remains in some sense a court poet without a court.[19] The idea of an independent laureate is in the last analysis a contradiction in terms.

What, though, of Jacobitism? Could not that have provided the answer: a set of norms, an alternative court? The question of Pope's putative allegiance to the exiled house of Stuart has been opened up again in this very volume. Whatever the nature and degree of his commitment, it is clear that Jacobitism was not substantial and central enough as a political and cultural alternative to be able to provide Pope with the full imaginative framework or the actual position of influence that his kind of poetry traditionally required.[20]

Despite his commitment to Bolingbroke and his early sympathy with the Patriots, the option of becoming an opposition laureate is not really open to Pope either, at least in the specifically political sense in which the phrase is used by Isaac Kramnick. The coming of party has discredited the whole political realm and simply to join the opposition is to allow the norms of the new age to dictate the agenda. As Christine Gerrard shows, Pope was earnestly beseeched to write on behalf of the Patriots in the late 1730s and to praise Frederick Prince of Wales as the hope of the future. But he had become far too suspicious of politics and royal myth-making to be comfortable with this role. Disgust with those who write in praise of the Hanoverians seems to have spilled over onto those who write in praise of *any* establishment, and even Horace and Virgil apparently have to be rejected now.[21]

Satire had been an option within the laureate tradition, though it was meant to be secondary to celebration. As we have seen, in Jonson's case the balance has already shifted, but he is able to preserve the saving grace that his satire itself depends on an acceptance of shared norms between patron and poet. But Pope goes much further. In his work celebration is in the end to be swallowed up entirely in satire. When Pope in *The Dunciad*, ii, 7–12 echoes the famous image from Davenant quoted previously, he ironically inverts the whole idea behind it. The beams of celebration in his passage refract themselves into the whole band of dunces; but where Davenant's 'lights' are 'Angelicall', Pope's allusion to the opening of book II of *Paradise Lost* gives them a satanic glow. For Pope, the whole ideological package has become unravelled. No longer can religious values, nationalism, classical ethics be linked up with the powers that be. The governors have lost the authority to govern and the legislators to legislate.

A conservative writer who comes thus to reject the sources of political authority in his society finds himself in as paradoxical a position as Archbishop Lefèvre. This situation, which Pope genuinely experienced as the truth, but also deliberately exaggerated, encourages him to use a powerful rhetoric of desperation, and in some ways he thrives on this. But desperation can hardly provide a total strategy. Since Pope, unlike Swift, continues to aspire to ambitious and elevated poetry, the question of where to find the ideological authority for such poetry becomes urgent. It is never entirely clear, for example, whether that authority is drawn from his own moral virtue and independence or from the more legitimate hierarchies of the past, from whose norms present power structures can be seen as deviant.[22]

One highly revealing aspect of Pope's campaign is the way that his confrontation with absurd modern laureates, and indeed with the whole idea of court and establishment writing, is in part carried out through invoking the shadowy presence of a true laureate – himself – absent and yet present at the same time, independent and yet the spokesman for an entire order, 'like Apollo . . . in the fulness of my Glory & Majesty, wanting nothing but the Laurel, which you may find at Cibber's'.[23]

In the *Epistle to Dr. Arbuthnot* Pope's strategy of setting himself up as the antithesis of Sporus–Hervey is obvious enough. But Sporus, a father of lies opposed to the truth-teller poet, is specifically a false poet-advisor to the royal family, 'at the Ear of *Eve*, familiar Toad' (319), who spits out rhymes along with all the other things. Here Pope's stance is primarily of independence. But in so far as he is identified as the antitype to Sporus, we are also made aware that the latter stands in the same relation to a false court as Pope would stand to a true.

It can hardly be denied that *Imitations of Horace, Epistle II i, To Augustus*, is one of the proudest and most resonant assertions of Pope's contempt for those that flatter kings, and one critic has gone so far as to say that all the poem's references to laureates from beginning to end intimate 'their enervating connection with monarchy'.[24] Yet the matter is not so simple. One of the sustained ironies in the poem is that Pope is in fact acting as an unpaid, unsolicited and indeed unwanted laureate poet to George II, despite saying that he is not. He steals an hour from his public labours (as the convention

53

was), tries to teach and advise him, and, of course, satirises him. He reminds him in traditional terms that 'a Poet's of some weight,/And (tho' no Soldier) useful to the State' (203-4) and explains among other less serious justifications that poetry can memorialise virtue and that in its satiric aspect it 'heals with Morals what it hurts with Wit' (262). The rich ironies of the poem would not be what they are without Pope's genuine belief in this role. He reveals, it has been said, an 'assertiveness concerning the writer's active role in state affairs' which is greater than Horace's.[25]

Yet, of course, this is a king Pope finds ridiculous and a court that has debased the whole idea:

> But most, when straining with too weak a wing,
> We needs will write Epistles to the King;
> And from the moment we oblige the town,
> Expect a Place, or Pension from the Crown;
> Or dubb'd Historians by express command,
> T' enroll your triumphs o'er the seas and land;
> Be call'd to Court, to plan some work divine,
> As once for LOUIS, Boileau and Racine.
>
> (368-75)

The irony becomes especially convoluted here. Pope is attacking this debased laureate tradition and the expectation of patronage in response to the flattery of such a court.[26] Yet he implies that George cares so little for poetry that he is now neglecting even this debased tradition, and so he archly gives him advice about how to fill the actual post of laureate: 'Or chuse at least some Minister of Grace,/Fit to bestow the Laureat's weighty place' (378-9). Like Swift in the *Argument against Abolishing Christianity*, there is a sense (in spite of his ironic tone) in which Pope is defending the nominal and debased modern version as at least better than total neglect. At the same time, despite Pope's mixed feelings about their example, the reference to Boileau and Racine offers a norm by which to measure the present decline, just as British ambivalence about Louis XIV does not prevent George from suffering by the comparison.[27]

We come finally to *The Dunciad*, a poem that begins, like its predecessor *MacFlecknoe*, with the appointment of a poet laureate of dullness. The main reason for the switch from Theobald to Cibber in the later version is surely that the latter actually is the reigning laureate.[28] Among other things this provides a poignant contrast between the positions of Pope and Dryden, who at the time of writing *MacFlecknoe* was himself the royal laureate. The tone of

Dryden's satire obviously comes in part from this regal assurance (it is a great historical irony that Shadwell was later to replace him under William and Mary) and the imagery has been shown to provide various positive allusions to true laureateship, true royalty and the link between literature and social order.[29] Pope writes, of course, in the radically different situation that he portrays as the collapse of social order. In his eyes it is the most extraordinary index of cultural debasement that the respective positions of Dryden and Shadwell are now reversed, and that Cibber is now the laureate, a genuine 'Antichrist of Wit' (ii, 16), like the buffoon laureate Querno whose coronation Pope sarcastically purports to regard as the origin of the institution.

It is against this antitype that Pope defines himself, though for once with curious impersonality. He is 'The Poet', 'The Muse' – 'O Muse! relate (for you can tell alone,/Wits have short Memories, and Dunces none)' (iv, 619–20). He is also the true historian set against the false 'historiographer royal', another role often combined with the laureate's, the two making up, Pope once wrote, the 'two greatest Lyers in Literature'.[30]

The point is underlined by the remarkable extent to which the poem preserves, though in inverted fashion, the framework of the traditional model while at the same time asserting its redundancy. This applies to the epic suggestion itself, but also to the way the fourth book incorporates the epistle on education from the *Opus Magnum* scheme. Pope uses the Scriblerian parody of learning to show what has gone wrong with the whole education of the nobility, the governors present and future, and it is precisely this education in the widest sense which is the true Renaissance laureate's responsibility.[31]

The fourth book thus moves carefully and chronologically through schooldays, university, the Grand Tour, and then to all the apparently harmless aristocratic pastimes of the virtuosi, gourmets and cricketers. What needs to be emphasised is that this last subject is not incidental satire. These pursuits may be trivial in themselves, but they represent a dereliction of duty on the part of a ruling class:

> The Cap and Switch be sacred to his Grace;
> With Staff and Pumps the Marquis lead the race;
> From Stage to Stage the licens'd Earl may run,
> Pair'd with his Fellow-Charioteer the Sun;
> The learned Baron Butterflies design,
> Or draw to silk Arachne's subtile line;
> The Judge to dance his brother Sergeant call;

The Senator at Cricket urge the Ball

(iv, 585–92)

These are upper class figures. They have allowed themselves to be distracted into this range of petty pastimes, but in so doing they have left responsibility for government to Walpole. In this they are joined by the monarch himself: 'nobly conscious, Princes are but things/ Born for First Ministers, as Slaves for Kings' (601–2). All this is the traditional laureate poet's concern, though here it is expressed paradoxically and in desperation.

It is important not to exaggerate here. *The Dunciad* is in one sense a poem about the *end* of a tradition. There is some truth in Damrosch's argument that this is a work in which the uniform, authoritative voice of the poet breaks down and we hear the very 'babel of contrary voices that rise from below', the voices of the age of the novel, in which a single voice of authority can no longer be imposed. But it is an over-simplification to say that Pope 'left the Renaissance behind and knew that he was doing so'.[32] It is a mark of Pope's continued conservatism that he persists in using this framework of a poet's concern for the education and guidance of a ruling class, and his despair, though real enough, is also rhetorically exaggerated, perhaps in the hope of an eleventh-hour conversion. The poem is an attack on a degenerate modern poet laureate, and the degeneration is so complete that Pope also rejects the very ideal that it debases. But the poem still discharges a true laureate's role and responsibility, and thus at the same time attempts to redefine such a tradition in more and more problematic circumstances. Pope makes a bold new claim for prophetic independence, but he continues to be haunted by his own and his predecessors' relationship to traditional power structures, and his paradoxical position brings out into the open contradictions that had always existed in the idea of the laureate poet.

Notes

1. Leopold Damrosch, Jr, *The Imaginative World of Alexander Pope* (Berkeley and Guildford, 1987), p. 76.
2. *The Dialogic Imagination*, cited by Damrosch, p. 284.
3. For a fine study, see Richard Helgerson, *Self-crowned Laureates: Spenser, Jonson, Milton and the Literary System* (Berkeley, 1983).
4. Sir William Davenant, preface to *Gondibert*, edited by David F. Gladish (Oxford, 1971), p. 38.
5. *Ben Jonson: Works*, edited by C. H. Herford and P. Simpson, 11 vols

(Oxford, 1925-52), viii, 565, cited by Helgerson, p. 50. Jonson is in part translating Vives.

6. *TE*, ix, 4-5; 'Preface to Shakespeare', *The Literary Criticism of Alexander Pope*, edited by Bertrand Goldgar (Lincoln, Nebraska, 1965), p. 164. In *The Dunciad*, iv, 175, however, Dulness expresses fond nostalgia for the 'pedant reign' of James I. James's court was, for Pope, in some respects already debased, despite the encouragement that the king had given Shakespeare. What we see here is a tendency which I comment on later for Pope's bitterness against Hanoverian courts to spill over into all courts, and this is obviously relevant to the controversy about Pope's Jacobitism.

7. Helgerson, p. 179.

8. For a history see Edmund K. Broadus, *The Laureateship: A Study of the Office of Poet Laureate in England* (Oxford, 1921). See also Robert Folkenflik, 'Patronage and the poet-hero', *Huntington Library Quarterly*, 48 (1985), 363-79. Roger Lund's paper at the Reading Renaissance conference (July 1989), '*Gondibert* and the failures of laureateship' also summarised the material well and mentioned Gray's refusal.

9. 'LXV, To My Muse', *Works*, viii, 48.

10. *Cynthia's Revels*, V, i. 35-7, 30-1, *Works*, iv, 131-2.

11. Isabel Rivers, *The Poetry of Conservatism* (Cambridge, 1973), p. 55.

12. Helgerson, p. 280.

13. Dedication to 'Georgics' (1697), Dryden, *Poems*, ii, 916.

14. 'A Letter to a Lady, Occasion'd by the Arrival of Her Royal Highness The Princess of Wales' (1714), 103-6, *John Gay: Poetry and Prose*, edited by V. A. Dearing and C. Beckwith (Oxford, 1974), i, 132.

15. For a good summary of the provenance of this piece see *Selected Prose of Alexander Pope*, edited by Paul Hammond (Cambridge, 1987), p. 213.

16. C. J. Rawson, ' "I the Lofty Stile Decline": self-apology and the "heroick Strain" in some of Swift's poems', *The English Hero, 1660-1800*, edited by Robert Folkenflik (Delaware and London, 1982), pp. 79-115.

17. Swift-Gay and the Duchess of Queensberry, 19 November 1730 (Sherburn, iii, 151).

18. Pope-Arbuthnot, 26 July 1734 (Sherburn, iii, 420).

19. Ian Jack, 'Pope and his audience from "The Pastorals" to "The Dunciad Variorum" ', *Studies in the Eighteenth Century*, IV, edited by R. F. Brissenden and J. C. Eade (Canberra, 1979), pp. 1-30, reprinted in *The Poet and his Audience* (Cambridge, 1984).

20. I am thinking of J. A. Downie's essay, '1688: Pope and the rhetoric of Jacobitism', ch. 1 of the present book. Even Douglas Brooks-Davies in *Pope's Dunciad and the Queen of Night, A Study in Emotional Jacobitism* (Manchester, 1985) does not argue that Jacobitism gave Pope a full cultural and political context.

21. Isaac Kramnick, *Bolingbroke and his Circle: The Politics of Nostalgia in the Age of Walpole* (Cambridge, Mass., 1968), p. 21; Christine Gerrard, 'Pope and the Patriots', ch. 2 of the present book; see Spence, i, 124, cited by Gerrard, n. 47. For the debate about positive and negative images of Horace in the period, see Howard D. Weinbrot, *Augustus Caesar in 'Augustan' England* (Princeton, 1978), especially p. 217, and

Howard Erskine-Hill, *The Augustan Idea in English Literature* (London, 1983), especially p. 308.

22. I have made further efforts at exploring this in *Politeness and Poetry in the Age of Pope* (Teaneck and London, 1989). I am grateful to Thomas Yoseloff of Associated University Presses for permission to summarise and recast a portion of my argument.
23. Pope–Countess of Denbigh [? 1742] (Sherburn, iv, 398).
24. Manuel Schonhorn, 'Pope's "Epistle to Augustus" ', *Tennessee Studies in Literature*, 16 (1971), 15–33, reprinted in *Pope: Recent Essays by Several Hands*, edited by Maynard Mack and James Winn (Brighton, 1980), pp. 546–64 (p. 548).
25. Malcolm Kelsall, 'Augustus and Pope', *Huntington Library Quarterly*, 39 (1976), 117–31 (p. 127).
26. Folkenflik, p. 373.
27. Compare *Imitations of Horace. Satire* II i, 111.
28. As Robert Folkenflik (p. 372) says, Pope may well have expected Theobald to become laureate.
29. Brooks-Davies, *Pope's Dunciad*, p. 92, n. 34; Earl Miner, *Dryden's Poetry* (Bloomington, Indiana, 1967), ch. 3; Michael Wilding, 'Allusion and innuendo in *MacFlecknoe*', *E C*, 355–70. There may also be, as Howard Erskine-Hill suggests in *The Augustan Idea in English Literature*, pp. 222–3, some satire of Charles II as a patron.
30. Pope–Earl of Orrery, 9 February 1743 (Sherburn, iv, 440).
31. There is an important treatment of the poem's whole topic of education by G. S. Rousseau, 'Pope and the tradition in modern humanistic education: ". . . in the pale of Words till death" ', in *The Enduring Legacy*, pp. 199–239; but Rousseau does not give enough weight to the fact that it is the contemporary *abuse* of humanistic learning that Pope is attacking.
32. Damrosch, pp. 285, 295.

4

Breaking decorums
Belinda, Bays and epic effeminacy

Carolyn D. Williams

Gender in classical epic

Few modern readers of *The Rape of the Lock* take Pope literally when
he maintains in the dedication to the book that:

> the ancient Poets are in one respect like many modern Ladies; Let an
> Action be never so trivial in it self, they always make it appear of the
> utmost Importance.

It is current critical practice to assume that in his comic epic Pope
presents two contrasting realms: the world of ancient heroes, whose
bold deeds and mighty rages have international repercussions; and the
feminine world of modern ladies, where nothing really matters and
the bitterest resentment is harboured in bosoms that are reassuringly
soft. Pope's alert contemporary readers, however, would have seen
this comment as alluding not only to the differences between heroic
and modern civilisations, but also to a tension between masculine and
feminine within epic itself. They would sense a rueful awareness on
Pope's part of a connection between classical epic's occasional
flirtation with the trivial or burlesque, and its tendency to allow
mistresses, mothers and goddesses not merely to influence the course
of events, but to intrude values which deny, frustrate or undermine
male heroics.

There is ample evidence that Pope, like many of his contemporaries, was uncomfortably aware of flaws in his classical models. A
timely reminder has appeared in an article by Howard D. Weinbrot,[1]
which shows how *The Rape of the Lock* and *The Dunciad* expose

embarrassing moments when Homer and Virgil allow the tone to slip below a level appropriate to heroic decorum. The fact that many such stylistic and ethical lapses are consistent with normal epic procedures only makes matters worse. Weinbrot notes that, 'the more characters in *The Rape of the Lock* embrace epic values and conventions, the less pleasant they are'.[2] Like most critics of the mock-heroic, Weinbrot has concentrated on allusions to excessive coarseness in the poet's epic models, and has ignored the dangers posed by excessive refinement – the quality that Pope defines as 'effeminacy'.[3] But Pope's dedication reveals a link between a wide range of comic indecorum and a feminine strain in classical epic.

Three related factors colour all Pope's encounters with epic: a dread of effeminacy as an insidious and protean evil that can crop up in the unlikeliest places; a conviction that the most effective way to teach manliness is a classical education, with plenty of Homer and Virgil; and the knowledge that critics from Plato[4] onwards have detected examples of, and possibly even incitements to, effeminacy in the fabric of epic itself. The object of this essay is to fit Pope's troubled and ambivalent perception of epic into a larger context. First, his views on sexuality in epic will be examined; then some observations on *The Rape of the Lock* and *The Dunciad* will show how he brings the dynamics of effeminacy to bear on his own compositions: they intensify the gravitational pull of the trivial and vulgar, drawing Pope's opening statement on the similarity between his own mock-heroic poetry and its great originals ever nearer to the literal truth – while the right-minded reader sees more and more reasons to wish the poet were only joking.

A comprehensive history of the Iliad, Odyssey and Aeneid, considered as handbooks on sexual orientation, is beyond the scope of a single essay, or even a single book.[5] This essay will concentrate on a few aspects of the Iliad and Odyssey.[6] To Pope and his colleagues, Homer's representation of sexuality is part of a wider educational programme, and they add their voices to a chorus of apologists who insist that Homer is not only the prince of poets, but an unremittingly conscientious moralist.[7] A problem arises, however, when women enter on the scene: heroic dignity and virtue become perilously fragile when the ladies deploy their wiles. The hapless warrior who yields to their influence finds his masculinity embarrassingly compromised whenever soft living and excessive heterosexual contact unleash his innate feminine propensities, impairing his courage, intellect and self-control. The rot can quickly spread from the fictitious hero to the living reader, who may be unable to distinguish

60

between a shining example and an awful warning. Pope and his team, acting as perceptive critics and responsible citizens, undertake a vitally important task: in their eyes, masculinity is far too complex and vulnerable to be taken for granted, and manly attitudes must be inculcated by a scrupulous interpretation of perilously enigmatic texts.

Renaissance precedents

Pope's response to Homer is further complicated and enriched by his experience of much intervening epic. He reads the Iliad and Odyssey not only through the spectacles of Virgil, but through those of Ariosto, Tasso, Spenser and Milton – not to mention a bevy of critics, commentators and translators. The effects are pervasive and profound: the most important for present purposes is a tendency to distort and magnify the role of the feminine.

Men are frequently drawn into sensuous effeminacy by alluring temptresses. An early and rather mild case is Virgil's Aeneas, who adopts a rich, oriental costume during his sojourn at Carthage; his purple cloak and sword with jewelled scabbard are presents from Dido.[8] Mercury calls him *uxorius*,[9] but Aeneas' misdemeanours are more political than sexual: he has not abandoned his empire-building prowess; he is simply building the wrong empire. In Dryden's *Aeneis* (1697), however, we see how unmanly Aeneas has come to appear. His costume has sunk from the glamorous to the frivolous:

> A Purple Scarf, with Gold embroider'd o're,
> (Queen *Dido*'s Gift) about his Waste he wore;
> A Sword with glitt'ring Gems diversify'd,
> For Ornament, not use, hung idly by his side.
> (*Virgil's Aeneis*, iv, 384–7)[10]

Dryden's Mercury addresses Aeneas as 'degenerate Man,/Thou Woman's Property' (iv, 389–90).[11] His Aeneas has been contaminated by association with his Renaissance predecessors.

A notorious example is Ariosto's Ruggiero. When he becomes the lover of the enchantress Alcina, his decadence shows in his costume:

> His armes that erst all warlike weapons bare,
> In golden bracelets wantonly were tide.
> (*Orlando Furioso*, vii, stanza 46, 3–4)[12]

The translator Sir John Harington glosses this passage as '*A description*

61

of an effeminate courtier.[13] Ruggiero's failure to maintain a properly masculine manner threatens his very identity:

> He had such wanton womanish behaviour . . .
> So from himselfe, beyond all reason led,
> By these inchantments of this am'rous dame,
> He was himselfe in nothing but in name.
>
> (vii, stanza 47, 3–8)[14]

Worst of all, by wasting his potency on an old, barren witch, Ruggiero is failing to beget legitimate heirs.[15] He is therefore a paradigm of the political, psychological and dynastic ravages of effeminacy. The tradition is maintained by Rinaldo in Tasso's *Gerusalemme Liberata* (1581), when he falls a prey to Armida's charms:

> His sword, that many a Pagan stout had shent,
>   Bewrapt with flow'rs hung idly by his side,
> So nicely decked that it seem'd the knight
> Wore it for fashion sake, but not for fight.
>
> (*Jerusalem Delivered*, xvi, stanza 30, 5–8)[16]

The most deplorably indecorous case in Spenser's *Faerie Queene* (1596) is Artegall, forced to wear woman's dress by the Amazon Radigund. But there are many other hapless young knights to keep him in countenance, from the herd of Acrasia's lover-victims to the Christian champion Redcrosse, who loses his 'manly forces' (i, stanza 6, 4) while paying court to Duessa.[17] As heir to all this – and Dryden too – Pope regards Homer's ladies with understandable suspicion, vigilant for the slightest sign of emasculation in any hero who has dealings with them.

Pope, however, cannot define women's role in epic as purely destructive. Femininity is a potent epic ingredient: dangerous but indispensable. He himself is an eager exponent of the chivalric tradition that makes female favour the inspiration for heroic masculine endeavour: witness his concern that the ladies will like his *Homer*.[18] Besides, women cannot be held ultimately responsible for male effeminacy – nor any other fault in men. Milton states this plainly in *Paradise Lost* (1667), when the Archangel Michael corrects Adam's crudely misogynist accusations with misogyny of a subtler kind:

> But still [says Adam] I see the tenor of man's woe
> Holds on the same, from woman to begin.

From man's effeminate slackness it begins,
Said the angel, who should better hold his place
By wisdom, and superior gifts received.

(*Paradise Lost*, xi, 632–6)

The chief purpose of epic, in Pope's eyes, is to teach the reader how to protect his 'superior gifts' from the assaults of temptation from without, and the even more dangerous sabotage of the enemy within.

Pope's Homer: laureate of patriarchy

First it is necessary to note the different educational methods of Homer's two epics. The Iliad is designed to teach its readers to be brave, hardy, pious, patriotic, contemptuous of orientals and amenable to military discipline. But its value is vitiated by Homer's choice of hero: Achilles' conduct is largely an object lesson in how *not* to behave, and undiscerning readers may pick up the wrong signals. Critics have long been scandalised by Achilles' reaction to the confiscation of Briseis, his concubine: he goes to the beach and cries to his mother, the sea goddess Thetis. Pope duly explains that these are 'Tears of Anger and Disdain' (Iliad, i, 458, and note)[19] provoked by slighted honour rather than a broken heart. All the same, Achilles is hard to defend. One problem is an early accretion of non-Homeric material which inevitably affects Achilles' image in the eyes of informed readers. His reputation for necrophilia, sodomy (active and passive), rape and satyriasis is carefully documented in Bayle's *Dictionary*. As for Thetis, she is beyond comparison the most embarrassing mother in classical mythology. She makes Achilles disguise himself as a girl in order to avoid the war: most people would assume that Homer knew of this episode, and read the Iliad accordingly.[20] Thetis' worst offence in Homer's text is advising Achilles to make love to his newly restored concubine – a course that he eventually adopts. Yielding to such a combination of excessive maternal solicitude and illicit sexuality is effeminacy with a vengeance. Pope does his best to palliate the offence. He provides an elegantly vague translation in which Thetis urges her son to 'indulge the am'rous Hour!' (*Iliad*, xxiv, 168).[21] He maintains that 'the whole Passage is capable of a serious Construction, and of such a Sense as a Mother might express to a Son with Decency'. But Pope is still 'of Opinion that this Passage outrages Decency'; he objects chiefly to 'the manner of the Expression, which must be allow'd to be almost obscene' (*Iliad*, xxiv, 168n).[22] Thetis tells Achilles to μίσγεσθ' (literally 'mingle') with Briseis. Pope invokes cultural relativity: 'as we are not competent Judges of what Ideas Words might carry in *Homer*'s Time, so we ought not entirely to condemn him, because it is possible the Expression might not sound so indecently in ancient as in modern Ears'.[23] But he does not like arguing in this fashion; the chief object of his Homeric exercise is to emphasise the relevance of his text to eighteenth-century society. This incident conforms to a pattern that recurs throughout Pope's *Homer*, and in his own mock-epics: masculine virtue is imperilled by sensual temptation, leading to effeminacy, in a context of linguistic indecorum. The exceptional element in this case is Pope's reluctance to condemn the culprit: he is too deeply impressed by Achilles' heroic personality.

The Odyssey here is a much safer guide because it tells the story of a virtuous man who behaves properly and is duly rewarded. In his Postscript, Pope observes that, 'In some points (and those the most essential to the Epic Poem) the Odyssey is confessed to excel the Iliad; and principally in the great end of it, the *Moral*'.[24]

Pope's Ulysses arrives at Ithaca with a heavy cargo of virtues, many of which cannot be found in Homer's original manifest. He is exemplary as king, hero, master, husband, father and son; an indefatigable worshipper of Zeus, the father of men and gods. The Popeian Odyssey is a spiritual journey, which the hero can complete only by the exercise of courage, humility and self-control. Ulysses' 'manliness' is for Pope not just the aggression, courage and general *machismo* commonly supposed to differentiate a man from a woman, but the wisdom, independence, maturity and emotional breadth that differentiate a man from a boy. In his encounter with the enchantress Circe, who changes her victims into swine, it also appears as the distinction between humans and animals. After he returns home Ulysses must direct his psychic energies outwards, reaching his full glory only when he exerts authority over his kingdom. Pope's team remain consistent in their treatment of Ulysses, from the carefully supplemented theodicy of the Pope/Fenton opening,[25] to the last line, which Pope proudly imports from Dryden's *Absalom and Achitophel* (1681): ' "And willing nations knew their lawful Lord" ' (*Odyssey*, xxiv, 631).[26] A literal-minded reader might be tempted to observe that this is very patriarchal, but you must not call it Homer.

Pope's Ulysses, in fact, sometimes seems a far cry from Homer's Odysseus, that wily sole survivor whose methods often cross to the shady side of the line between wisdom and cunning. Homer's original seldom displays the authoritative aggression we expect from a patriarch in action. He is predominantly an underdog. Now and then his brute strength and military prowess come in useful, but he is usually placed in situations where a straight fight, like the Iliad's climactic duel between Achilles and Hector, is out of the question. It is typical of the Odyssey's low, even domestic, tone that the only single combat is Odysseus' boxing match with the beggar Irus, for a haggis. Dignity is one of the many luxuries that Homer's Odysseus must do without. He lies, flatters, manipulates, and makes words do the work of muscle; he takes advantage of his physical attractions to obtain favours from influential members of the opposite sex, but manages to avoid committing himself in marriage. He swallows his pride, bears exploitation and insult patiently, but never loses hope that he will get his own back.

Similar strategies are employed by Odysseus' wife Penelope; indeed Homer's imagery draws suggestive parallels between their predicaments. When Odysseus hears a bard singing of the Trojan wars, he weeps as bitterly as a woman bereaved of her husband in battle:

> Thus while he sung, *Ulysses'* griefs renew,
> Tears bathe his cheeks, and tears the ground bedew:
> As some fond matron views in mortal fight
> Her husband falling in his country's right:
> Frantic thro' clashing swords she runs, she flies,
> As ghastly pale he groans, and faints, and dies;
> Close to his breast she grovels on the ground,
> And bathes with floods of tears the gaping wound;
> She cries, she shrieks: the fierce insulting foe
> Relentless mocks her violence of woe,
> To chains condemn'd as wildly she deplores,
> A widow, and a slave, on foreign shores!
>
> (*Odyssey*, viii, 569–80)

Such is the fate that Penelope has been struggling for twenty years to avert. Broome feels obliged to argue that Ulysses' reaction detracts nothing from his manliness:

> This is undoubtedly a very moving and beautiful comparison; but it may be ask'd if it be proper to compare so great a Heroe as *Ulysses* to a woman, the weakness of whose sex justifies her tears? . . . Tears discover a tender, not an abject spirit. *Achilles* is not less of a Heroe for weeping over the ashes of *Patroclus*, nor *Ulysses* for lamenting the calamities and deaths of thousands of his friends.[27]

When Penelope finally acknowledges her husband, the simile

65

describing her joy recalls Odysseus' shipwrecks on voyages to and from Ogygia:

> As to the shipwreck'd mariner, the shores
> Delightful rise, when angry *Neptune* roars,
> Then, when the surge in thunder mounts the sky,
> And gulph'd in crouds at once the sailors dye,
> If one more happy, while the tempest raves
> Out-lives the tumult of conflicting waves,
> All pale, with ooze deform'd, he views the strand,
> And plunging forth with transport grasps the land.
> The ravish'd Queen with equal rapture glows,
> Clasps her lov'd Lord, and to his bosom grows.
>
> (*Odyssey*, xxiii, 249–58)[28]

The events of the narrative have brought Ulysses, sacker of cities, and the chastely domestic Penelope onto common ground.

The double sexual standard, often invoked to the disadvantage of women in the Odyssey, ironically allows Homer to inflict one ordeal on Odysseus that Penelope must be spared. His hero spends seven years as an unwilling lover to the goddess Calypso, when he would rather be at home, ruling his kingdom: 'But by night he had to lie down beside her in the hollow caves: he did not want to make love; she did.' (Odyssey, v, 154–5.) As Odysseus labours under direct female domination and other associated indignities, it becomes increasingly difficult to focus on the eighteenth-century ancients' vision of the Odyssey as the unified masterpiece of an instructor in patriarchal values, whose work is intended 'for Eternity to please and instruct Mankind'.[29] In fact, this remark provokes a characteristically reductive riposte from that arch-modern, Richard Bentley:

> Take my word for it, poor Homer, in those circumstances and early times, had never such aspiring thoughts. He wrote a sequel of Songs and Rhapsodies, to be sung by himself for small earnings and good cheer, at Festivals and other days of Merriment; the *Ilias* he made for the Men; the *Odysseis* for the other Sex.[30]

Although Pope and his team of ancients ignore the theory that the Odyssey may have been aimed at a female audience, they frequently reveal an uneasy sense that control and containment of the feminine within the text presents awkward problems to Homer and his hero alike. It is with considerable relief that they turn their attention to an episode where Odysseus' masculinity can be thoroughly vindicated.

Effeminacy in action

According to received wisdom, Homer recommends manliness not only by showing rugged heroes in victorious action, but by contrasting them with examples of feeble effeminacy. In the Iliad, the Greeks are masculine, the Trojans effeminate.[31] In the Odyssey, commentators single out the Phaeacians, the hero's kindly and honourable hosts, as feminised foils to his masculinity. At first sight, it is hard to tell what they have done to deserve such treatment. One reason is that, like the Trojans, they are a doomed race who have incurred divine resentment. Since the reasons given by Homer for Poseidon's hostility towards the Phaeacians are manifestly unfair, and it would be impious to attribute injustice to a god, there must have been – it is assumed – some other cause. Luckily, there is plenty of evidence to support an alternative charge – part of it provided by Homer, but most of it diligently manufactured by generations of critics: Pope makes his own contributions, for example by letting Poseidon call the Phaeacians 'soft' and 'degenerate' (*Odyssey*, xiii, 151)[32] when there is no warrant in the original. Whom the gods wish to destroy, the commentators pronounce effeminate.

The Phaeacians' chief crime is that they have found some activities more satisfying than military training, or even war, and are not ashamed to say so:

> To dress, to dance, to sing our sole delight,
> The feast or bath by day, and love by night.
> (Odyssey, viii, 285–6)

Broome hastens to reassure the disgusted reader that

> *Eustathius* rightly observes that the Poet does not teach that we ought to live such lives, but only relates historically what lives were led by the *Phaeacians*; he describes them as a contemptible people, and consequently proposes them as objects of our scorn, not imitation.[33]

The antithesis between 'scorn' and 'imitation' is decisive: there can be no neutral relativism, no wistful hankering, no compromise of any kind – too much is at stake. This attitude is at least a thousand years old in the days of Eustathius.[34] Horace refers contemptuously to *Alcinoique/in cute curanda plus aequo operata iuventus* (*Epistle I ii*, 28–9): 'Alcinous' young blades, who devoted an inordinate amount of attention to skin care'. Bearing in mind the high priority Horace gave to keeping his own skin intact at the battle of Philippi, when he

Carolyn D. Williams

dropped his shield and ran, is he perhaps trying to shore up his own sense of manliness by sneering at the Phaeacians? They are, in any case, a suspiciously soft target.

The Phaeacians incur further rebukes in the course of a necessary service to Homer's structural plan. Their most important function is to provide an occasion for the tale of Odysseus' wanderings. Generations of critics, unable to tell a Homeric fiction from an Odyssean lie, berate them for their ignorant credulity. Broome adds a sexual slant to their condemnation:

> Ulysses . . . knew that the *Phaeacians* were simple and credulous; and that they had all the qualities of a lazy people, who admire nothing so much as romantic adventures: he therefore pleases them, by recitals suited to their own humour: but even here the Poet is not unmindful of his more understanding Readers, and the truth intended to be taught by way of moral is, that a soft and effeminate life breaks the spirit, and renders it incapable of manly sentiments or actions.
>
> (*Odyssey*, vi, 12n)[35]

How can credulity and simplicity be included in any definition of effeminacy, however broad? Broome is responding to the perceived presence of these qualities against a background of luxury and refinement. He uses the concept of effeminacy to make Phaeacian gullibility more intelligible, as well as finding in it a further proof of their depravity. He draws a powerful, if implied, analogy between this legendary race of privileged degenerates and the women any eighteenth-century gentleman could expect to meet every day. Given the widespread belief that women were intellectually inferior to men, and the custom of educating them down to their station, it is not surprising that Broome should classify intelligence, wisdom and knowledge of the world as masculine characteristics, while finding folly and superstition more likely to occur among women.

The Phaeacians, however, are not universally condemned. Pierre Bayle, although mildy ironic, is on the whole approving ('the people loved good cheer, and the conveniences of life, which did not hinder the men from being active and very good seamen')[36] and one French cantata represents Louis XIV as an Alcinous who has made war only '*pour mieux affermir le repos de la terre*'.[37] The Phaeacians also receive a few kind words from Lady Mary Wortley Montagu, who finds Alcinous more of a hero than Achilles, and recommends him as an example for Frederick the Great.[38] She probably feels less inhibited because of her sex: however assiduously she supports Alcinous, no one will reproach her for deficient masculinity.

68

Even in Pope's *Homer*, the Phaeacians receive some praise – partly because Pope's team finds it strategically necessary at one point, when Odysseus himself commends their mode of living and remarks that a banquet is the most delightful thing in the world (*Odyssey*, ix, 11). Plato denounces this incitement to intemperance (*Republic*, iii, 390 B); Athenaeus (*Deipnosophistae*, xii, 513 B–C) thinks Odysseus is being tactfully disingenuous; Rapin believes he is drunk.[39] This throws Pope and Broome into a mighty flutter: the attack is not aimed at the expendable Phaeacians, but at Ulysses himself, their ideal once-and-future king. In this emergency they justify their hero's opinion by setting the Phaeacians, for once, in a good light. Pope's translation at this point adds a moral and political dimension to Odysseus' compliment, which becomes a tribute to the joys of 'a peaceful reign' (*Odyssey*, ix, 3), and Broome annotates in the same vein: 'it is certainly the most glorious aim of a King to make his subjects happy, and diffuse an universal joy thro' his dominions'.[40]

One incident at Alcinous' court, however, draws into single focus indecorum, moral dubeity and effeminacy. In the Olympian high comedy of Demodocus' lay of Ares and Aphrodite, the goddess of love commits adultery with the god of war, and after the guilty pair are trapped in bed by the jealous husband, the gods assemble to pass appropriate comments.[41] This is one of the jewels of the Odyssey: Pope mentions it to Broome as an inducement to encourage him to translate book VIII,[42] yet Broome implies that he has undertaken this task with repugnance. He notes that commentators have traditionally been appalled to see deities treated with so little reverence: this book 'has been more severely censur'd by the Critics than any in the whole *Odyssey*' (*Odyssey*, viii, Argument, note).[43] Frantic efforts have been made to vindicate the respectability of Homer and his gods, often by demonstrating that this ostensibly offensive story is allegorical,[44] and Broome records some of these attempts. He prefers, however, to lay the blame on Phaeacian moral debility-as-effeminacy:

> We must consider that it is neither the Poet, nor his Heroe, that recites the story: but a *Phaeacian* sings it to *Phaeacians*, a soft effeminate people, at a festival. . . . The Moral we are to draw from this story is, that an idle and soft course of life is the source of all criminal pleasures; and that those persons who lead such lives, are generally pleas'd to hear such stories, as make their betters partakers in the same vices.
> (*Odyssey*, viii, Argument, note)[45]

Phaeacian narrative, therefore (Broome implies), can be separated out from its stylistic and moral context, and be allowed to accommodate

Carolyn D. Williams

the indecorous, immoral and effeminate without contaminating the Homeric epic norm. The moral that a judicious reader of Pope's *Odyssey* will draw is not from the story of Ares and Aphrodite in isolation, but from the nexus of indecorum, immorality and effeminacy exemplified by the Phaeacians themselves.

The episode also makes a stylistic shift, and for this Broome must hold Homer responsible, repeating Rapin's charge that as sexual intrigue raises its unheroic head Homer adandons his customary 'grandeur and majesty' and sinks into 'a familiar way of talking' (*Odyssey*, viii, Argument, note).[46] With this, the court of Alcinous takes on a disconcerting resemblance to another court where 'Thou, Great *Anna*! whom three Realms obey,/Dost sometimes Counsel take – and sometimes *Tea*.' (*The Rape of the Lock*, iii, 7–8.)

'Trivial Things'

The preponderance of female interest in Pope's mock-epics is no arbitrary distortion of source material: it arises from perceived conflicts between masculine and feminine values within epic itself. In origin and purpose, this device has much in common with Pope's use of low and trivial elements, and all three are often closely connected. Pope's prefatory comparison between ancient poets and modern ladies is promptly borne out in the opening lines of *The Rape of the Lock*:

> What dire Offence from am'rous Causes springs,
> What mighty Contests rise from trivial Things,
> I sing . . .
>
> (i, 1–3)

The poem's title, and the tone of its introduction, have prepared readers for something in the burlesque or mock-heroic line, so they will be quick to assume that 'dire' and 'mighty' are absurd exaggerations. This poem will deal with fine ladies' vanity and flirtations in high society: the important business of politics and warfare will find no place in its pages. But, despite their cosily miniaturising context, these lines are a reminder that epic struggles can have deplorably petty causes. The Trojan War started with a crooked beauty contest and an adulterous love affair. It is unexpectedly difficult to draw a firm distinction between important and trivial, epic and mock-epic, even masculine and feminine domains.

70

Femininity in *The Rape of the Lock* is often associated with intellectual deficiencies which, while charmingly appropriate to beautiful young ladies, would be unacceptable in men. Thus female superstition is treated as a form of amiable weakness, filtered with indulgent gallantry through Ariel's statement that 'The Fair and Innocent shall still believe' (i, 40). For Fair read 'effeminate', for Innocent read 'ignorant', and you have the Phaeacians. But Belinda, being a woman, is not rebuked for excessive credulity. Furthermore, she inhabits a mock-epic where the most blatant fiction may turn out to be true. Belinda is Pope's gateway to an alternative poetic universe. As Emrys Jones observes:

> If gentlemen, or 'wits', were creatures of modern enlightenment, women could be regarded as belonging to the fabulous dark ages. Accordingly what women, or women of this kind, provided for a poet like Pope, a poet working in a *milieu* of somewhat narrow and dogmatic rationalism, was a means of entry to a delightful world of folly and bad sense.[47]

The Rape of the Lock provides access to forbidden pleasures: readers can revel in the joys of naivety, their wonder at the marvellous untrammelled by conscientious comparisons with the probable. But femininity, whether in epic or mock-epic, is dangerous when it inhibits masculine activity (the paradigm being Odysseus' imprisonment in Calypso's caves), as at the moment when a male heroic rage can hardly pull itself free of female resentment:

> Not youthful Kings in Battel seiz'd alive,
> Not scornful Virgins who their Charms survive,
> Not ardent Lovers robb'd of all their Bliss,
> Not ancient Ladies when refus'd a Kiss,
> Not Tyrants fierce that unrepenting die,
> Not *Cynthia* when her *Manteau*'s pinn'd awry,
> E'er felt such Rage, Resentment and Despair,
> As Thou, sad Virgin! for thy ravish'd Hair.
>
> (iv, 3–10)

Pope seems at first to be contrasting the heroic passions proper to epic with the petty concerns of modern fashionable ladies, but much of his material is a *reductio ad absurdum* of conflicts already present in his epic models. Indeed, through the collision between public and domestic, sublimely heroic and ridiculously concrete, he is carefully and decorously inviting the reader to separate issues that a true epic often brings together: he never hints that youthful kings, and even

71

tyrants fierce, may get their come-uppance as a result of female desire, vanity and frustration.

Such cases, though common in epic and tragedy, are rare in real life. The most usual way to inhibit masculinity is not to subject a man to violence or restraint, but to seduce him, so that his manly qualities become vitiated by his own effeminacy. Soft, swooning femininity looks like a harmless complement to thrusting, energetic virility, but it can easily become infectious. Sickly Affectation, an obvious danger to women, produces an equally deleterious effect on those men who fail to see through her act as she 'Faints into Airs, and languishes with Pride' (iv, 34). Like Belinda, the Baron is destined to be dissolved by Umbriel's vial of 'fainting Fears,/Soft Sorrows, melting Griefs, and flowing Tears' (iv, 85–6). He has already been sucked dangerously deep into a world where no use is made of manly weapons, and all significant conflicts are carried on by means of 'Sword-knots' (i, 101). True, the Baron's courage is roused during his duel with Belinda:

> Nor fear'd the Chief th'unequal Fight to try,
> Who sought no more than on his Foe to die.
>
> (v, 77–8)

But Pope's naughty pun emphasises the self-destructive nature of the Baron's project, and the reader might be forgiven for wondering if, in any case, he is really up to it. According to Michael Seidel, 'An exhausting and sterile sexual strategy controls the poem: union of any kind is a sort of castration. . . . The Baron, too, cuts when he cannot penetrate.'[48]

Usurpation of masculinity follows, and it is the feminine which fills the power vacuum. When Belinda draws her 'deadly *Bodkin*' (v, 88), the Baron has no weapon with which to defend himself. (He could not even cut her lock without borrowing a woman's implement.) The bodkin's ancestry condemns a degenerate culture: it began its career as 'three *Seal-Rings*', used to place the patriarchal authority on the letters of Belinda's 'great great Grandsire' (v, 91, 90). Appropriately 'melted down' (v, 91), it has passed into female ownership, becoming successively 'a vast *Buckle* for his Widow's Gown' (v, 92) – how sincere, one wonders, was her mourning? – an infant's toy, and a hair ornament. The entire metamorphosis is a diminution of an epic precedent, 'the progress of *Agamemnon's* Scepter in *Homer*' (v, 89ff n). How are the mighty fallen. The weapons of war have descended into the possession of viragoes like the Amazonian Thalestris.

72

Neither man nor woman can prosper under this dispensation: *The Rape of the Lock* ends happily only because Pope can foresee a swift restoration of the balance of power.

The 'Mighty Mother'

In *The Dunciad* Pope predicts a much less welcome restoration, a return of 'native Anarchy' (i, 16) when:

> Dulness o'er all possess'd her ancient right,
> Daughter of Chaos and eternal Night

> (i, 11–12)

This formidable embodiment of the eternal feminine is not a pretty young mistress, but a ponderous matriarch, 'Laborious, heavy, busy, bold, and blind' (i, 15). Her subjects are not lovers but sons, whose lack of independence, integrity and intelligence indicates that they have never been adequately differentiated from that matrix which gave them birth. The king of the Dunces, her favourite son, nestles drowsily in her lap – a privilege he has attained after destroying his own literary progeny on a sacrificial pyre. True dunces can neither father viable offspring, nor support themselves by the exercise of creative ingenuity: they have little to lose by destroying the fruit of their own potency. Their limited reproductive energies are directed towards motherhood. Bays is surrounded by 'much Embryo, much Abortion' (i, 121); Annius bears Mummius' coins in 'this our paunch before' (iv, 388) to await their 'second birth' (iv, 386) with the aid of Douglas' 'soft, obstetric hand' (iv, 394). At the climactic enthronement of Dulness, Bays acquires countless companions, as the goddess exerts the combined attractive forces of mother, queen bee and gravitational black hole (iv, 73–86). Her final irresistible yawn engulfs the entire work, an exploit hideously appropriate to the entity who was once the maternal source from which everything arose, and to which, given sufficient moral and intellectual inertia, all must entropically return. In this sense it is both sinister and inevitable that the *Ur*-epic should have been a Dunciad.[49]

Pope uses Homeric and Virgilian allusions to emphasise the effeminating powers of Dulness, and to reinforce Martinus Scriblerus' claim that *The Dunciad* is a true epic. Further mighty mothers are invoked, including Thetis and Venus. Thetis' appearance at Achilles' funeral games (where she 'proposed the prizes')[50]

73

Carolyn D. Williams

gives a precedent for Dulness to preside at the coronation games, which are also held in honour of a goddess's favoured son. Whereas the occasional slip-ups in the Iliad and Aeneid struck eighteenth-century readers as jarringly indecorous, Dulness's maternal presence focuses and justifies the obscenities of book II. Under her protective shadow, the games become systematic displays of unselfconscious infantilism.[51] As Dulness's children strip and play before her, they may not lose their adult vigour (Curll, for example, is a seasoned whoremaster whose burning urine indicates venereal disease), but they lack the dignity and responsibility that should accompany true manhood. The games themselves are also suspiciously safe: no boxing, wrestling or weapons. In this respect, in fact, the Phaeacians are more 'manly'. Smedley, the only dunce who might have come to grief, has a lovely time with the mud-nymphs – the baser they are, the softer they fall. 'Soft' is a key word in this episode, linking the charm of yielding femininity with the texture of excrement; effeminacy, which appeared exclusively as excessive refinement in *The Rape of the Lock*, can now be dragged into the dirt:

> First he relates, how sinking to the chin,
> Smit with his mien, the Mud-nymphs suck'd him in:
> How young Lutetia, softer than the down,
> Nigrina black, and Merdamante brown,
> Vy'd for his love in jetty bow'rs below,
> As Hylas fair was ravish'd long ago.
>
> (ii, 331–6)

The reference to Hylas, widely believed to be Hercules' catamite, depicts Smedley as emasculated lover. These heroic games have extended the progress of effeminacy by opening a direct route between boudoir and sewer.

More elegantly effeminate is the 'young Aeneas' (iv, 290) who pays homage to Dulness on his return from the Grand Tour. In eighteenth-century terms he is a textbook case: idle, ignorant, fashionable, sensual, cowardly and potentially corrupt. The last three qualities are conveyed by the following laconic couplet:

> Stol'n from a Duel, follow'd by a Nun,
> And, if a Borough chuse him, not undone.
>
> (iv, 327–8)

He is (over)protected by a trinity of maternal figures: Dulness, Venus and his doting mother, who successfully 'begg'd the blessing of a Rake' (iv, 286). Here Venus, like Thetis, provides a precedent for Dulness: in this case by sheltering Aeneas in a 'kind cloud' that keeps him 'Safe and unseen' (iv, 289–90). The note on this passage does not mention the incident in the Iliad when Venus rescues her son Aeneas from battle (Iliad, v, 311–7); nevertheless, the lurking implication remains that perhaps Aeneas, too, is a mother's boy. Pope's classical parallels often work like this: he debases modern fops and dunces, not by contrasting them with ancient heroes at their best, but by alluding to moments when he feels he has caught Homer and Virgil bending. He uses this technique so skilfully that his victims look more effete than ever. The 'young Aeneas' of *The Dunciad* begins where his great original leaves off: even the Phaeacians could learn from this accomplished youth, who has 'gather'd ev'ry Vice on Christian ground' (iv, 312). The musical requirements of the Roman Catholic Church and Italian opera led to the wholesale production of *castrati*, and the juxtaposition of 'the smooth Eunuch and enamour'd swain' (iv, 310) suggests that these ambiguous creatures may meet other needs. Literally emasculated themselves, they promote effeminacy in others by perverting the (comparatively) healthy course of natural heterosexual desires.[52] Such couplets recall the confusion of that 'Chaos dark and deep' (i, 55) where 'Farce and Epic get a jumbled race' (i, 70). No one should be surprised by inadequate sexual discrimination in the realm of Dulness, when she is so strongly opposed to discrimination in any form.

Vital differences

For Pope, discrimination is all-important; he is forever clarifying differences between right and wrong, wise and foolish, serious and trivial. In the most simple and damning of all his antitheses, he justifies his entire career as satiric poet by appealing to 'The strong Antipathy of Good to Bad' (*Epilogue to the Satires*, ii, 198). It is easy enough to see how manliness and effeminacy fit into Pope's moral scheme. It would be a dangerous mistake, however, to ignore the complexity of Pope's sexual terminology: as this essay has shown, his notions of manlinesss carry a moral, intellectual and political charge that cannot be generated by mere maleness alone. Nor is Pope the uncritical heir of an unchanging monolithic 'masculist' tradition: in their different ways, the Baron, Bays and Ulysses all illustrate the standards of masculinity as interpreted by Pope and his coadjutors. Pope's manly men show their strength of character by their ability to transmute tender passions into motives for noble action. Lesser mortals are debased by desire. The distinction is clearly drawn in 'Martinus Scriblerus his Prolegomena and Illustrations to the Dunciad':

> Thus it being agreed that the constituent qualities of the greater Epic Hero, are *Wisdom*, *Bravery*, and *Love*, from whence springeth *Heroic Virtue*; it followeth that those of the lesser Epic Hero, should be *Vanity*, *Impudence*, and *Debauchery*, from which happy assemblage resulteth *heroic Dulness*, the never-dying subject of this our Poem.[53]

Unfortunately, the conduct of the greater epic heroes is not always so exemplary in epic itself. Nevertheless, Pope is confident that, with appropriate guidance, his readers will be able to distinguish between virtuous pleasure and vile effeminacy. True manliness strikes a balance between the claims of love and battle, so that they are revealed as complementary, not conflicting. It is important to remember that Pope is working within a tradition that sees 'feminine' concerns as an integral, albeit secondary, part of epic. Even Thomas Hobbes, one of Homer's least suave translators, acknowledges the function of epic as a sentimental education for both sexes: 'the work of an Heroick Poem is to raise admiration (principally) for three Vertues, Valour, Beauty, and Love; to the reading whereof Women no less than men have a just pretence'.[54] The ease and resourcefulness with which Pope has adapted this tradition to his own poetic purposes should not be allowed to obscure the significance of his achievement.

Notes

1. Howard D. Weinbrot, '*The Rape of the Lock* and the contexts of warfare', in *The Enduring Legacy*, pp. 21–48.
2. Weinbrot, p. 30.
3. For mock-heroic as a critique of epic coarseness, see Geoffrey Tillotson, *The Rape of the Lock*, introduction, *TE*, ii, 106–7. For the moral and political dangers of effeminacy, and the efficacy of the classical syllabus and the public school system as preservatives of masculine potency, see Jonathan Swift, *The Intelligencer*, 9 (1728). The best introduction to the eighteenth-century concept of the classics as manly learning is Penelope Wilson, 'Classical poetry and the eighteenth-century reader', in *Books and their Readers in Eighteenth-century England*, edited by Isabel Rivers (Leicester, 1982), pp. 69–96.
4. See, for example, Plato, *Republic*, iii, 386ff. He fears that Achilles' description of the afterlife (Odyssey, xi, 487–91) will reduce Homer's

readers to cowards and slaves, because they will believe that there is no such thing as a fate worse than death.

5. Although no systematic examination of epic as a guide to sexual discrimination has yet been published, much useful material related to this subject can be found. Studies that I have not directly quoted, but which were indispensable in the writing of this essay include: Reuben Brower, *Alexander Pope: The Poetry of Allusion* (Oxford, 1959) and *Mirror on Mirror: Translation, Imitation, Parody* (Cambridge, Mass., 1974); Howard Clarke, *Homer's Readers: A Historical Introduction to the 'Iliad' and Odyssey'* (Newark, London and Toronto, 1981); Douglas Knight, *Pope and the Heroic Tradition: A Critical Study of his Iliad* (New Haven, 1951); H. A. Mason, *To Homer through Pope* (London, 1972); Steven Shankman, *Pope's 'Iliad': Homer in the Age of Passion* (Princeton, 1983); Hans-Joachim Zimmermann, *Alexander Popes Noten zu Homer: Eine Manuskript- und Quellenstudie* (Heidelberg, 1966).

6. Pope's *Homer*, *Iliad* and *Odyssey* are italicised; Homer's Iliad and Odyssey are not so distinguished. Pope's close collaboration with his assistants makes it both convenient and just to refer to their joint production as 'Pope's *Homer*'.

7. See *TE*, ix, 4–5.

8. See Aeneid, iv, 261–4.

9. Aeneid, iv, 266.

10. Dryden, *Poems*, iii, 1154.

11. Dryden, *Poems*, iii, 1155.

12. Ludovico Ariosto, *Orlando Furioso in English Heroical Verse*, translated by Sir John Harington (London, 1634), p. 52. (Translation of *Orlando Furioso* [1532], vii, stanza 54, 3–4.)

13. Harington, p. 52.

14. Harington, p. 52 (Ariosto, vii, stanza 55, 3, 5–8).

15. Harington, vii, stanza 52, 5–8, p. 53 (Ariosto, vii, stanza 60, 4–8).

16. Torquato Tasso, *Jerusalem Delivered*, translated by Edward Fairfax (London, 1962), p. 400. (Translation of *Gerusalemme Liberata*, xvi, stanza 30, 5–8.)

17. Edmund Spenser, *The Faerie Queene*, edited by Thomas P. Roche, Jr, with the assistance of C. Patrick O'Donnell, Jr (Harmondsworth, 1978), p. 120).

18. See, for example, Pope's declaration in his preface: 'If my Author had the *Wits* of After Ages for his Defenders, his Translator has had the Beauties of the present for his Advocates; a Pleasure too great to be changed for any Fame in Reversion.' (*TE*, vii, 25, n. 2.)

19. *TE*, vii, 109.

20. The fullest treatment of eighteenth-century reactions to this topic is Yvonne Noble, 'Sex and gender in Gay's *Achilles*', in *John Gay and the Scriblerians*, edited by Peter Lewis and Nigel Wood (London, 1988), pp. 184–215.

21. *TE*, viii, 542 (*Iliad*, xxiv, 130–1).

22. *TE*, viii, 543.

23. *TE*, viii, 543.

24. *TE*, x, 385.

25. *Odyssey*, i, 1–40, *TE*, ix, 25–31.

26. *TE*, x, 378.
27. *TE*, ix, 293 (translation of Odyssey, viii, 521–31).
28. *TE*, x, 335 (translation of Odyssey, xxiii, 233–40).
29. Anthony Collins, *A Discourse of Free-Thinking, Occasioned by the Rise and Growth of a Sect call'd Free-Thinkers* (London, 1713), p. 9. Collins does not support patriarchal authority – or indeed authority of any kind. This does not, however, detract from his belief in the perfection and durability of Homer's works.
30. Richard Bentley, *Remarks upon a Late Discourse of Free-Thinking* (London, 1713), p. 18.
31. See, for example, Thomas Blackwell, *An Enquiry into the Life and Writings of Homer* (London, 1735), p. 301, where the Greeks are inhabitants of 'a free Country, wide and warlike' pitted against 'another of more effeminate manners'.
32. *TE*, x, 13. Compare Odyssey, xiii, 130.
33. *TE*, ix, 278 (translation of Odyssey, viii, 248–9).
34. Eustathius, Archbishop of Thessalonika, and author of voluminous commentaries on Homer, died c.1193.
35. *TE*, ix, 204.
36. Pierre Bayle, *A General Dictionary* (10 vols) translated by John Bernard, Thomas Birch *et al.* (London, 1734–41), s.n. 'Alcinous' (i, 452).
37. The cantata is published in *Cantates françaises* (Paris, 1715), fol. 3e *Cantate*. Quoted in Naomi Hepp, *Homère en France au XVIIᵉ Siècle* (Paris, 1968), p. 594.
38. Lady Mary Wortley Montagu–Count Francesco Algarotti, 30 December 1756 (*The Complete Letters of Lady Mary Wortley Montagu*, edited by R. Halsband, 3 vols (Oxford, 1965–7), iii, 117–18).
39. René Rapin, *Comparaison d'Homère et de Virgile*, in *Oeuvres*, 2 vols (The Hague, 1725), i, 123.
40. *TE*, ix, 298, 300–1. (Compare *Odyssey*, ix, 5–7.) For other instances of favourable presentation of the Phaeacians in Pope's *Homer*, see the Introduction to Pope's *Homer*, *TE*, vii, ccxv–ccxvii.
41. See *Odyssey*, viii, 264–366.
42. 'The tale of Mars and Venus will suit your gay genius, and be such a comfort to you, that I would not have it any other man's property for the world.' (Pope–Broome, 14 July [1723] (Sherburn, ii, 182).
43. *TE*, ix, 260.
44. See *Odyssey*, viii, 307n, *TE*, ix, 280.
45. *TE*, ix, 260–1.
46. *TE*, ix, 261.
47. Emrys Jones, 'Pope and Dulness', *Proceedings of the British Academy*, 54 (1968), 231–63 (p. 242).
48. Michael Seidel, *Satiric Inheritance. Rabelais to Sterne* (Princeton, 1979), p. 231.
49. 'The first Dunciad was the first Epic poem' ('Martinus Scriblerus, of the Poem', *Dunciad Variorum*, *TE*, v, 48).
50. 'Dunciados Periocha: or, Arguments to the Books' (*Dunciad Variorum*, *TE*, v, 55).
51. See Jones, pp. 253–5.
52. A useful starting-point for investigating conventional eighteenth-

century wisdom on homosexuality is G. S. Rousseau, 'Discourses of sexual difference: Beau Wilson and the mythologies of homosexual love', in *Studies in Eighteenth-century Culture*, xix (1989) pp. 289–323. The bibliography is particularly recommended.

53. 'Ricardus Aristarchus of the Hero of the Poem' (*Dunciad, TE*, v, 256).
54. *The Iliads and Odysses of Homer, Translated out of Greek into English, by Tho. Hobbes of Malmesbury* (3rd edn, London, 1686), 'To the Reader. Concerning the Vertues of an Heroick Poem', [A3]v. For further study of Pope's approach to a female readership, see Penelope Wilson, 'Engendering the Reader: "Wit and Poetry and Pope" Once More', in *The Enduring Legacy*, pp. 63–76.

5

'Let Blood and Body bear the fault'
Pope and misogyny

Steve Clark

I

Until recently the issue of misogyny had received little attention in Pope studies. Even when addressed, it tended to be relegated to a minor aspect of a more general misanthropy. The balance-sheet would run something like this: on the debit side, Pope is perceived as harbouring an ultimately disdainful condescension towards Belinda in *The Rape of the Lock*; he produces some consistently unflattering portraiture in *Epistle to a Lady*, and attaches some murkily foetal imagery to the 'Mighty Mother' of Dulness in *The Dunciad* ('How hints, like spawn, scarce quick in embryo lie' (i, 1, 59)). Against this is set the interest in a specifically female sensibility shown in his excursions into elegy and heroic epistle, the affectionate and respectful intimacy of his addresses to the Blount sisters, and his wide-ranging awareness of the forms and conventions through which women in his culture were 'by Man's oppression curst' (*Epistle to a Lady*, 213).

This consensus has been forcefully challenged in recent books by Laura Brown, Felicity Nussbaum and Ellen Pollak.[1] Nussbaum's *The Brink of all We Hate* provides an illuminating generic study of anti-feminist satire between 1660 and 1750. She convincingly demonstrates that this is an appropriate context (though not perhaps the only one) in which to situate such poems as *The Rape of the Lock* and *Epistle to a Lady*. No attempt is made, however, to break with the canon as traditionally conceived: it is assumed that the virulence of this tradition is mitigated through the capacity of literary artistry to 'add nuance to convey the ambivalence inherent in the female sex' (p. 2). Thus Pope's verse need not be condemned as 'finally misogynist' but can be partially redeemed as 'ambiguous and complex in its use of eighteenth-century conventions and commonplaces about the sex' (p. 140). In contrast, Brown's *Alexander Pope* and Pollak's *The Poetics of Sexual Myth* adopt a more strongly iconoclastic position: 'Pope must be scrutinised, doubted and demystified' and his 'explicit values . . . critically and remorselessly questioned' (Brown, p. 3). Each accepts 'the premise that both the aesthetic and the mythic or conventional are functions of ideology', so that within the literary text 'the illusion of complexity' may be no more than 'a sophisticated rhetorical strategy for obscuring an ideological simplicity' (Pollak, pp. 194, 218). Whatever reservations one might hold about their respective approaches[2] (which must, of course, be seen not as a single homogeneous entity but as a diverse context of argument), their work makes it impossible to regard Pope as writing poems 'about women' which establish an impartial taxonomy of an external object of study; it must now be acknowledged that the masculine attitude of ratiocination is necessarily bound up with issues of desire and control. Statements about women are best read as statements by men, with the ultimate function of reconfirming the authority of a masculine poetic voice. I wish to take this new stringency of assessment for granted, and try to move beyond the issue of Pope's reinforcement or qualification of cultural stereotype. I shall begin by examining the ambivalence provoked by his body in the critical reception of his work, and go on to look briefly at its presence in his own writing; then analyse the depiction (or, more accurately, annulment) of the female mind in *The Rape of the Lock* and elsewhere; and conclude by considering the covert reinstatement of a vocabulary of gratified desire in *Epistle to a Lady*.

II

'A Parallel of the Characters of Mr. Dryden and Mr. Pope'[3] has been a virtual set-piece of English criticism for over two hundred years, a sub-genre with its own distinctively sexualised co-ordinates. Matthew Arnold compares these 'two men of such admirable talent, both of them, and one of them, Dryden, a man on all sides, of such energetic and genial power':[4] notice the stress on 'man' (the lack of any parallel term sets up an implicit opposition to non-man or subman) and also on 'genial'. Johnson defines the primary meaning of the term as 'that which contributes to propagation', a sense vividly brought out in De Quincey's remark that, 'Dryden followed, genially, an impulse of his healthy nature. Pope obeyed spasmodically, an overmastering febrile paroxysm'.[5] The contrast is between an essentially virile verse (Saintsbury talks of Dryden's 'infinite "body" '[6]) and an emasculated, though fastidious, dexterity; or, in Johnson's illustration, between the 'varied exuberance of abundant vegetation' and a 'velvet lawn, shaved by the scythe'.[7] The image of tumescence underlying the spatial metaphors in such formulations as T. S. Eliot's, 'When Pope alters, he diminishes. . . . But the effect of the portraits of Dryden is to transform the object into something greater'[8] becomes at times almost comically explicit. Leigh Hunt, for example, contrasts the 'delicate pungent nature' of Pope, 'a genius of a less masculine order', to the 'robuster' Dryden whose 'trenchant sword . . . demanded stoutness in the sheath';[9] in this context it becomes hard not to see a specifically sexual allusion in Leslie Stephen's comment, 'his emotion came in sudden jets and gushes, instead of in a continuous stream'.[10]

Even taking the historical fluctuation of connotation into account, there has been a remarkably consistent gender-reversal in the characterisation of Pope's poetic voice. As early as 1722 he was praised for his 'Female lines';[11] in 1759 Edward Young found the 'masculine melody' of Homer betrayed by Pope's *'effeminate* decoration', which 'put *Achilles* in petticoats a second time';[12] in 1856 George Gilfillan mentioned 'the *feminine* element' that 'mellowed and modified his feelings';[13] and Maynard Mack's 1985 biography referred to 'that quality of his sensibility that some critics have called feminine for lack of an exacter term'.[14] The *locus classicus*, or rather *reductio ad absurdum*, is supplied by Francis Thompson:

The gods are in pairs, male and female; and if Dryden was the Mars of English satire, Pope was the Venus – a very eighteenth-century Venus, quite as conspicuous for malice as for elegance. If a woman's satire were informed with genius and cultivated to the utmost perfection of form by lifelong and exclusive literary practice, one imagines it would be much like Pope's. His style seems to me feminine in what it lacks: the absence of any geniality, any softening humour to abate its mortal thrust. It is feminine in what it has, the malice, the cruel dexterity, the delicate needle point which hardly betrays its light and swift entry yet stings like a bee. Even in his coarseness – as in *The Dunciad* – Pope appears to me female. It is the coarseness of the fine ladies of that material time, the Lady Maries and the rest of them. Dryden is a rough and thick-natured man, cudgelling his adversaries

83

Steve Clark

with coarse speech in the heat and brawl and the bluntness of his
sensibilities; a country squire, who is apt to use the heavy end of his
cutting whip; but when Pope is coarse he is coarse with effort, he goes
out of his way to be nasty, in the evident endeavour to imitate a man. It
is a girl airing the slang of her schoolboy brother.[15]

The direct link is via his comment on 'that sense of unrelieved cruelty
which repels one in much female satire'. Thus Pope is cast as our
Lady of Pain. In terms of an inherited critical iconography it becomes
appropriate to think of him as the victim as well as the perpetrator of
sexist stereotyping. His attention to the nuances and conveniences of
domestic life (Saintsbury describes his verse as 'swept, garnished,
polished)'[16] is regularly denigrated as testimony to a restricted range
of experience. Johnson says of *The Rape of the Lock*: 'the whole detail
of the female-day is here brought before us', a routine 'from which
we have a thousand times turned fastidiously away'. (The idleness,
consumption and display of Belinda's routine are unhesitatingly
regarded as wholly representative.) In discussing Pope the invalid's
'perpetual need of female attendance', Johnson even transforms his
sex: 'he expected that every thing should give way to his ease or
humour, as a child whose parents will not hear her cry has an
unresisted dominion in the nursery'. This is immediately preceded by
a reference to Pope's will as 'polluted by a female resentment', and
followed by a phrase adapted from Young's satire on women: 'He
hardly drank tea without a stratagem'.[17] Hazlitt seems more generous: though 'his Muse . . . grew somewhat effeminate through long
ease and indulgence', Pope's 'retired and narrow' life-style also
helped produce a refined sympathy for 'the sentiments and habitudes
of human life, as he felt them within the little circle of his family and
friends'. Yet this effectively reinforces the association of femininity
with illness, and therefore malice: 'his enmity is effeminate and
petulant from a sense of weakness . . . his delicacy often borders on
sickliness'.[18]

Given the general tenor of anti-Pope polemic, his sexual capacities
would not pass unremarked. Ruffhead tried desperately to hold the
line: 'his constitution was too infirm and delicate to sustain the violent
agitations of licentious pleasures: so that his tender frame preserved
him from those modes of intemperance, to which genius, in
particular, has often proved a victim'.[19] But this in turn simply
provides further ammunition: Edward Ward sneers in *Apollo's
Maggot in his Cups* that the muses 'dab'd on just an Inch of Stuff,/
Enough to show the Gender';[20] the anonymous writer of *Sawney and
Colley* adds 'As impotent in *Spite* as *Love*';[21] and Lady Mary Wortley

84

Montagu cruelly reverses his own line: 'No more for loving made, than to be lov'd'.[22]

The most vivid and notorious instance of 'the delicate little creature' being 'sickened at habits and company which were quite tolerable to robuster men'[23] occurs in Colley Cibber's *Letter to Mr. Pope*. In response to the line 'And has not *Colley* still his Lord, and Whore' (*Arbuthnot*, 97) Cibber recounts his visit to 'a certain House of Carnal Recreation, near the *Haymarket*' in the company of Pope and a 'young Nobleman':

> where his Lordship's Frolick propos'd was to slip his little *Homer*, as he call'd him, at a Girl of the Game, that he might see what sort of Figure a Man of his Size, Sobriety, and Vigour (in Verse) would make, when the frail Fit of Love had got into him; in which he so far succeeded, that the smirking Damsel, who serv'd us with Tea, happen'd to have Charms sufficient to tempt the little-tiny Manhood of Mr. *Pope* into the next Room with her: at which you may imagine, his Lordship was in as much Joy, at what might happen within, as our small Friend could probably be in Possession of it: But I (forgive me all ye mortified Mortals whom his fell Satyr has since fallen upon) observing he had staid as long as without Hazard of his Health he might, I,
>
> > *Prick'd to it by foolish Honesty and Love,*
>
> As *Shakespear* says, without Ceremony, threw open the Door upon him, where I found this little hasty Hero, like a terrible *Tom Tit*, pertly perching upon the Mount of Love! But such was my Surprize, that I fairly laid hold of his Heels, and actually drew him down safe and sound from his Danger.[24]

A fine comic anecdote, and a palpable hit for Cibber. But the episode must also have possessed a powerful emblematic significance to justify being illustrated in four separate broadsheet engravings. It brings out the double nature of the 'Figure' of Pope, his 'Size, Sobriety and Vigour (in Verse)' belied by an actual 'little-tiny Manhood', subject to the officious intervention of nurse-surrogates. But note how 'fell Satyr', combines with 'fallen upon', to stress unexpectedly his poetic virility: '*Tom Tit*, pertly perching upon the Mount of Love' may be an absurd spectacle, but Pope may remain a 'Hero' in his verse provided it is able to repress, eradicate or transform all corporeal reference.[25]

III

Pope took enormous care in constructing 'a willed highly controlled projection . . . of his person into posterity' through the medium of portraiture: of over sixty distinct types, only one (an unauthorised sketch by William Hoare) displays his bodily shape.[26] Within his verse, a similar screening occurs. There is little or no sense of situated perspective even within the later, more elaborately developed, autobiographical persona. Does Eloisa's voice emanate from her cell, from the convent, from the wilderness or from some realm of mystic meditation? Where (indeed who) is the speaker of the *Elegy to the Memory of an Unfortunate Lady* – lover, relation, or supposedly impartial onlooker? Is the tour offered in *Epistle to a Lady* of a supposedly real gallery or does it occur in a purely textual dimension? Everywhere in Pope, even in an explicitly topographical poem such as *Windsor-Forest*, we find tricks of phantasmagoria through abrupt condensation and lack of syntactical connection. As Hazlitt says: 'the little is made great, and the great little',[27] primarily through rapid transitions of scale which make it virtually impossible to establish a fixed centre of sentience.

It is the later satires which introduce a new tactic of brandishing 'the libel'd Person, and the pictur'd Shape' (*Arbuthnot*, 353). The pre-emptive poignancy of lines such as, 'In me what Spots (for Spots I have) appear' (*Satire* II i, 55), 'I cough like *Horace*, and tho' lean, am short' (*Arbuthnot*, 116), and 'Weak tho' I am of limb, and short of sight' (*Epistle* I i, 49) heightens the impact of the pervasive vocabulary of martial valour, and Pope's repeatedly declared willingness to 'perish in the gen'rous Cause' of moral and literary ideals (*Satire* II i, 117). The effect is well caught in a line from Statius quoted in one of Pope's contributions to *The Guardian*:[28] *major in exiguo regnabat corpore virtus* (great courage was sovereign in that tiny frame), and lies behind the famous proclamation:

> Ask you what Provocation I have had?
> The strong Antipathy of Good to Bad.
> When Truth or Virtue an Affront endures,
> Th'Affront is mine, my Friend, and should be yours.
> Mine, as a Foe profess'd to false Pretence,
> Who thinks a Coxcomb's Honour like his Sense;
> Mine as a Friend to ev'ry worthy mind;
> And mine as Man, who feel for all mankind.
> *Fr.* You're strangely proud.
>   *P.* So proud, I am no Slave:
> So impudent, I own myself no Knave:
> So odd, my Country's Ruin makes me grave.
> Yes, I am proud; I must be proud to see
> Men not afraid of God, afraid of me:
>   (*Epilogue to the Satires*, Dialogue Two, 197–209)

The persuasiveness of this 'Heroical disposition'[29] depends in large measure on its capacity both to carry and suppress a negative connotation of actual physical prowess. This is particularly evident in 'strong Antipathy', which can perhaps be glossed as 'the physically weak possess strength in the cause of good', but this sense must admit the counter-possibility of 'strong in antipathy but in nothing else and therefore probably not even in that'. It is because this risk is faced so directly that the pose comes across as something other than ludicrous charade.

But this proclaimed ethical virility can be turned inside out by stressing its powerful neo-platonic implications. Howard Weinbrot notes that, 'one essential aspect of Pope's self-defence both before and after *The Dunciad* was his insistence upon the brave and masculine spirit chained within his warped body';[30] the rhetoric of righteous corporeal struggle can easily be transposed to ascetic renunciation, with souls becoming 'Dull sullen pris'ners in the body's cage' and spirits distilled from their 'kindred dregs' (*Unfortunate Lady*, 18, 25–6). Thus in *Eloisa to Abelard*, Abelard's situation becomes emblematic of that of the poetic voice, the castrated male as recipient of the tribute of female passion and hence deemed worthy of elevation into godhead.[31] In *The Rape of the Lock*, the power of the Baron can be seen as deriving as much from a gesture of symbolic self-emasculation as from actual possession of the lock;[32] and in *Epistle to a Lady* Martha Blount will be idealised as a 'softer Man' (272). In Pope's satiric verse, the most vivid example of this repudiation of the desiring body is undoubtedly the portrait of Sporus.

One is immediately struck by how much of the detail is applicable to Pope himself. 'Ass's milk' (306) was fed to invalids; Johnson comments on Pope's difficulty with personal hygiene (a 'painted Child of Dirt' (310)), and on his beautiful features as a child ('A Cherub's face, a Reptile all the rest' (331));[33] the 'familiar Toad' (319) recalls Dennis's famous gibe of 'hunch-backed Toad'.[34] It is difficult also to see how Pope's own exploitation of 'Antithesis' can be distinguished from that for which Sporus is condemned. If anything, it would appear to imply an unlikely equality between their respective compositions:

> His Wit all see-saw between *that* and *this*,
> Now high, now low, now Master up, now Miss,
> And he himself one vile Antithesis.
> Amphibious Thing! that acting either Part,

87

The trifling Head, or the corrupted Heart!
Fop at the Toilet, Flatt'rer at the Board,
Now trips a Lady, and now struts a Lord.
Eve's Tempter thus the Rabbins have exprest,
A Cherub's face, a Reptile all the rest;
Beauty that shocks you, Parts that none will trust,
Wit that can creep, and Pride that licks the dust.

(323-33)

The original Sporus, Nero's slave boy and catamite, was castrated.
Pope, in contrast, insists on the voluptuous prowess of the
'Amphibious Thing'. 'Thing' must necessarily have the habitual play
on genitals,[35] 'amphibious' in that it partakes of opposed elements, and
in 'acting either Part' possesses knowledge of the enjoyment of both
'Lady' and 'Lord'. The 'reciprocating motion'[36] of 'see-saw' takes on a
specifically erotic connotation, as do the chiming thrusts of 'now
Master up, now Miss'. Even 'Half Froth, half Venom, spits himself
abroad' becomes a paradoxical tribute to ejaculatory capacity (320);
'*Eve*'s Tempter', after all, engaged in a famously successful seduction.
(This is further reinforced both by 'trips' (usually taken as a mannered
gait, but also suggesting both a literal and metaphorical fall to the
ground) and by the secondary erectile sense of 'strut': 'to swell; to
protuberate' (Johnson 2).) Wherein then lies Pope's superiority?

Not Fortune's Worshipper, nor Fashion's Fool,
Not Lucre's Madman, nor Ambition's Tool,
Not proud, nor servile, be one Poet's praise
That, if he pleas'd, he pleas'd by manly ways;

(334-7)

'Manly ways' may appear to set up an unequivocal opposition to
Sporus's 'florid Impotence' (317) (what has been called Pope trying
to pass himself off as 'the phallus for the poetry of the age'.[37] Yet the
Sporus-figure is sufficiently indeterminate in gender to assimilate the
erotic experience of both sexes: Pope seeks to establish not a virile but
a wholly desexualised poetic voice, one whose authority depends on
its own incapacitation, its distance from this carnally proficent
simulacrum of his own bodily deformity.[38]

IV

This ambivalence of gender also extends to Pope's two most intimate
renditions of female desire, the *Elegy to the Memory of an Unfortunate
Lady* and *Eloisa to Abelard*. The Lady's suicide demonstrates, as Brean
Hammond says, her 'essentially *virile*' character.[39] In acting the

88

'Roman's part' she displays not 'too tender' but 'too firm a heart' (7–8), and an 'ambition' that elevates her to the rank of 'Kings and Heroes' (13, 16). It is the masculine narrator whose soul 'now melts in mournful lays' (77). Eloisa's monologue in fact incorporates numerous statements that Pope's direct source attributed to her emasculated lover. In Hughes it is Abelard whose passion 'grows furious by Impotence' in the 'dark Cells of the House'; who laments 'the Tumult of my Senses, and that Contrariety which reigns in my Heart' through the power of the 'Jealous God'; who describes himself as 'a distracted Lover, unquiet in the midst of Silence and restless in this abode of Peace and Repose'; who finds it 'difficult in our Sorrow to distinguish Penitence from Love', and who begs Heloise to 'thrust your self between God and me, and be a Wall of Separation'.[40] The superimposition of voices in Pope's pert and impudent close – 'He best can paint 'em, who shall feel 'em most' (366) – also insists on the function of female emotion as 'sad similitude' of the 'griefs' of a 'future Bard' (359–60), and by extension, any male reader.[41]

Much of the critical argument surrounding *Eloisa to Abelard* – particularly on the questions of dramatic progression and ironic distance – has been triggered by a sense of Eloisa as a kind of conduit for a passion ultimately extraneous to her situation and character. In this, I would argue, she is wholly representative of Pope's characterisation of women: the 'craving Void' (94) becomes the site of a double movement – an annulment of mental activity, and an introjection of uninhibited desire. My most contentious premiss is that this displaced physical passion need not be seen as a specifically female attribute, and in fact is best understood in the context of Pope's more general repudiation of the desiring body.

It will here be useful to look at some examples of how the erotic subtext functions in *The Rape of the Lock*. Ariel threatens that any spirit found 'careless of his Charge' (ii, 123):

> Shall feel sharp Vengeance soon o'ertake his Sins,
> Be stopt in *Vials*, or transfixt with *Pins*;
> Or plung'd in Lakes of bitter *Washes* lie,
> Or wedg'd whole Ages in a *Bodkin's* Eye:
> *Gums* and *Pomatums* shall his Flight restrain,
> While clog'd he beats his silken Wings in vain;
> Or Alom-*Stypticks* with contracting Power
> Shrink his thin Essence like a rivell'd Flower.
> Or as *Ixion* fix'd, the Wretch shall feel
> The giddy Motion of the whirling Mill,
> In Fumes of burning Chocolate shall glow,
> And tremble at the Sea that froaths below!
>
> (ii, 125–36)

Steve Clark

The envisaged 'Vengeance' involves three distinct levels of sexual anxiety: engulfment ('stopt in', 'plung'd in', and 'clog'd'; also 'the Sea that froaths below'), detumescence ('contracting', 'shrink', and 'rivell'd'; 'Stypticity', the power of stanching blood (Johnson 1)), and castration ('sharp', 'Pins', 'Bodkin', and especially the 'whirling' blades of the coffee 'Mill'). Though the urbanely surreal lyricism of the passage may qualify these punitive undertones, it does not detract from the central point: Ariel's assertion of authority and delegation of duties is reinforced rather than undermined by the underlying sexual reference, and as such is representative of masculine discourse in the poem.

In contrast, female speech is continually demeaned through a presumably unconscious stratum of erotic innuendo. Dennis commented that Pope 'could not forbear putting Bawdy into the Mouth of his own Patroness',[42] and this accurately reflects the sense, not of innate impulses surfacing through cultural repression, as some recent critics may have it, but of an insidious form of control exerted through the implanting of a conveniently submissive anatomical destiny.

The Rape of the Lock immediately announces its subject as 'am'rous Causes' (i, 1), but this is quickly broken down into a further division of spheres of volition:

> Say what strange Motive, Goddess! cou'd compel
> A well-bred *Lord* t'assault a gentle *Belle*?
> Oh say what stranger Cause, yet unexplor'd,
> Cou'd make a gentle *Belle* reject a *Lord*?
>
> (i, 7–10)

The latinate puns – 'assaults' or leaps on (*adsulto*), 'rejects' or pushes off (*reicio*) – appear to suggest that both parties are equally subject to the impulses that arise from 'Things below' (i, 36). The Baron's behaviour, however, is dignified by 'Motive' ('that which determines the choice' (Johnson1)), whereas Belinda is to be rendered intelligible by disclosing a 'Cause, yet unexplor'd'. The opposition has become one of the commonplaces of modern analytic philosophy: she is placed in a physical universe of predetermined cause and effect: he belongs to a human realm of free decision.[43] It may seem anachronistic to accentuate the opposition between these terms; but this distribution of intentionality is consistent throughout: for example, the coffee that dulls Belinda's alertness 'Sent up in vapours to the *Baron*'s Brain/New Stratagems' (iii, 119–20), and in ii, 29–32 he is

90

endowed with more mental activity in two couplets than she displays throughout the entire poem.

'*Belinda* smil'd, and all the World was gay', but only because a sylph is available to take on the burden of all 'careful Thoughts' (ii, 52, 54). The implications of this recurrent deflection have generally been overlooked. Alastair Fowler, for example, stresses that Pope's machinery 'has the originality of being thoroughly interiorised'.[44] At no time, however, is the opposite possibility considered: that the function of the sylphs is not to endow the heroine's mind with a lyrical grace and emotional complexity, but to effect an elaborate displacement of volition which allows it to be presented as a virtual interior void. What is the residue once the machinery has been removed? There are many examples of a curious double motion whereby episodes that should enlarge the range of Belinda's mental activity actually suggest its nullity. Ariel inquires somewhat doubtfully: 'If e'er one Vision touch'd thy infant Thought' (i, 29), and his scepticism as to the attention span of his charge proves fully justified, since his warning immediately vanishes from her head (i, 120). The question, 'What guards the Purity of melting Maids' (i, 71) is answered by ' 'Tis but their *Sylph*, the wise Celestials know' (i, 77), and there is a similar denial of agency in 'oft, in Dreams, Invention we bestow' (ii, 99), or in Belinda's own inquiry: 'What mov'd my Mind with youthful Lords to rome?' (iv, 159).

As Dennis noted, the 'Machines . . . do not in the least influence that Action; they neither prevent the Danger of *Belinda*, nor promote it, nor retard it', citing in particular Umbriel's journey in the fourth canto: 'How absurd was it then for this *Ignis Fatuus* to take a Journey down to the *central Earth*, for no other Purpose than to give her the *Spleen*, whom he left and found in the Height of it'.[45] The sheer oddity of this procedure has been insufficiently acknowledged: Belinda is frozen in a histrionic tableau while her 'Rage, Resentment and Despair' (iv, 9) are imported from elsewhere. In similar fashion, the poetic voice imperiously decrees when her fictive existence shall be terminated, 'Then cease, bright Nymph! to mourn thy ravish'd Hair' (v, 141), and commands that she shall be henceforth placated by the lock's stellification (though, in one last twist, into a constellation vulgarly known as 'Bernice's Bush').[46]

In consequence, critical commentary on Belinda has tended to be a perpetual speaking for: it is always someone else who stocks the 'moving Toyshop' of her heart (i, 100). The absence of any assertive self-consciousness within the poem results in an almost irresistible impulse on behalf of the reader to deflect agency away from her onto some other causal factor that precludes choice or dissent. David Fairer, for example, remarks that, 'Any censure of coquettish "levity" of heart is deflected onto the sylphs who "contrive it all" (i, 104)'.[47] The alternative candidate for this role of determining principle is what Cleanth Brooks calls 'congeries of biological processes'.[48] Murray Krieger, for example, notes that 'the unaesthetic world of biological and domestic facts always lurks beneath';[49] and Pat Rogers finds 'a profoundly physical, even biological, cast to many areas of the text', commenting that Belinda's 'outrage at the Baron's assault is all the greater because it represents what subconsciously she has been wishing for and inviting all along'.[50] One need not endorse the tendency of recent feminist criticism to read the 'rape' as an actual 'violent defloration of chastity' to find these remarks injudicious. It is surely misguided, however, to pillory individual critics for such remarks: instead what should be stressed is the way in which the poem itself solicits this kind of extrapolation. As Hugo Reichard puts it: 'Pope has established the conflict of his scene not in the consciousness of the coquette but in the insight of the reader';[51] and so the pleasure of the text should be seen not as an amoral jouissance (' 'Tis a sort of writing very like tickling'[52]) but in the gratification to be derived from a discursive mastery.

Where Restoration satire tends to be wholly unconcerned with the mental processes of women (John Oldham's *Satyr upon a Woman*, Robert Gould's *Love Given O're*, and Richard Ames's *The Folly of Love*, for example, are all heavily reliant on a simple correlation between seductive appearance and inner corruption – 'Within a gawdy Case a nasty Soul'[53]), Pope introduces at least the possibility of a far more nuanced inference of female personality from exterior gesture. He is prepared to acknowledge that 'Motions, Looks, and Eyes' (*RL*, iii, 15) might disclose 'Th' exactest traits of Body or of Mind' (*Epistle to a Lady*, 191), and something distinctive comes into English anti-feminist satire with this desire to master by explaining rather than by chiding, berating, denouncing. But the oft-noted imagery of fragile enclosure in *The Rape of the Lock* – the 'painted Vessel' on the Thames (ii, 47), the 'frail *China* Jar' (ii, 106), and the 'Silver Bound' and 'wide Circumference' of the petticoat (ii, 121–2) – implies that the female mind has no 'imprison'd Essences' to 'exhale' (ii, 94), and many of the poem's most celebrated effects, such as the complex transformations between sun, eyes and gaze, depend on the play between internal and external allowed by its luminous void. The authorial privilege of absolute insight (which itself represents an internalisation of the recurrent injunction in anti-feminist satire to penetrate the boudoir's private space: 'Open her secret Boxes'[54]) is rewarded by the spectacle of a 'vacant Brain' crowded by 'gay Ideas' that are externally derived and controlled (i, 83). This mental vacancy manoeuvres almost any critical commentary into a position of implicit condescension – of explaining what Belinda cannot comprehend, her own motives and desires – and allows it the satisfaction of expounding them from the perspective of an omniscient masculinity.

V

It has frequently been noted, particularly in relation to the enervation of Sir Plume and the narcissism of the Baron, that Belinda is herself the most virile figure in the poem: 'an arrant Ramp and a Tomrigg', as Dennis observed.[55] The best-known instance occurs in the Homeric parallels to the dressing table scene, where 'awful Beauty puts on all its Arms' (i, 139). But similar power is evident in Belinda's authority to summon forth 'The various Off'rings of the World' (i, 130), in her bellicosity at cards, where she 'Burns to encounter' her opponents and 'decide their Doom' (a prospect which 'swells her Breast with Conquests yet to come' (iii, 25-8)), and the readiness of the 'fierce Virago' to command 'To Arms' (v, 37) (an epithet linking her to the passion of 'fierce *Othello*' who 'in so loud a strain/Roar'd for the Handkerchief that caus'd his Pain' (v, 105-6)). When Ariel peers into the 'close Recesses of the Virgin's Thought', he sees an 'Earthly Lover lurking' in an otherwise transparent 'Mind' (iii, 140-44). Though customarily interpreted as the sender of the morning's *billet-doux* or as a subconscious yearning for the Baron's assault, this figure may also be read as signifying the presence of a masculine desire within Belinda herself.[56]

This seemingly bizarre suggestion can be usefully related to the famous couplet in *Epistle to a Lady*: 'Men, some to Bus'ness, some to Pleasure take;/ But ev'ry Woman is at heart a Rake' (215-16). 'Rake' is emphatically a masculine term: Johnson defines it as 'a loose, disorderly, vicious, wild, gay, thoughtless fellow, a man addicted to pleasure', citing this usage from Pope. So the second line could be glossed as 'every woman is at heart a man' – or at the very least a potent desiring body. The force of the singular term overpowers the comparatively vague and etiolated 'Bus'ness' and 'Pleasure' of the anonymous mass of 'Men'. Notice how much weaker the more logical version of the same sentiment is in, for example, Gould's line,

'Thus if they durst, all Women would be Whores', or the direct paraphrase offered in *Sawney and Colley*, 'For *ev'ry Woman*, you are sure,/ Is in her *Heart* a *very Whore*'.[57]

The precedent of Rochester as rake and wit hangs heavily over Pope's erotic vocabulary ('we must with Wilmot own,/ The Cordial Drop of Life is Love alone' (*Epistle I vi*, 126–7)),[58] a point which is neatly brought out in 'On lying in the Earl of Rochester's Bed at Atterbury':

> With no poetick ardors fir'd,
> I press the bed where *Wilmot* lay:
> That here he lov'd, or here expir'd,
> Begets no numbers grave or gay.
>
> (1–4)

'I press' seems a sadly forlorn and solitary activity in a location far more suitable for expiring in 'ardors' of a different kind – an exclusion made poignantly explicit in the verb 'begets'. Pope's customary attitude to Rochester is more censorious,[59] yet the persona of 'The gayest Valetudinaire,/Most thinking Rake alive' ('A Farewell to London', 39–40, *TE*, v, 128–32) appears with some frequency in the correspondence. The most sustained poetic exercise in this vein comes in *Sober Advice from Horace*, which prompted Thomas Bentley to comment: 'What an *Erection* of Wit, what a *Tentigo* of Parts in his Notes! How he triumphs, and dashes his Sp(erm) about him!'[60] A few couplets give the general flavour:

> When sharp with Hunger, scorn you to be fed,
> Except on *Pea-Chicks*, at the *Bedford-head*?
> Or, when a tight, neat Girl, will serve the Turn,
> In errant Pride continue stiff, and burn?
> I'm a plain Man, whose Maxim is profest,
> 'The Thing at hand is of all Things the *best*'.
>
> (149–54)

This is Pope playing 'Philosopher and Rake' (158) with some panache, though without quite living up to Bentley's billing.[61] There is none of the personal risk, the plaintive vulnerability, the fear of betrayal by the body, which for Rochester is the condition of encountering another's desire. Instead, for all the implied camaraderie of the stews, there is a certain star-struck gloating over the spectacle of self-destructive aristocratic excess:

And pity Men of Pleasure still in Pain!
Survey the Pangs they bear, the Risques they run,
Where the most lucky are but last undone.

(50–2)

But the 'Men of Pleasure' undergo some unexpected metamorphoses. Bentley observes that 'our *Sober Adviser*, finding *Fufidius* in HORACE, turns him into *Fufidia*, and then persecutes the poor imaginary Woman with the most *horrid* and *brutal ribaldry* for which there's not the least Foundation in the original'.[62] This is not an isolated instance: Pope himself draws attention to his consistent tactic of gender-reversal in his opening Bentleian footnote: 'Why Imitated? . . . A Metaphrast had not turned *Tigellius*, and *Fufidius*, *Malchinus* and *Gargonius* . . . into so many LADIES. *Benignus, hic, hunc*, &c. all of the Masculine Gender: Every School-boy knows more than our Imitator' (*TE*, v, 74).

In his preface to Juvenal's *Sixth Satire*, Dryden observes that 'my author makes their lust the most heroic of their vices', and that 'to bid us beware of their artifices, is a kind of silent acknowledgement that they have more wit than men'.[63] The competitive and aggressive sexuality of the central sequence of portraits in *Epistle to a Lady* is likewise identified with this quality of wit-as-aggression: Calypso (48), Philomedé (76), Flavia (87), and Atossa (127); even Narcissa seeks to 'pique all mortals, yet affect a name' (61). So 'Turn then from Wits' (101) may seem to be the central injunction of the poem. But what exactly does this entail? Should we regard 'Wit' here as a disastrous imbalance of the imaginative faculty, the scandalous appropriation of a masculine prerogative, or 'inexorably a sign both of its own absence and of the absence of the presence it usurps' and thus 'no wit at all'[64]? I would prefer, however, to relate the term in more direct fashion to Pope's Restoration predecessors: Flavia's credo, 'while we live, to live' (90), is surely that of a libertine intellectual:

Wise Wretch! with Pleasures too refin'd to please,
With too much Spirit to be e'er at ease,
With too much Quickness ever to be taught,
With too much Thinking to have common Thought:
Who purchase Pain with all that Joy can give,
And die of nothing but a Rage to live.

(95–100)

(The attributes of 'Spirit', 'Quickness', 'Thinking', 'Pain', 'Joy', and 'Rage' make the preceding accusation of 'Impotence of mind' (93) almost ludicrously inappropriate.) Similarly, Narcissa (53–68) is a 'fool to Pleasure' in whom 'Passion burns'; she is governed by whim, prone to debt, aristocratically disdainful of 'Good-nature', and drawn towards 'Atheism' and 'Heathen' behaviour. And it is tempting to see in 'Sin in State, majestically drunk', with a 'barren Bride' though 'frank to all beside' (69–72), at least a passing reference to Charles II (whose name occurs six lines later).

With Atossa (115–50), as with Sporus, the problem of duplication is particularly acute. It has often been observed that she occupies Pope's own position as satirist. Endowed with 'Fury', 'Rage', and 'Hate', she 'shines, in exposing Knaves, and painting Fools' (recalling 'I must paint it' (16), and anticipating 'our Scorn of Fools' (276)); she 'Finds all her life one warfare upon earth', powerfully, almost blatantly, echoing his own words, 'The Life of a Wit is a Warfare upon Earth'.[65] How can such a tempestuous figure possibly be reconciled with the initial proposition, 'Most Women have no Characters at all' (2)? Perhaps because female 'character' as something *composed* (in the various senses of the word) is being ideally embodied in the malleable, mute and somewhat abjectly acquiescent Martha Blount. For all the initial insistence on 'great Atossa's mind', she is depicted as incapable of any directed intellectual activity: 'No Thought advances, but her Eddy Brain/ Whisks it about, and down it goes again' (121–2).[66] One may even, in the light of what was said earlier about Belinda, choose to regard her mental life as a series of quasi-allegorical forces manifesting themselves through, rather than possessed by, her. But once the key emotional and psychological terms of her portrait are assembled – 'Passion', 'Rage', 'Fury', 'Wit', 'Pleasure', 'Scandal', 'Revenge', 'Violence', 'Hate', 'Gratitude', 'Passion', 'Love', 'Spirit', 'Warmth', and 'Wealth' – it surely becomes difficult to deny *her* the title of 'bolder man' (130).[67]

Thus Pope's discursive authority ('Fine by defect, and delicately weak' (44)) yet again appears to be constituted through an exorcism of desire: in this case, the object of repudiation has become a female body invested with a masculine potency. These gender terms themselves may now appear hopelessly indeterminate in relation to his work. Perhaps, though, we may come to regard this as one of its greatest strengths.

Notes

1. Felicity A. Nussbaum, *The Brink of All We Hate: English Satires on Women, 1660–1750* (Lexington, 1984); Laura Brown, *Alexander Pope*

(Oxford, 1985); Ellen Pollak, *The Poetics of Sexual Myth: Gender and Ideology in the Verse of Swift and Pope* (Chicago, 1985). See also the introduction to *The New Eighteenth Century*.

2. Briefly, Nussbaum's lack of a clearly oppositional voice (rectified in her later work) leads to numerous local collusions (Martha Blount, for example, becomes 'both the subject of panegyric and precariously like the sisters whom *we* all find morally repugnant' (p. 156)); Brown presents Pope 'as a consistent advocate of the beliefs and ambitions of the capitalist landlords and of an imperialist consensus' (p. 3), thereby positing a monolithic mercantilist ideology that wholly subsumes the actual political divisions between Walpole's government and the Tory opposition; and Pollak never satisfactorily reconciles the considerable finesse of her rhetorical criticism with the ponderous determinism of a globally conceived patriarchal order.

3. The title of W. H. Dilworth's fourteen-page itemised balance-sheet, appended to *The Life of Alexander Pope* (London, 1759), pp. 138–51.

4. Introduction to *The English Poets*, edited by T. H. Ward, 4 vols (London, 1880), p.xxxviii; reprinted as 'The study of poetry', in *Essays in Criticism*, Second Series (London, 1888).

5. 'Lord Carlisle on Pope', *Tait's Edinburgh Magazine*, April–July 1851; *The Collected Writings of Thomas De Quincey*, edited by David Masson, 14 vols (Edinburgh, 1889–90), xi, 119.

6. George Saintsbury, 'Pope and the later Couplet', *A History of English Prosody*, 3 vols (London, 1908), ii, 456.

7. 'Pope', *Lives of the Poets*, edited by G. B. Hill, 3 vols (Oxford, 1905), iii, 82–276 (pp. 222–3).

8. 'John Dryden', *TLS*, 9 June 1921, reprinted in *Selected Essays* (3rd edn, London 1951), pp. 305–16 (p. 310).

9. *Wit and Humour, Selected from the English Poets* (London, 1846), p. 281; preface to *Poetical Works* (London, 1832), p. xxiii.

10. Leslie Stephen, 'Epistles and satires', *Alexander Pope* (London, 1880), p. 189. Compare De Quincey: 'all his thinking proceeded by isolated and discontinuous jets', *North British Review*, August 1848, *Works*, xi, 63.

11. Thomas Gilbert, *Poems on Several Occasions* (London, 1722), p. 110.

12. *Conjectures on Original Composition, in a Letter to the Author of Sir Charles Grandison* (London, 1759), p. 59.

13. 'Satire and satirists', *Scottish Review*, January 1856, p. 22.

14. Maynard Mack, *Alexander Pope: A Life* (New Haven, 1985), p. 29.

15. Francis Thompson, 'Pope', *A Renegade Poet and Other Essays* (Boston, 1910), pp. 191–200 (pp. 197–9).

16. Saintsbury, ii, 451.

17. *Lives*, iii, 234, 197, 198, 200: 'For her *own* breakfast she'll *project a scheme*/Nor take her *Tea* without a *stratagem*', *Love of Fame, the Universal Passion*, Satire VI (187–8).

18. 'On Dryden and Pope', *Lectures on the English Poets*, in *The Complete Works of William Hazlitt*, edited by P. P. Howe, 21 vols (London, 1930–34), v, 68–85, (pp. 71, 69). The most detailed analysis of Pope's medical history is Marjorie Nicolson and G. S. Rousseau, *'This Long Disease, My Life': Alexander Pope and the Sciences* (Princeton, 1968), pp. 7–82. For

recent shorter summaries, see Mack, 'The least Thing like a Man in England', *'Collected in Himself'; Essays Critical, Biographical, and Bibliographical on Pope and some of his Contemporaries* (Delaware, 1982), pp. 372–92; and *Alexander Pope*, pp. 153–8; Brean Hammond, *Pope* (Brighton, 1986), pp. 9–13; and Leopold Damrosch, Jr, *The Imaginative World of Alexander Pope* (Los Angeles, 1987) pp. 19–24.

19. Owen Ruffhead, *The Life of Alexander Pope* (London, 1769), p. 20.

20. *Apollo's Maggot in his Cups* (London, 1729), p. 19.

21. *Sawney and Colley, a Poetical Dialogue: Occasioned by A Late Letter from the Laureat of St. James's, To the Homer of Twickenham* (London, 1742), p. 7.

22. *Verses address'd to the Imitator of the First Satire of the Second Book of Horace. By a Lady* (London, 1733) 62; cf. *Epistle to a Lady*, 166.

23. 'Prior, Gay, and Pope', *The English Humorists of the Eighteenth Century*, lecture 4 (London, 1853), p. 214.

24. *A Letter from Mr. Cibber to Mr. Pope, Inquiring into the Motives that might induce him in his Satyrical Works, to be so frequently fond of Mr. Cibber's Name* (London, 1742), pp. 47–8.

25. For other tributes to Pope's poetic virility, see *A True Character of Mr. Pope, and his Writings*, May 1716, in *The Critical Works of John Dennis*, edited by Edward Niles Hooker, 2 vols (Baltimore, 1939–43), ii, 103–4 ('The grosser part of his gentle Readers believe the Beast to be more than Man; as Ancient Rusticks took his Ancestors for those Demy-Gods they call *Fauns* and *Satyrs*'; and more recently Allen Tate's 'Mr Pope', *Collected Poems 1919–1976* (New York, 1977), p. 6: 'Ladies leaned out more out of fear than pity/ For Pope's tight back was rather a goat's than a man's' (3–4).

26. David Piper, *The Image of the Poet: British Poets and their Portraits* (Oxford, 1982), p. 58.

27. Hazlitt, *Works*, v, 72.

28. 'The Club of Little Men', *The Guardian*, edited by James Calhoun Stephens (Lexington, 1982), no. 92 (26 June 1713), p. 328.

29. Appendix I, *TE*, v, 205: 'the Heroical disposition and high courage of the Writer, who dar'd to stir up such a formidable, irritable, and implacable race of mortals'.

30. Howard D. Weinbrot, *Alexander Pope and the Traditions of Formal Verse Satire* (Princeton, 1982), p. 143.

31. 'Abelard's being rendered impotent by the cruelty of Eloisa's friends, did not in the least abate the warmth of her passion for him, but seemed rather to increase it' (Dilworth, p. 33).

32. In the famous couplet, iii, 147–8, 'spread. . . wide' appears to identify the *'Forfex'* with Belinda herself, (di)splayed for the Baron's pleasure. ('Spread' signifies sexual availability throughout the misogynist tradition: for example, 'What care our Drunken Dames to whom they spread', *The Satires of Decimus Junius Juvenalis* no. 6, 421, in Dryden, *Poems*, iii, 694–719.) But the image also allows a possible reversal of power: the threat of castration carried by the equation of woman with 'Sheers' is borne out by the subsequent fate of the sylph 'clos'd' within the 'fatal Engine' and 'cut. . . in twain' by the 'meeting Points' of blades, legs, vaginal lips (iii, 149–53). See Ellen Pollak's fine discussion of these

lines, *The Poetics of Sexual Myth*, pp. 100–2.
33. 'His face was not displeasing, and his eyes were animated and vivid'; 'His weakness made it very difficult for him to be clean', *Lives*, iii, 197.
34. 'As there is no Creature in Nature so venomous, there is nothing so stupid and so impotent as a hunch-back'd Toad', *Reflections Critical and Satyrical, upon a late Rhapsody, call'd, An Essay on Criticism, Works*, i, 415. Dennis also refers to 'that Angel Face and Form of his', *True Character*, ii, 105.
35. *OED* 11c: 'privy member, privy parts'. Played upon interminably in *Sober Advice from Horace* (90, 103, 136, 154). Edward Ward mocks Pope's 'poor thingless Body', *Apollo's Maggot*, p. 19.
36. Johnson 1. Compare Lovelace on 'what can be done by the *amorous see-saw*', Samuel Richardson, *Clarissa or The History of a Young Lady*, edited by Angus Ross (Harmondsworth, 1985), letter 108, p. 424.
37. Hammond, *Pope*, p. 159.
38. For more on Sporus as Pope's 'antiself', see Dustin Griffin, *Alexander Pope: The Poet in his Poems* (Princeton, 1978), pp. 178–88, especially on 'Sporus' perverted sexuality and Pope's virtual sexlessness' (p. 187).
39. *Pope*, p. 173.
40. *Letters of Abelard and Heloise* (3rd edn, London, 1713), pp. 74–8. The significant adaptations are nearly all from Abelard's third letter (pp. 72–85).
41. For biographical parallels with Pope's own correspondence, see James A. Winn, 'Pope plays the rake: his letters to ladies and the making of the *Eloisa*', *The Art of Alexander Pope*, edited by Howard Erskine-Hill and Anne Smith (London, 1979), pp. 89–118; Patricia Meyer Spacks, 'imaginations warm and tender: Pope and Lady Mary', *South Atlantic Quarterly*, 83 (1984), 207–15; and Mack, *Alexander Pope*, pp. 326–31.
42. *Remarks upon Mr. Pope's Translation of Homer, Works*, ii, 130. For fuller discussion, see Earl Wasserman, 'The limits of allusion in *The Rape of the Lock*, *JEGP*, 65 (1966), 425–44; Wolfgang E. H. Rudat, 'Belinda's "Painted Vessel"': allusive technique in *The Rape of the Lock*', *Tennessee Studies in Literature*, 19 (1974), 49–55; and, more sceptically, Penelope Wilson, 'Engendering the reader: "Wit and poetry and Pope" once more', in *The Enduring Legacy*, pp. 63–78.
43. According to the *OED*, 'cause' can still be used of human volition, although its primary meaning would be 'that which produces an effect' in the physical realm. Pope's psychological usages regularly imply determination by an external force: for example, Belinda's dream 'That ev'n in Slumber caus'd her Cheek to glow' (i, 24); the Gnomes 'caus'd Suspicion when no Soul was rude' (iv, 73); and Othello roars for 'the Handkerchief that caus'd his Pain' (v, 106). Other notable usages are 'The same Self-love, in all, becomes the cause' (*Essay on Man*, iii, 271), and 'Something as dim to our internal view,/ Is thus, perhaps, the cause of most we do' (*Epistle to Cobham*, 49–50). For further discussion, see Rebecca Ferguson, *The Unbalanced Mind: Pope and the Rule of Passion* (Brighton, 1986), pp. 32–63. Dennis's objection that 'The Word *compel* supposes the Baron to be a Beast, and not a free Agent', presupposes that, unlike Belinda, he initially possesses choice (*Remarks on Mr. Pope's Rape of the Lock. In Several Letters to a Friend*, May 1714, published

1728, *Works*, ii, 350).
44. Alastair Fowler, 'The paradoxical machinery of *The Rape of the Lock*' in *Alexander Pope: Essays for the Tercentenary*, edited by Colin Nicholson (Aberdeen 1988), pp. 151–70 (pp. 152, 164–5).
45. *Remarks on Mr Pope's Rape of the Lock*, *Works*, ii, 337.
46. Fowler, p. 159.
47. David Fairer, *Pope's Imagination* (Manchester, 1984), p. 64.
48. Cleanth Brooks, 'The Case of Miss Arabella Fermor', *The Well-Wrought Urn* (New York, 1947), pp. 74–93 (p. 74).
49. Murray Krieger, 'The "Frail China Jar" and the rude hand of chaos', *Centennial Review of Arts and Sciences*, 5 (1961), 176–94 (p. 184).
50. Pat Rogers, *An Introduction to Pope* (London, 1975), pp. 37, 39.
51. Hugo M. Reichard, 'The love affair in Pope's *The Rape of the Lock*', *PMLA*, 69 (1954), 887–902 (p. 894).
52. Pope–Mrs Marriot, 28 February [1714] (Sherburn, i, 211).
53. Oldham, *A Satyr upon a Woman, who by her Falshood and Scorn was the Death of his Friend* (London, 1678), 72; Gould, *Love given O're: Or, a Satyr Against the Pride, Lust, and Inconstancy of Women* (London, 1682); Ames, *The Folly of Love* (London, 1691).
54. Ames, p. 22.
55. *Works*, ii, 331, 334.
56. Sylphs, it should be remembered, were themselves originally 'inclos'd in Woman's beauteous Mold' until undergoing their 'soft Transition' into a form capable of receiving the 'most intimate Familiarities' with the 'Fair Sex' (i, 48–50 and Preface).
57. *Love given O're*, p. 5; *Sawney and Colley*, p. 11.
58. Pope is referring to Rochester's 'A Letter from Artemisia in the Town to Chloe in the Country', 44, (see *TE*, vi, 380).
59. Pope is reported by Joseph Spence as calling him a 'holiday writer' and 'of a very bad turn of mind, as well as debauched': *Observations, Anecdotes and Characters of Books and Men*, edited by James M. Osborn, 2 vols (Oxford, 1966), pp. 469, 470 (i, 201). Details of the annotations in Pope's copy of Rochester's *Poems on Several Occasions* (London, 1696) are given in Mack, *Collected in Himself*, pp. 384–5.
60. *A Letter to Mr. Pope, Occasion'd by Sober Advice from Horace, &c.* (London, 1735), p. 16.
61. For examples of common idiom, and perhaps direct sources, compare 'Happy Minute' (22) with the 'lucky minute' of 'As Chloris full of harmless thought' (23) and the 'livelong Minute' of 'Love and Life' (14); '*Rufa*'s at either end a Common-Shoar' (29) with 'Her belly is a bag of turds,/And her cunt a common shore' ('On Mrs Willis, 19–20); 'Me naked me, to Posts, to Pump they draw' (173) with the closing curses of 'The Imperfect Enjoyment' (62–72); and 'Give me a willing Nymph . . . Extremely clean' (162–3) with the exhortation to 'cleanly sinning' delivered in 'By all Love's soft yet mighty Powers' (14).
62. Bentley, p. 5.
63. Preface, 32, 9–10, Dryden, *Poems*, iii, 694.
64. See Fairer, pp. 99–106; Susan Gubar, 'The female monster in Augustan satire', *Signs*, 3.2. (1977), 380–94; Pollak, p. 114.
65. 'The preface of 1717', *TE*, i, 6.

66. Compare Ames, 'That fatal Gulph we call a *Common Whore*' (p. 13), and Gould, 'That Whirl-pool Sluice which never knows a Shore' (p. 5). For another example of the underlying iconography, compare Ames's couplet, 'Who without horrour, or amazement, can/Survey that hideous *Precipice of Man?*' (p. 12) with Pope's famous description of Calypso as 'the brink of all we hate' (52).

67. Compare Johnson's 'Some of the female characters may be found perhaps more frequently among men; what is said of Philomedé was true of Prior', *Lives of the Poets*, iii, 245; and Brown's almost plaintive question about these 'ghosts of men': 'If women stand for men in this poem, then where are the "real" women to be found?' (*Alexander Pope*, p. 106). The final gibe, 'To Heirs unknown descends th'unguarded store' (149), also refers to a specifically masculine trauma of inheritance.

6

'*Matter too soft*'
Pope and the women's novel

Susan Matthews

I

Late eighteenth-century women writers seem necessarily to be readers, or misreaders, of Pope. *The Rape of the Lock* and *Epistle to a Lady* of course work within an existing discourse of femininity; but the authority that Pope's poetry acquires gives to his most famous accounts of femininity a status and power which lift them out of their original contexts and allow them to take on a range of new meanings. The Popeian accounts of women enter the culture of later women writers in forms which may bear little resemblance to the complex meanings apparently present to twentieth-century readers of Pope. Yet Pope functions as an authority controlling the options available to women writers. Their writing necessarily has to confront the language to which his poetry gives rise. This essay sets out to contrast a series of twentieth-century feminist responses to Pope's discourse of femininity with those of eighteenth- and early nineteenth-century writers, looking at allusions and reworkings of Pope's images of women in Fanny Burney's *Camilla* and *Cecilia*, Maria Edgeworth's *Belinda* and in the work of Mary Wollstonecraft and Hannah More.

The opening lines of *Epistle to a Lady* present in a peculiarly concentrated form a number of the key ideas which surround the notion of woman.[1] Yet the criticism is interestingly presented as being spoken by a woman, Martha Blount, the exception who proves the rule. The charge of lacking character therefore is brought by a woman against women:

103

Nothing so true as what you once let fall,
'Most Women have no Characters at all'.

(1-2)

Pope appeals to female authority, yet it is the poet who confirms and authorises Martha Blount's judgement.[2] The terms used are highly loaded: in these lines, 'character' is a word belonging within a particular tradition of literary 'characters'; but it is a term which also carries the meaning of moral character, and which links identity, morality and writing. A character is both 'the individuality impressed by nature or habit on man or nation' and 'a letter of the alphabet'. In denying identity to women, Pope is simultaneously denying them morality and access to language.[3] The third line ('Matter too soft a lasting mark to bear') picks up the earliest sense of character from the Greek χαρακτηρ, 'a distinctive mark impressed, engraved or otherwise formed; a brand, stamp', and in doing so brings with it the suggestion of women as slaves or animals which cannot be branded satisfactorily with the identifying mark of the owner. Resisting the identity of mark or line, women are differentiated in terms of colour, a secondary characteristic in the terms of contemporary aesthetic theory.[4] Pope's poem insists also on women's ability to change themselves, a point picked up and developed in the following account of the 'characters' that women adopt for their portraits. The emphasis on inconsistency and lack of fixity becomes even stronger in Pope's gloss: 'That their particular Characters are not so strongly mark'd as those of Men, seldom so fixed, and still more inconsistent with themselves.' Femininity and 'character', then, are seen as being somehow incompatible: women are thereby denied access to the kind of subjectivity bestowed on men by the public discourse of civic humanism, within which character does not describe individual personality but profession or social position.[5] Women are differentiated by the roles they adopt in masquerade, the costumes they put on for their portraits.

Two distinct strategies seem to be adopted by twentieth-century feminist critics in response to this account of femininity. Perhaps the most familiar, and that implied in my own account of the opening lines of *Epistle to a Lady*, charges Pope with denying identity to women through a modified version of a standard misogynist charge. Thus Ellen Pollak, in *The Poetics of Sexual Myth*, compares Pope and Swift in their construction of ideas of woman.[6] For her, Pope's

104

apparently chivalrous defence of femininity is part of the century's attempt to contain femininity within an oppressive order, whilst Swift's apparent misogyny in fact liberates subversive images of woman. In other words, she sees Pope as constructing woman within a language of fancy, colour, softness. And she goes on to claim that Pope 'was the progenitor of the new literary patriarchy that made its greatest impact in the eighteenth-century feminocentric novel'.

But it would be equally possible to show the continuity between Pope's apparent misogyny and a different kind of feminism. Reverse the valuation, and Pope's denial of character becomes a form of liberation. The difference, put in fashionably Lacanian terms, is between a feminism which claims for women a place within the symbolic order and one which rejects the symbolic order as masculine and finds true feminism within the imaginary. When Pope claims that women have no character, no identity, he is denying them a place within the symbolic order. From this perspective Pope's account seems to prefigure one approach of post-modern feminism. We could find a recent parallel in Cindy Sherman's photographs – likewise an examination of female identity. In the series *Untitled Film Stills*, in what appears in each case to be a frame from an old B-movie, the artist appears in a new guise in each photograph. It might well seem that Sherman's photographs of herself present an analysis of femin-inity-as-masquerade which replicates Pope's eighteenth-century account. In a move characteristic of contemporary feminism, the critic Judith Williamson sees Sherman's photographs as a means of forcing the spectator to recognise the process by which he or she ascribes meaning to female appearance: 'by presenting a whole lexicon of feminine identities, all of them played by "her", she undermines your little construction as fast as you can build them up'.[7] The recognition that female identities are not innate but constructed by the viewer ('All how unlike each other, all how true!') seems to open up a way for us to revalorise Pope's account of the multiple images of women. Determinedly unhistorical, we could in fact celebrate his recognition – anti-essentialist as it might seem – that female identity is not innate, but a series of roles offered by the symbolic order. We thus make Pope seem to pre-date the Lacanian notion that sexuality is chosen in masquerade.

It is a strategy of this kind which Terry Castle uses in *Masquerade and Civilisation*, her study of masquerade-culture in the eighteenth century which discusses a number of women's novels.[8] For Castle, the conventional masquerade scene functions as a means of liberating women from the symbolic order, providing access to a female imaginary. Castle, of course, is school of Bakhtin, and her association of femininity with the multiple identities of the masquerade, and both with positive meanings, rests on the idea that the masquerade, in its kaleidoscopic show of images taken from the symbolic order, offers entry into a space outside that order, the female imaginary. The problem (one that she gets round brilliantly) is that neither of the two women's novels she chooses to discuss embraces the masquerade topos wholeheartedly. Fanny Burney's *Cecilia*, as Castle stresses, offers a controlled and moralised image of masquerade, whilst Elizabeth Inchbald's *A Simple Story* places little emphasis on its masquerade scene.

Castle writes that the female writer 'may begin by acknowledging' the masquerade as 'the space of her own desire'. But, overwhelmingly, this is just what the female writer in the eighteenth century does not do. If we place behind these eighteenth-century women's novels Pope's language of femininity, rather than the Bakhtinian masquerade, we begin to understand the resistance of women writers to the idea of female characterlessness. Female changeability, for them, is already contained within a moral discourse which presents it as a charge against women. It is the shift in the meaning and value of sexuality within modern discourse which enables Castle, Williamson or Tassie Gwilliam[9] to valorise female changeability. For the eighteenth-century woman writer, however, the notion is always coloured and weighted. And whereas the image of the masquerade may offer a means of imaginatively escaping this prohibition, the Popeian charge that women have no character in fact encourages women to respond with claims to innate character, which for them of course means innate virtue. For women writers, as we shall see, lack of character is linked quite specifically with *Epistle to a Lady*, as well as with the pleasures of the masked ball. The space of the masquerade has therefore already been co-opted by Pope into a male discourse. Female writers, alert to the hierarchy of genre, eager to borrow a little male authority, often allude to Pope. *Epistle to a Lady* and *The Rape of the Lock* echo through the women's novel, at every level from explicit reference to the recreation of Popeian scenes and images.

II

In Pope's epistle the moral indictment is not explicit, in that the traditional accusation of inconstancy turns into the milder one of lacking character. Yet the buried charge of sexual infidelity can always be disinterred – such is the instability of the discourse within which Pope writes. In 1767, J. H. Fuseli writes: 'A man has a character, and dares to do no more than what becomes a man; but women, they say, have none, and therefore are never out of their sphere.'[10] Here 'character' becomes a form of moral guide or constraint, even though the allusion to *Macbeth* might seem highly inappropriate in such a context. Fuseli's youthful work crudely spells out the hidden charge of Pope's text:

> Let temples, sacraments, honour, nature, misery; let life, stript of all feminine endearments, vanity, delicacy, pride; let mangled conscience and hag-ridden disease; let hatred, jealousy, revenge – bar her gates, dispute her every inch of ground, fulminate her ear, assail her with torrents of tears, intangle her way with silken nets, or strew it all with daggers; – if a woman is bent on a purpose, swift as the thoughts of love, or lewdness, or fury, 'tis all one – she will throw herself headlong, and palpitate ecstasy on the bosom of perdition! – – She will break your heart, or have her's broken. (pp. 45–6)

It seems that it is Fuseli's sentence rather than the woman which rushes 'headlong' to its conclusion. The feverish declaration draws in its wake a series of misogynistic charges. Fuseli echoes Pope's claim that 'ev'ry Woman is at heart a Rake', and Pope's epistle merges with Hamlet's soliloquies to express a male fear of female desire. Female lack of character, woman's supposed ability to metamorphose herself into countless shapes, becomes a statement of desire. If it is the man, the father, lover or husband who rightly imposes form and identity on feminine softness, then the ability to change signals the need for countless shaping men.

It is perhaps easy to think of reasons why male discourse should valorise hardness and fear softness. The surprise is that this same opposition reappears in the writing of women. Mary Wollstonecraft offers a specific attack on the Popeian image in *A Vindication of the Rights of Woman*. Yet her writing, just as much as that of Pope, values 'character'. Her sharpest insight is contained in the charge that the softness of female character, used by male writers as a charge against women, is in fact a male creation, a move which eroticises women and forms them according to the shifting forms of male desire. If one woman becomes a multiplicity of desirable objects, these changes are created in response to the demands of men. She asks why it is that female beauty is considered to be at its height at twenty and male beauty at thirty, and answers that at twenty the countenance does not express character. Women are valued as a blank slate onto which male desire and male identity can be written:

> Strength of body, and that character of countenance which the French term a *physionomie*, women do not acquire before thirty, any more than men. . . . The French, who admit more of mind into their notions of beauty, give the preference to women of thirty. I mean to say that they allow women to be in their most perfect state, when vivacity gives place to reason, and to that majestic seriousness of character, which marks maturity or the resting point.[11]

In *A Vindication* Wollstonecraft quotes Pope on women no less than four times, saving her fiercest irony for the Popeian image of woman as 'Matter too soft'. For Wollstonecraft, Pope's image is that of sadomasochism, of flesh that can endure 'the most cruel wounds' and still function as an erotic object:

> If women are to be made virtuous by authority, which is a contradiction in terms, let them be immured in seraglios and watched with a jealous eye. Fear not that the iron will enter into their souls – for the souls that can bear such treatment are made of yielding materials, just animated enough to give life to the body.
>
> > Matter too soft a lasting mark to bear,
> > And best distinguish'd by black, brown, or fair.
>
> The most cruel wounds will of course soon heal, and they may still people the world, and dress to please man – all the purposes which certain celebrated writers have allowed that they were created to fulfil. (p. 208)

Pope's couplet is here revealed as focusing on woman-as-matter, a borderline state 'just animated enough to give life to the body', but infinitely resilient to the force of men. Yet in finding women insufficiently soft, Wollstonecraft believes, male sexual perversity seeks a softer object of desire:

> So voluptuous, indeed, often grows the lustful prowler, that he refines on female softness. Something more soft than women is then sought for; till, in Italy and Portugal, men attend the levees of equivocal beings, to sigh for more than female languor. (p. 152)

Wollstonecraft's response attacks Pope's text as an eroticisation of women's bodies which ignores their minds, and one which finally displaces their bodies in a search for ever more provoking erotic objects. Her reading seems quite different from that which Fuseli constructs as an expression of male fears of female desire. Yet in their search for the definition of character they share a fear of mutable softness as expressive of sexuality.

The conservative moralist Hannah More shares Wollstonecraft's repudiation of soft changeableness, but unlike Wollstonecraft she writes as a dutiful daughter of Pope, invoking his writings on women in order to bestow the authority of male poetry on her female prose.[12] As if intimidated by the literary standing of her precursor text, she tries to adopt a Popeian wit, whilst introducing the explicit moral expected of female writing:

> With 'mysterious reverence' I forbear to descant on those serious and interesting rites, for the more august and solemn celebration of which, Fashion nightly convenes these splendid myriads to her more sumptuous temples.
>
> (viii, 196)

'Fashion' proves threatening to Hannah More because its 'rites' destroy identity and character, particularly the distinctions of rank, creating a world in which:

> the wise and the weak, the learned and the ignorant, the fair and the frightful, the sprightly and the dull, the rich and the poor, the patrician and plebeian, meet in one common and uniform equality; an equality as religiously respected in these solemnities, in which all distinctions are levelled at a blow, (and of which the very spirit is therefore democratical) as it is combated in all other instances.
>
> (viii, 197)

There follows a quotation from *The Rape of the Lock*, iii, 37–44 ('Behold, four *Kings* in Majesty rever'd . . . Draw forth to Combat on the Velvet Plain') by which Pope's authority is used to counter the democratic spirit she discerns in the world of Fashion. The realm of Fashion, More suggests, relies upon appearance to create identity. It is therefore not surprising that she quotes directly from *Epistle to a Lady* at the point where Pope defines feminine identity in terms of appearance:

> Society too is a sort of magic lanthorn; the scene is perpetually shifting.
> In this incessant change we must
>   Catch, e'er she fall, the Cynthia of the minute; –
>
> (viii, 58)

The negative associations of feminine changeableness are used to condemn the shifting identities of society, the antithesis to More's values of stability and innate nature. But she also significantly misquotes Pope's original 'Catch, ere she change, the Cynthia of this minute', replacing 'change' by 'fall'. Not only does the moral charge become explicit in this rewriting but the change from 'the Cynthia of this minute' to 'the Cynthia of the minute' also suggests the way in which Fashion multiplies Cynthias, mass producing identity as well as destroying stable identity. In yet another echo of Pope, she transfers this criticism from women to men. In the dangerous world of the male club, she warns, men can lose the moral security of defined character as easily as women:

> In this society a young man loses his natural character, which, whatever it might have been originally, is melted down and cast into the one prevailing mould of Fashion; all the strong, native, discriminating qualities of his mind being made to take one shape, one stamp, one superscription!
>
> (viii, 183)

The phrase 'natural character' is of course significant, stating the claim that it is nature that creates individuality. Within the setting of the male club it is Fashion that operates in the terms conventionally ascribed to femininity, obscuring the quintessentially masculine 'strong, native, discriminating qualities of his mind'. Despite her respect for the Popeian model, Hannah More effects a modification of the stereotype by shifting the mutable, metamorphosing power from women to Fashion. The home, formed by the stable identity of the virtuous married woman, is freed from the Popeian charge of fickleness.

More, like Wollstonecraft, rejects the charge that female identity lies in appearance. The *Epistle to a Lady* notoriously (and traditionally) defines female identity in the opening lines in terms borrowed from painting. But Hannah More rejects just this analogy:

> If, indeed, women were mere outside, form and face only, and if *mind* made up no part of her composition, it would follow that a ball-room was quite as appropriate a place for choosing a wife, as an exhibition room for choosing a picture. But, inasmuch as women are not mere portraits, their value not being determinable by a glance of the eye, it follows that a different mode of appreciating their value, and a different place for viewing them antecedent to their being individually selected, is desirable.
>
> (viii, 178–9)

But as Hannah More continues the comparison between women and pictures, she finds it rather to the advantage of pictures:

The two cases differ also in this, that if a man select a picture for himself from among all its exhibited competitors, and bring it to his own house, the picture being passive, he is able to *fix* it there: while the wife, picked up at a public place, and accustomed to incessant display, will not, it is probable, when brought home, stick so quietly to the spot where he fixes her; but will escape to the exhibition-room again, and continue to be displayed at every subsequent exhibition, just as if she were not become private property, and had never been definitively disposed of.

(More's emphasis) (viii, 179)

Not being passive, a wife is more difficult to fix, although it is clearly the function of marriage to fix female identity.

Hannah More's revision of Pope's model is typical of the ways in which many female novelists adopt this discourse. The horror of soft changeableness remains, but the charge shifts from women to men and takes on specific political meanings. Feminism, accepting the terms offered by Pope, simply passes on the misogynist charge. Women writers, rather than accepting female changeableness and turning it to positive ends, like some of their late twentieth-century readers, try to establish themselves within the Popeian discourse, endorsing an innate and more stable definition of 'character'. And yet within the women's novel, the perception of woman as changeable has a tendency to return, creating a reading of Pope which allows the complexity of later readings.

III

The woman's novel typically challenges Pope's verdict on women whilst remaining within the same framework of assumptions. The heroine of a woman's novel is usually, like Martha Blount, the exception who proves the rule, the woman of character whose firm identity is contrasted with the masquerade-women around her. For in rejecting Pope's charge, the female novel often also accepts its terms. To those around them, Clarissa, Evelina, Cecilia, Camilla, Belinda all appear to alter, but in (the fictional) reality they remain true to their character of virtue. It is the women that surround them who are more likely to provide images of change.

To some extent the search for a stable identity is successful in the woman's novel. The fiction in fact provides an authority for stable identity which is lacking in the social world. The defining text for the heroine is the novel itself, so often named after her, and freeing her

111

from the compromising definition of a father's or husband's name. Whereas Joseph Andrews becomes *Joseph Andrews* and Tom Jones becomes *Tom Jones*, Clarissa Harlowe, Cecilia Beverley, Camilla Tyrold and Belinda Portman become simply *Clarissa, Cecilia, Camilla* and *Belinda*. Yet the loss of the surname also by implication seals off these created identities from the social world. Pope's *Epistle to a Lady* points out in an authorial note that:

> The poet's politeness and complaisance to the sex is observable in this instance, amongst others, that, whereas in the *Characters of Men* he has sometimes made use of real names, in the *Characters of Women* always fictitious.

Similarly, John Duncombe's *The Feminiad*, a verse epistle in praise of women writers, presents a roll-call of Orinda, Cleora, Ardelia, Cornalia, Flavia, Florimel, Delia and Eugenia.[13] The true names of these female poets are provided in footnotes. This device could be seen as a conscious emancipation from a system of naming which labels a woman as belonging either to father or husband. But it also effectively seals off female literary achievement from social reality, allowing the female writer to preserve her daughterly or wifely identity unscathed.

This strategy is echoed in the typical structure of the woman's novel. Characteristically, the heroine is separated from her parents: orphaned like Cecilia, or like Clarissa disowned or ignored. In the case of *Evelina* it is not only the heroine but the novel itself which seems to lack parents. Burney published the novel anonymously and writes in the Advertisement to *Cecilia*:

> The indulgence shown by the public to *Evelina* which, unpatronized, unaided, and unowned, past through Four Editions in one year, has encouraged its Author to risk this *second* attempt.[14]

In a happy revision of Hamlet's ghost, *Evelina* becomes an object undefined by any parental identification, just as its heroine herself lacks social definition. She has no true surname, and concludes her first letter to her guardian:

I am,
With the utmost affection,
gratitude and duty,
Your

EVELINA – ——

I cannot to *you* sign *Anville*, and what other name may I claim?[15]

At her first ball, Evelina hears herself discussed as a 'nobody'. Near the end of the novel, Burney's Cecilia, delirious and seemingly on the point of death, is lost in London, unknown to those around her, not knowing her own name. Cecilia's wealth is hers only on condition that she keeps her own name on marriage, but Burney's narrative batters her into a state in which her only mark of identity is her obsession with her lover's name. Her friend Henrietta discovers her through an advertisement:

> The advertisement in the newspapers had at once brought her to town, and directed her to the house: the mention that the lost lady *talked much of a person by the name of Delvile*, struck her instantly to mean Cecilia . . .
>
> (p. 891)

Yet when Henrietta sees Cecilia she scarcely recognises her:

> 'Oh, who would know her! what have they done to you, my beloved Miss Beverley? how have they altered and disfigured you in this wicked and barbarous manner?'
>
> (p. 892)

Suffering rather than the pursuit of pleasure has turned Cecilia into yet another example of the protean woman.

But if female identity is fictional not natural, this conclusion is one of which most female writers seem afraid. They wish to ground it in something more stable. Just as Hannah More invokes an idea of 'natural character' and Wollstonecraft appeals to 'soul' to authorise individuality, so the woman's novel asserts the 'natural' identity of the central characters. Their novels repeatedly show the extent to which female identity is dependent on external forces, on education, family and social recognition, on reputation and on money. But the explicit conclusion is usually that the heroine at least has a character which could exist unchanged in any circumstances. Both *Evelina* and *Camilla* present us with heroines whose behaviour seems to all around them to embody changeability. The more they remain faithful to their own aims, the more they seem to others to change. Only the reader and the heroine are included in the secret of the heroine's consistency until the end of the novel. Camilla is falsely seen by her lover's respected tutor, Dr Marchmont, as a type of inconstant womanhood. Dr Marchmont warns:

113

'With all the charms she assembles, her character seems too unstable for private domestic life. When a few years more have blunted the wild vivacity, the floating ambition, the changing propensities which now render her inconsistent to others, and fluctuating even to herself, she may become as respectable, as she must always be amiable.'[16]

The narrative tells of the process by which Camilla's fidelity is finally demonstrated to those around her. Yet *Camilla* also reveals, as if by accident, the contradictory nature of the role demanded of women. Consistency and stability are required qualities, but the education of women at the same time demands of them a degree of plasticity.

Changeability, lack of character, appear in the *Epistle to a Lady* as a charge against women. Yet as Pope's poetry is also aware, these qualities are also precisely those which are demanded of them. In so far as women function as a means of exchange between men, it is necessary that they should be adaptable. Suitably enough, in the *Epistle to Bathurst* women appear in the context of a discussion of money. In Pope's fantasy of the replacement of money by goods, women take their place in just the role Levi-Strauss would expect:

> To White's be carried, as to ancient games,
> Fair Coursers, Vases, and alluring Dames.
> Shall then Uxorio, if the stakes he sweep,
> Bear home six Whores, and make his Lady weep?
>
> (57–60)

If women are a means of exchange, the danger is perhaps that they will have too much character; their value must depend to some extent on their uniformity of identity, their relative lack of character which allows them to be passed from one owner to another. Thus anonymity, far from offering the escape from the symbolic order which Castle suggests, is instead one of the attributes demanded of women.[17] The trouble is that women are supposed to function as money at the point of exchange in marriage, but then to cease to have an exchange value. Exactly this perception of the necessary adaptability of female character forms a central didactic message of Fanny Burney's *Camilla*. In a sermon addressed to the heroine, her father writes:

> The temporal destiny of woman is enwrapt in still more impenetrable obscurity than that of man. She begins her career by being involved in all the worldly accidents of a parent; she continues it by being associated in all that may environ a husband . . . (p. 356)

114

Female identity, it seems, inevitably shifts with the move from father to husband. The problems of female education, Mr Tyrold explains, derive from 'this doubly appendant state'. A parent must accommodate a daughter both to the father's social status and to whatever status the husband may occupy. 'What parent yet has been gifted with the foresight to say, "I will educate my daughter for the station to which she will belong"?', he laments. Mr Tyrold's sermon was later excerpted from the novel and published with one of the most popular conduct books for women, John Gregory's *A Father's Legacy to his Daughter* (a work to which Wollstonecraft takes particular exception).[18] The discourse of femininity thus contains a central contradiction: lack of character is both the quality which marks women's inferiority to men *and* that which is demanded of them. After all, the last canto of *The Rape of the Lock* provides an image of transformation: the lock is metamorphosed into a star. Belinda has to learn the importance of *not* remaining a maid. This contradiction is masked in part by the different meaning which 'character' bears when used for men and for women. The moral meaning of 'character' allows a constant identity for women which survives changes of marital status. Yet 'character' also confusingly refers to identity, to all those meanings suggested at the opening of *Epistle to a Lady*.

Often, the more dangerous Popeian female images are presented as secondary figures set in contrast to the heroine. In Burney's *Camilla*, Pope's characterisation is marginalised and used for the older woman, Mrs Arlbery, the transgressive figure or temptress who threatens to lead astray the heroine by offering an entrée into the world of Fashion, of appearances, masquerade, goods and luxury where innate character is lost. Camilla is assured by Mrs Arlbery that, 'inconsistency in a woman was as flattering, as in a man it was tedious and alarming' (p. 495). Mrs Arlbery, a sharp critic of characterlessness in men, finds her own character in the female stereotype of inconsistency. Detecting a rare lapse into consistency, Sir Sedley Clarendel reproves her:

> 'My dear madam!' exclaimed he, in a tone of expostulation, 'who can think of the same scheme two days together? Could you possibly form a notion of anything so patriarchal?' (p. 400)

Ironically, to claim the character of inconsistency is one way of achieving a stable and self-created identity.

In *Cecilia*, Burney provides an even more traditional comic form of character-drawing when Mr Gosport creates a taxonomy of fashionable women:

'The TON misses, as they are called, who now infest the town, are in two divisions, the SUPERCILIOUS, and the VOLUBLE. The SUPERCILIOUS, like Miss Leeson, are silent, scornful, languid, and affected, and disdain all converse but with those of their own set; the VOLUBLE, like Miss Larolles, are flirting, communicative, restless, and familiar, and attack, without the smallest ceremony, every one they think worthy their notice. But this they have in common, that at home they think of nothing but dress, abroad, of nothing but admiration, and that everywhere they hold in supreme contempt all but themselves.' (p. 37)

These divisions do not provide *character*: the 'ton misses' are seen as imitating character – trying it on rather than owning it. Their true character is simply that of 'women', and the underlying verdict is just the same as that of Pope's *Epistle to a Lady*: most women have the character of 'woman', unstable, obsessed with winning admiration, taking on a character only in masquerade. Burney and Hannah More here join with Mary Wollstonecraft in defining the arena of fashion, the world in which it might seem that meanings are primarily made by women, as a language without meaning, appearance without character. In *A Vindication*, Wollstonecraft writes:

The air of fashion, which many young people are so eager to attain, always strikes me like the studied attitudes of some modern pictures, copied with tasteless servility after the antiques; the soul is left out, and none of the parts are tied together by what may properly be termed character. (p. 108)

Fashion and soul are seen as incompatible opposites. Indeed, Wollstonecraft could be providing a gloss to the opening lines of *Epistle to a Lady*.

Burney's witty Mrs Arlbery in *Camilla* seems to provide a prototype for Maria Edgeworth's Lady Delacour in *Belinda*.[19] Lady Delacour characteristically assures Belinda that it is 'never too late for women to change their minds, their dress, or their lovers' (p. 14). But Edgeworth also uses Lady Delacour as a means to explore some of the more disturbing implications of Pope's Belinda. One of the types of human vanity in the face of age, physical decay and death is traditionally provided by the old woman trying vainly to obliterate decay with cosmetics. Part of the resonance of Belinda at her dressing table in *The Rape of the Lock* comes from the suppressed memory of Hamlet's warning in the graveyard: it is woman who acts as a

116

memento mori. Narcissa in *Epistle to Cobham* (242–7) and 'Sappho at her toilet's greasy task' in *Epistle to a Lady* restore the association of cosmetics with old age and a sinister concealment. We might expect the woman's novel to reject this image, but death returns to the dressing table in Edgeworth's *Belinda*, a novel whose title shows its obsession with Popeian images of women. Here Edgeworth contains the disturbing implications of Belinda by transferring qualities associated with her to another character – the figure of Lady Delacour. Edgeworth's Belinda represents innate character, not masquerade, reality not appearance. Yet in the masquerade scene near the opening of the novel, Belinda and Lady Delacour swap identities. In the mode of Gothic, Edgeworth's attempt to clean up Pope's Belinda fails, and the separated identities merge. Lady Delacour is a creation of art not nature, and she invites her young friend into her dressing room with the words:

> 'Let me see you in my dressing-room, dear Belinda, as soon as you have adored
>
> "With head uncover'd the cosmetic powers".
>
> But you don't paint – no matter – you will – you must – every body must, soon or later.' (p. 26)

Her quoting of *Rape of the Lock* i, 124 confirms that this is Pope's Belinda invited to revisit the site of her beauty and power. Swift's ironic revisitings of Belinda's toilette (*The Progress of Beauty* and *A Beautiful Young Nymph Going to Bed*) are outdone by the horror awaiting Edgeworth's Belinda:

> The room was rather dark, as there was no light in it except what came from the candle which Lady Delacour held in her hand, and which burned but dimly. Belinda, as she looked round, saw nothing but a confusion of linen rags; vials, some empty, some full, and she perceived that there was a strong smell of medicines.
> Lady Delacour, whose motions were all precipitate, like those of a person whose mind is in great agitation, looked from side to side of the room, without seeming to know what she was in search of. She then, with a species of fury, wiped the paint from her face, and returning to Belinda, held the candle so as to throw the light full upon her livid features. Her eyes were sunk, her cheeks hollow; no trace of youth or beauty remained on her death-like countenance, which formed a horrid contrast with her gay fantastic dress.
> 'You are shocked, Belinda,' said she; 'but as yet you have seen nothing – look here,' – and baring one half of her bosom, she revealed a hideous spectacle. (pp. 23–4)

In drawing on a misogynist image of woman, Edgeworth also puts it

117

to a new use in a description which horrifyingly embodies a fear of breast cancer. Yet her discourse nevertheless remains within the moralised context of Pope's discourse. Edgeworth joins Pope's Belinda with his 'Sappho at her toilet's greasy task' from the *Epistle to a Lady*. Lady Delacour, rotting within from breast cancer, nevertheless shines in society, a typical example of woman as a temporary creation of art. Her present identity is just one of her transformations; in the words of another society lady:

'I have been informed, and upon *the best authority*, that Lady Delacour was not always the unfeeling, dissipated, fine lady she now appears to be. This is only one of the transformations of fashion – the period of her enchantment will soon be at an end, and she will return to her natural character.' (p. 91)

The character to which Lady Delacour will return is that recommended by the conduct books: 'when she is tired of the insipid taste of other pleasures, she will have a higher relish for those of domestic life, which will be new and fresh to her' – this we are told by the novel's exemplary mother, Lady Anne Percival. Meanwhile Lady Delacour's attempt is to form Belinda into the glittering and unreal figure of Pope's creation. Again with specific reference to *The Rape of the Lock*, she promises Belinda that 'a new star shall appear in the firmament of fashion, and it shall be called Belinda' (p. 71). The difference between stars in the firmament of fashion and in the sky is that the former are rather more short-lived. Belinda, like any other heroine of a woman's novel, proves the exception to the rule, the woman of nature not art. It is Lady Delacour who echoes Pope's Belinda; Edgeworth's Belinda redeems her namesake – as even Lady Delacour recognises when she says to her: 'I cannot help believing you, because you never yet deceived me, even in the merest trifle: you are truth itself Belinda.'

Fanny Burney's *Camilla* is typical of many female novels in that it asserts the consistency of character revealed by the heroines. They, unlike all the world around them, male and female, are consistent, and act from character and principle. Mrs Arlbery in *Camilla*, lamenting the loss of character in men and women, says:

'We are almost all, my good General, of a nature so pitifully plastic, that we act from circumstances, and are fashioned by situation.' (p. 398)

But the novel ends with the authorial assertion that character is innate, not determined by circumstances or education. Women, according to Fanny Burney, are creatures of nature not art. *Camilla* returns at the end to the novel's subtitle, a 'Picture of Youth'. Like Hannah More, Burney rejects the idea that a woman can be represented by a painting, for the painting only represents what is inessential to Camilla's character, the qualities associated with her youth not with her true and continuing identity:

> And Dr. Marchmont, as he saw the pure innocence, open frankness, and spotless honour of her heart, found her virtues, her errours, her facility, or her desperation, but A PICTURE OF YOUTH; and regretting the false light given by the spirit of comparison, in the hypothesis which he had formed from individual experience, acknowledged its injustice, its narrowness, and its arrogance. What, at last, so diversified as man? what so little to be judged by his fellow? (p. 913)

Light and colour were the secondary characteristics which Pope associated with femininity in *The Rape of the Lock* and *Epistle to a Lady*. But Burney rejects the 'false light given by the spirit of comparison' as well as the 'Picture of Youth' as themselves secondary to the portrait supplied by her novel. Camilla, in other words, has her own character, which is 'diversified' from that of others, yet true and unchanging to its own rules or virtue. The conclusion contradicts both Pope's charges against women and Mrs Arlbery's cynical extension of the charge to include 'almost all'.

The female fear of the Popeian charge against women narrows the options for many female novelists, shutting their novels to the explicit admission of the flexibility of social identity of which their own fictions are paradoxically aware. Deeply imbued as they are with the Popeian charge against women, their desire is to swap places with men and to take on the claim to a natural identity unthreatened by time and social change. Fearing the mutability which female roles may bring, they moralise the masquerade and often see it as a place which is threatening to the heroine. For Pope's eighteenth-century women readers, the emphasis on change in his account of female character is not a liberating one, but carries the traditional charges against women that it seems to suppress.

Notes

1. See also Ellen Pollak, *The Poetics of Sexual Myth* (London, 1985) pp. 109–15.

2. Compare Fielding, 'An Essay on the Knowledge of the Characters of Men', in *Miscellanies*, 3 vols (London, 1743) which omits the discussion of female character as a separate science in which he is not skilled:

> I do by no means hint at the various Laughs, Titters, Tehes, etc. of the Fair Sex, with whom indeed this Essay hath not any thing to do; the Knowledge of the Characters of Women being foreign to my intended Purpose as it is in Fact a Science, to which I make not the least Pretension. (i, 194–5)

3. See also Felicity Nussbaum, 'Heteroclites: the gender of character in the scandalous memoirs', in *The New Eighteenth Century*, pp. 144–67, especially pp. 146–50.
4. The same assumptions are found in civic humanist aesthetic theory, and in William Blake's emphasis on the 'wiry line of rectitude' and the denial of the importance of colour.
5. See Thomas Gisborne, *An Enquiry into the Duties of the Female Sex* (4th edn, London, 1799), pp. 2–3.
6. Pollak, p. 180.
7. See Judith Williamson, 'A piece of the action: images of "woman" in the photographs of Cindy Sherman', in *Consuming Passions* (London and New York, 1986), pp. 91–113.
8. Terry Castle, *Masquerade and Civilisation: The Carnivalesque in Eighteenth Century English Culture and Fiction* (London, 1986).
9. Tassie Gwilliam, ' "Like Tiresias": metamorphosis and gender in *Clarissa*', *Novel*, 19 (1986), 110–17.
10. *Remarks on the Writings and Conduct of J. J. Rousseau* (London, 1767), p. 45.
11. *A Vindication of the Rights of Woman* (London, 1929 reprinted 1982) p. 73.
12. 'Strictures on the modern system of female education', in *The Works of Hannah More*, 8 vols (London, 1801), VII–VIII.
13. John Duncombe, *The Feminiad; or Female Genius* (London, 1751).
14. Fanny Burney, *Cecilia*, introduced by Judy Simons (London, 1986).
15. Fanny Burney, *Evelina*, edited by Edward A. Bloom (Oxford, 1982), p. 24.
16. Fanny Burney, *Camilla or a Picture of Youth*, edited by Edward A. Bloom and Lillian D. Bloom (Oxford and New York, 1983), p. 725.
17. See Jane Spencer, *The Rise of the Female Novelist* (Oxford, 1986), p. 167.
18. *A Father's Legacy to his Daughter . . . To which is added, Mr Tyrold's Advice to his daughter from 'Camilla' by Mrs d'Arblay* (Poughnill, 1809).
19. Maria Edgeworth, *Belinda*, introduced by Eva Figes (London, 1986).

7

Missing parts
Voice and spectacle in Eloisa to Abelard

Stephen Bygrave

Pope's poetry comes with a freight of possible contexts: dedications, footnotes, arguments and glosses, to say nothing of letters, biographies, memoirs, reviews and parodies, and even the more evident intertexts provided by its imitated or parodied sources. The interpretative problems of those contexts are often so large in themselves as to forestall their use as keys for texts to which they might have been presumed ancillary. (Is *A Key to the Lock* a pre-emptive defence against political misappropriation or is it, rather, by forestalling a reading which otherwise would be all too plausible, an elaborate double bluff?) There is a problem then of the criteria for relevance, which is a problem also intrinsic to the texts themselves: what sustains, resides in, or is the residue of texts which are able to incorporate so much? The ambition to recuperate or appropriate Pope's texts, shared by some of the best of his critics, must take account of a kindred ambition in those texts. Throughout them there is evidently an appropriative energy, which might be called a rhetoric of incorporation. Attempts to appropriate them risk falling into one of two traps: either of falling into the waiting maw of 'commentary' or of mimicking Pope's own appropriation of such commentary. In terms of the concern here, is it that Pope provides the context for *Eloisa* or vice versa?

This essay is concerned with pre-empting a movement in recent criticism to appropriate some of Pope's early poetry as exemplary proto-feminist text; or, if not to pre-empt, to enter the caveat that such a movement depends on reading those texts against the grain or in terms of their unconscious. Exemplariness would then rest more explicitly in the encounter of past text and present reading, in the

Stephen Bygrave

appropriation itself.[1] This is not to say that there is a disinterested
core-reading of those texts as monolithically conservative, of which
various kinds of interested reading would be partial and deviant
variations. Nor are these early poems versions of a progressive,
feminising discourse that Pope subsequently suppresses; they are
versions, rather, of a strategy for incorporating such a discourse. It is
incorporated most evidently into the self-consciously constructed
oeuvre of the 1717 *Works* in which *Eloisa to Abelard* and the *Verses to
the Memory of an Unfortunate Lady* first appeared. The claim is that
such apparently private discourse impinges upon and may subvert the
ideology of the private sphere produced and reproduced by the later
poems. Such a claim must rest on the demotion of that later context
('Pope' coming to signify different texts from those to which other
criticism has paid most attention). Alternatively, it must demonstrate
that the private discourse, far from being subsumed by the *oeuvre*,
remains at an antagonistic distance from it, living an after-life of
critique. Thus in the last part of this essay I shall suggest how making
public an ostensibly private, feminine discourse might relate to the
different (not wider) context of an understanding of Pope as a career
or as a single text.

Having sketched one binary opposition which is disposable though
analytically useful, I now want to sketch a second such opposition. I
want to offer a reading of *Eloisa to Abelard* in terms of a paradigm of
'voice' and 'spectacle' which is assumed by much recent criticism of
Pope: 'spectacle' as the visual arrangement of a scene, requiring a
spectator (who may also be represented in the poem), and 'voice' as a
function which can seem to have escaped from such arrangement and
to provide a kind of exemplary self-expression. A version of this
paradigm is provided in a rich and subtle recent book by Lawrence
Lipking which traces the appropriation and reappropriation of
Sappho as text and as exemplary past poet by, among others, Pope
and his model for *Eloisa to Abelard*, Ovid. For Lipking, Ovid is the
poet of Sappho's fall. Where the poet Sappho of the Second Ode
watches her lover, Ovid's Sappho watches herself loving. Thus the
distinction between the 'historical' Sappho and Ovid's Sappho is a
proleptic version of Schiller's distinction of naive from sentimental, a
distinction in Lipking's words 'between direct presentation of a
subject or emotion and the self-dramatising effort to load that subject
with personal significance'.[2] The distinction is analytically useful,
despite that questionable confidence in a founding 'direct presentation' (recalling Schiller less than it recalls Arnold or Auerbach)
because this can only be a paradigm for ways of reading. (As Lipking

himself points out, the original 'direct presentation' is itself an appropriation: Sappho's Second Ode comes down to us only through its citation by Longinus.) Lipking's citation of Schiller is significant because the model of origin and version, innocence and corruption, organicism and self-consciousness, which implies the redemptive possibility of recovering the first term in each pair, is familiar in Romantic aesthetics. It is Romantic aesthetics which justifies the kind of reading that stresses the prevalence of voice over spectacle; stresses, that is, the disruption of the poem's ideological form by a self-authenticating discourse of original and innocent representations. The poem can become an exemplary site of subversion, what *Eloisa to Abelard* calls 'an altar for forbidden fires' (182). Against this, I want to argue that the kind of pre-emptive or forestalling tactics I have invoked are also the tactics of Pope's poetry and that if it is to be appropriated this must be done through what it has appropriated. The voice/spectacle paradigm of some recent criticism is one which Pope forestalls and incorporates. Though Lipking stresses the visual terms of *Eloisa to Abelard* over its ostensible voice, he does so in order to reassert an opposition of voice and spectacle. Pope continues the movement of Ovid's epistles in which Sappho is silenced in order to be spoken for.

The critique of Pope as corrupting and misappropriating his original depends on a familiar kind of Romanticisation (a making Romantic) of the eighteenth century. This is a process well under way by the time Joseph Warton specifies for praise a tender, sensible and pathetic Pope in the first volume of his *Essay on the Genius and Writings of Pope* in 1756. *Eloisa to Abelard* has become a prime exhibit in the back-projection of Romantic aesthetics onto the earlier eighteenth century. I shall be looking at the procedures of that poem, along with two others to which it is related: the *Elegy to the Memory of an Unfortunate Lady* and *Sapho to Phaon*, the early translation from Ovid. I want however to begin with a couplet in Pope's translation from the French of François de Malherbe (*TE*, vi, 71–2), published in the same year as the *Elegy* and *Eloisa*:

> As children birds, so men their bliss pursue,
> Still out of reach, tho' ever in their view.
>
> (5–6)

Thus out of context the couplet might seem a staging-post in a Romantic quest-lyric. While in context it is no more than an item in a list of aspirations all of which are vanity, out of context it might seem a statement of aspiration to a Romantic sublime. What interests me here is not the pursuit but the 'view', the notion that the object of desire is a visual object. 'Men' in that couplet is generic ('so men their bliss pursue'), but more than twenty years later Pope reworks the couplet in the *Epistle to a Lady*:

> Pleasures the sex, as children Birds, pursue,
> Still out of reach, yet never out of view.
>
> (231–2)

The 'follies' here are specifically female follies, not the generalised vanity of the earlier couplet. Women are associated with the visual sense, but they do not become spectators: pleasure is simply something always within the field of vision of 'the sex'. What is to be viewed is disposed by the poet, who casts himself here as a painter: 'If Folly grows romantic, I must paint it' (16). I shall return to the *Epistle to a Lady*, but I want here to stress these pictorial metaphors in *Eloisa to Abelard*. The earlier poem seems misread as a dramatic monologue. It is often read too in terms of the kind of process associated with the Romantic lyric rather than in terms of the static image. It has been read, specifically, as offering a model for female discourse. I shall argue simply that the control exercised by the (male) spectator remains more crucial than the notion of Eloisa as exemplary female voice. Then I shall suggest the priority of a metaphor of spectacle over a metaphor of 'voice' in Pope's corpus. The management of competing discourses and the claim for an economy of public and private within that corpus make such a suggestion consequential. I shall try to show that *Eloisa to Abelard* is a paradigm for such procedures.

Pope's poem is a heroic epistle, ostensibly written by Eloisa from the convent to which she has retired. It works by a series of synecdoches, the figure by which the absent is made present through naming of a part.[3] Thus Abelard is a mere 'name', the male made present through reading a letter not addressed to the female: 'That well-known name awakens all my woes' (30). Eloisa too is in bits, a series of invocations of eyes, heart, tears, hands, and so on. And even these bits are in bits: 'No happier task these faded eyes pursue,/To read and weep is all they now can do' (47–8). This fragmented absence is set against a dream or memory of fulfilled desire in which 'All then is full, possessing, and possest' (93) and Abelard functions as 'father, brother, husband, friend!' (152).[4] Self-construction is by a chain of association which constructs the other. Fulfilment becomes a matter of having the parts reassembled:

124

> Still on that breast enamour'd let me lie,
> Still drink delicious poison from thy eye,
> Pant on thy lip, and to thy heart be prest;
> Give all thou canst – and let me dream the rest.
>
> (121–4)

Warton calls these 'luscious ideas'.[5] We are invited to complete the chain of association which would end in the full presence of Abelard: 'I can no more; by shame, by rage supprest,/Let tears, and burning blushes speak the rest' (105–6).

The metonymy in the line, 'Come thou, my father, brother, husband, friend!' runs from sacred to profane: from 'father' and 'brother' as the public terms of the Paraclete to the private claim of relationship. To many critics the poem has seemed to be about the tension between these two sets of terms.[6] Much of the criticism of Pope sees the poem as an earnest debate between the conflicting claims of the cloister and the impossible object of desire, 'the struggles of grace and nature, virtue and passion' as Pope's 'Argument' has it.[7] In the poem itself, 'their unfortunate passion' becomes 'those restless passions' (82), a dialectic of part and whole, vacuum and plenum. The opposition of flesh and spirit is one of the symptoms of passion deriving from Ovid, like that of freezing and burning – to which I would add the division between these bodily symptoms and their spectator. Lipking draws attention to Eloisa's visualisation of two visualising figures in the opening lines, 'Contemplation . . . whose eyes roll upward toward heaven; and the black goddess Melancholy . . . who broods upon the darkness or a letter'.[8] Even from the start, then, voice is succeeded by spectacle, or rather voice is incorporated by spectacle as these elements are conjoined rather than disjoined by the antitheses: 'I view my crime, but kindle at the view' (185); 'I hear thee, view thee, gaze o'er all thy charms/And round thy phantom glue my clasping arms' (233–4). Certainly the proximity to blasphemy would produce a sublime *frisson*:

> Fill my fond heart with God alone, for he
> Alone can rival, can succeed to thee.
>
> (205–6)

But this follows an imperative of parallel impossibility, the desire for emptying-out:

> oh teach me nature to subdue,
> Renounce my love, my life, my self – and you.
>
> (203–4)

125

Love and selfhood are complementary.[9] The landscape 'pants' and
'quivers' (159–60). In such a sexually overdetermined frame we
begin to have doubts as to whether everything is a *double entendre*:
'soft intercourse' (57), 'swelling organs' (272). Warton praises the
delicacy by which Abelard's castration is alluded to, and Pope's
early biographer Owen Ruffhead admires 'the oblique and delicate
allusions with which [Eloisa] glances at the nature of her lover's
deplorable disaster'.[10] Pope's 'Argument' does not mention this
'disaster', thus the poem depends on prior knowledge of the story.
'All is not Heav'n's while *Abelard* has part' (25), yet Abelard has a
missing part, and this is crucial because it means that Eloisa's desire
must be heroic because incapable of being tawdried by fulfilment in
other than ideal terms. W. B. Carnochan's description of the poem
as a 'rhapsodic fantasy of masturbation and release'[11] is exceptional;
but even this fails to describe the way in which that release is
displaced. It does not occur within Eloisa's discourse. The close of
the poem invokes 'some future Bard' whose sensitivity is then
praised: 'He best can paint 'em, who shall feel 'em most'.

We seem then to be invited to follow a movement outside the
poem, into the biography of the poet. In 1716 Pope writes to
Martha Blount:

> I am here studying ten hours a day, but thinking of you in spight of
> all the learned. The Epistle of Eloise grows warm, and begins to have
> some Breathings of the Heart in it, which may make posterity think I
> was in love. I can scarce find it in my heart to leave out the
> conclusion I once intended for it – [12]

Then, sending a wooden box containing his works to Lady Mary
Wortley Montagu in Constantinople, Pope says that she will not
have seen *Eloisa to Abelard*: 'in which you will find one passage, that
I can't tell whether to wish you should understand, or not?'[13] It
might be thought that it was the final lines to which Pope was
calling attention in both these letters. However, Hagstrum has
suggested that Pope's coyness to Lady Mary in the letter of June
1717 is because 'Lady Mary may perceive an identification between
himself and the emasculated Abelard'.[14] In any case, what is
suggested by these letters from Pope is that *Eloisa* is less obsessively
private utterance than it is a sort of *poème à clef* for the coterie. This
is what Warton comes to assume in hinting at a biographical link
with the *Elegy to the Memory of an Unfortunate Lady*.

The *Elegy to the Memory of an Unfortunate Lady*, which shared its
own second edition with the second edition of *Eloisa to Abelard* in

1719, is rhetorically similar. The opening lines offer a Gothic tableau. We move first from a partial to a fuller view and from yes/no questions to 'wh-' questions. A curse is placed on the lady's family for their failure of sensibility: 'all, whose breast ne'er learn'd to glow/For others' good, or melt at others' woe' (45-6). The lady remains anonymous, but following the funerary inscription at the end of the poem there is a similar turn as that at the end of *Eloisa to Abelard*. The spectator is again revealed as not only the rhetorical necessity of the opening lines but as a dramatised poet-figure: 'Poets themselves must fall, like those they sung'. And his 'soul now melts', unlike those of the lady's family.

Commentary on the *Elegy* at first assumed it to be without the kind of public or quasi-historical basis provided by the letters of Abelard and Heloise. Eloisa's question, 'Canst thou forget that sad, that solemn day . . .?' (107), is a rhetorical question not just because there is no interlocutor but because the dramatic context was familiar and Pope adverts to it. For similar reasons *Eloisa to Abelard* continues to be read as the public dress of Pope's private desires, or even as his dressing in drag. In the first edition of his *Essay* Warton says that *Eloisa* ought to have ended at line 358,

> For the eight additional ones, concerning some poet, that haply might arise to sing their misfortunes, are languid and flat, and diminish the pathos of the foregoing sentiments. They might stand for the conclusion of almost any story.[15]

This is consistent with Warton's principle that language should be 'the particular and unalienable property of the person who uses it'; and he quotes lines 241-6, suggesting that they lack 'a VISION of some such appropriated and peculiar distress, as could be incident to none but Eloisa; and which could be drawn from and have reference to, her single story'.[16] However, this principle of propriety can easily be transposed from Eloisa to Pope. The second edition (1762) adds, 'at first it appears' and 'it should seem' to the dismissal of the coda, and then Warton adds the assurance that the 'circumstance' of the poem is that loss also recorded in the *Elegy to the Memory of an Unfortunate Lady*. Johnson too will offer, in his life of Pope, a lengthy gloss on the background or stimulus to which the 'Elegy' is the foreground or response. Warton says, 'the recollection of this circumstance will add a beauty, and a pathos to many passages in the poem, and will confirm the doctrine delivered above concerning the choice of subject'.[17] That 'doctrine', adduced from the *Elegy to the Memory of an Unfortunate Lady*, is that 'if this ELEGY be so excellent, it may be ascribed to this cause; that the occasion of it was real'.[18] The difference to him. So, discussing the trope of personification, one recent critic says that:

> Eloisa's 'Melancholy' with its gloomy and transforming presence does not divert us from Eloisa's response but adds to it, and makes us feel not only that Eloisa can try to half-objectify a subjective sensation but also that she is herself so rich a person as to give rise to – or split off into – intensely apprehended and active aspects of psychic life.[19]

As though personification were about revealing rather than creating 'persons', this psychic apprehension and activity is deemed to be that of the fictional Eloisa. It is apparent that this relies on the same premiss as Warton had stated in his *Essay* two and a half centuries ago.

So if, as another critic has claimed, 'in this poem, Pope discovers a voice for women in English poetry'[20] he does so by throwing his own voice. The claim needs the disclaimers about ventriloquising the female, about women being spoken *for*, which modify similar claims made for another piece of epistolary sentiment, Richardson's *Clarissa*. The claim derives from an influential article on the heroic epistle by Gillian Beer, which argues that the anglicisation of Ovid's *Heroides* from Drayton on provided later female Gothic not only with an iconography but also with an authority to represent a version of female sensibility, of the voice of a heroine. In her words, 'if the narrative pattern prepared women for martyrdom, the rhetoric restored power to the powerless'.[21] For Gillian Beer, *Eloisa to Abelard* is the telling instance of such a restorative and enabling rhetoric. Her response to the caveat just raised deserves quoting at length:

> The form did function to extend the rhetorical possibilities of language for its male authors – but this extension relied upon an appeal to the authority of women, who were assumed to be naturally learned in the realms of erotic knowledge and suffering. So the claims of the art-form have a mimetic basis: the primary 'author' or authority is conceived as the experiencer; the actual author-writer casts himself as secondary, a concealed scribe recording the actualities derived from women's experience. . . . Heroic epistle takes as its pre-condition the enforced passivity of women: formally and in narrative the poems rely upon sequestration. But the sense of enforcement means that these are poems which sustain a constant protest against the conditions which produce the form.[22]

Beer's own reading of Pope's poem, however, does not notice the way Pope's 'concealed scribe' breaks cover at the end. That the form was capable of appropriation by female writers and readers does not make the form itself somehow progressive, and however we read the end of *Eloisa to Abelard* we are reminded that the female voice comes to us mediated, translated. Eloisa is distanced from herself, a third person – 'In vain lost *Eloisa* weeps and prays' (15) – but the last lines make it explicit that her voyeurism takes place under the voyeuristic eye of the poet. What is ostensibly the voice of Eloisa is succeeded by what is certainly Pope's picture: 'He best can *paint* 'em who shall feel 'em most' (italics mine). In these final lines Eloisa appeals outside the poem to the poet who writes it. Some critics have seen the final 'sad similitude' as their conjunction, or even copulation. This, I think, is merely to extend the 'mimetic basis' that Beer describes. The questions to ask, rather, are: how far does the form's 'mimetic basis' commit us to remain within that context? *Whose* 'protest' is it? And is it not the case that voice is succeeded or superseded by spectacle? Carnochan writes of the poem as an instance of an eighteenth-century concern with the construction of boundaries. Boundaries can be transgressed only in verbal or ideal terms: 'All my loose soul unbounded springs to thee' (228).[23] Fantasy is permitted such liberties, but the close of the poem is a reminder that this liberty should not become licence, anarchy. It remains, in other words, a male fantasy.[24]

Pope's version of the heroic epistle goes further in insisting that fantasy remain private. *Sapho to Phaon*, his translation of the fifteenth letter of Ovid's *Heroides*, which was published in a collaborative volume in 1712, predates many of the techniques of *Eloisa to Abelard*, for example in the insistent synecdoche of the opening and the initial claim that desire is expressed because it has to be expressed:

> Pride of thy Age, and Glory of thy Race,
> Come to these Arms, and melt in this Embrace!
> The Vows you never will return, receive;
> And take at least the Love you will not give.
> See, while I write, my Words are lost in Tears;
> The less my Sense, the more my Love appears.
>
> (105–10)[25]

This is succeeded by the claim for ideal fulfilment – here, in dreams –

> O Night more pleasing than the brightest Day,
> When Fancy gives what Absence takes away,
> And drest in all its visionary Charms,

129

Restores my fair Deserter to my Arms!

(145–8)

– only for this liquefying of boundaries, which suggested that the utterance could be instrumental, to harden:

> Alas! the *Muses* now no more inspire,
> Untun'd my Lute, and silent is my Lyre,
> My languid Numbers have forgot to flow,
> And Fancy sinks beneath a Weight of Woe.

(228–31)[26]

The poem ends with a resolve for action which the poem cannot include. There is nothing in it comparable with the coda to *Eloisa to Abelard* or the *Elegy* – nor is there in John Hughes's translation of the letters of Abelard and Heloise (1713). For reasons I have suggested, Abelard is the occasion for desire rather than the object of desire. Hence even good critics of the poetry miss the point in insisting that the poem reveals or creates Eloisa's 'character'. There can be no such insistence about Abelard, who exists explicitly as 'Idea'. As such, the poem can continually promise and defer the reconciliation of those conflicts it presents. Abelard's 'Lov'd Idea' lies 'mix'd with God's' in Eloisa's heart (11–12).[27] Thus completion must occur outside the containing 'relentless walls' of the convent and of Eloisa's obsessive discourse. The last lines function like the prologues and epilogues to plays in which the author dramatises a figure who steps outside the play to deliver a speech without costume or make-up, as first viewer of the spectacle which such an activity frames.[28] Eloisa invites us to consider her as spectacle – 'see in her Cell sad *Eloisa* spread . . . See my lips tremble, and my eye-balls roll . . . See from my cheek the transient roses fly!/See the last sparkle languish in my eye!' (303, 323, 331–2) – and the last lines provide us with a frame, with a position for the spectator. The last lines return us to a sociable, even demotic world: out of the 'darksom round' and into the light. This enlightenment can be set against the 'universal darkness' which indulgence in the private discourses of enthusiasm and melancholy has produced at the end of *The Dunciad*.[29]

Edward Said describes a comparable moment in Swift's 'Verses on the Death of Dr. Swift', which anticipates the reception of Swift's own death in the mouths of his acquaintances. By doing so, Swift 'constructed the continuity he wished to perpetuate . . . Swift's death is transformed from a variety of gossipy stories into an event'. But it is an event only within the disparate accents of gossip – and 'nowhere else'. Such an 'event' however, though contained within 'the transcendent judgement of history', gives its own terms to history: 'It becomes Swift's problem . . . to show language as the arena in which fictions battle each other until only the most worthy remain. What remains of Swift can only be described, a long time later, by an impartial, anonymous voice that . . . understands Swift as a man who was *too much* for his own time'. As I understand it, this single, retrospective voice contrasts with the dispersal of meanings among the trivial words and pastimes of the idle urban bourgeoisie and is closer to the 'objective chronology' of historic time, two movements which are gathered together triumphantly by the movement of the poem. The poem is a synthesis which transcends such chat, and can control it, because 'this conversation belongs neither to the public nor to the private world but to an entirely independent verbal order that obliterates every worthwhile distinction'.[30] The poem – this 'powerful verbal structure' – literally makes history, and the subject – Swift – supplements the particular time of his existence. Said argues for the deconstruction of an opposition of public to private through the maintained panache of taking the one (which is impossible) for the other (which is credible). The term 'continuity' is an important one: for Said it is an extrapolation from this single text by Swift to a writing career which is continuous with the political career – must indeed take over its capacity for political action. Rightly distrustful of notions of 'development', critics must therefore look for continuities by which later work does not cancel earlier. They must strain to do so since in the case of Pope a more apparent movement is that by which the exquisite private sensibility of the convent or the bedroom becomes the nightmare carnival of the public streets.[31] Fancy abandons Sapho but Pope abandons fancy: at the very end of the *Essay on Man*, addressing Bolingbroke he says, 'That urg'd by thee, I turn'd the tuneful art/From sounds to things, from fancy to the heart' (iv, 391–2).[32] Pope's own epilogue within *Eloisa* can be read as closing off a voice which has the potential to subvert or usurp the opposition of public and private if it were to break the bounds of its enclosure. It reasserts the present and a transmissible patriarchal voice.

Of course this raises major questions, not just about techniques within a single poem but about the ways in which we predicate a canon, or a literary history. I want to offer a last few instances of the relations between female voice, self-construction and subjection that I have sketched in *Eloisa to Abelard*. The heroic antinomies of that poem become mere contraries in the antithetical technique of the picture gallery in the later *Epistle to a Lady* (1732–4). 'Woman's at best a Contradiction still' (270) which, 'at best', is a variant, 'a softer Man' (272). Thus what is an ethos of plain view for the male world is an ethos of appearance, of concealed substance for the female:

> But grant, in Public Men sometimes are shown,
> A Woman's seen in Private life alone:
> Our bolder Talents in full light display'd,
> Your Virtues open fairest in the shade.
> Bred to disguise, in Public 'tis you hide;
> There, none distinguish 'twixt your Shame or Pride,
> Weakness or Delicacy; all so nice,
> That each may seem a Virtue, or a Vice.
>
> (199–206)

Women enter public discourse as appearance. Where men are 'shown' there, women are best 'seen' in private where they can be visualised without the difficulty of distinction that public discourse imposes. Their consolation for this is that though paler they can be visualised as more 'mild', 'sober', and 'serene'.

> Ah Friend! to dazzle let the Vain design,
> To raise the Thought and touch the Heart, be thine!
> That Charm shall grow, while what fatigues the Ring
> Flaunts and goes down, an unregarded thing.
> So when the Sun's broad beam has tir'd the sight,
> All mild ascends the Moon's more sober light,
> Serene in Virgin Modesty she shines,
> And unobserv'd the glaring Orb declines.
>
> (249–56)

The production of 'Thought' and an organic growth of 'Charm' is valorised over the 'dazzle' of the publicly visible, but Pope cannot think himself outside of the visual terms. The superiority of the private idea of the female is a visual superiority: all eyes turn from the sun to the moon, and all eyes are male. It is in the public world of males that 'Thought' and 'Charm' have exchange value. A discourse that is apparently double resolves itself as actually unitary.

I hope to have demonstrated that the apparent vacillations of *Eloisa to Abelard* are prospective versions of a figuration common in Pope's texts: not *either* the one *or* the other but *both* the one *and* the other, with the other always subordinate in a hierarchy. If there are always only appearances, then those who are defined by appearance are better kept within the bounds of a discourse where appearance and substance can (appear to) coincide – provided that even there the watchful poet will be present. Voice is succeeded by spectacle. Less abstractly, this distinction between appearance and substance, this insistence on two worlds, is what makes possible *The Rape of the Lock*, for example. Placing Belinda where the hero would be in an epic enables the distinction to be exploited comically; and even Queen Anne is subject to it. The famous double vision of the poem – is Belinda celebrated or condemned? – insists on Belinda's beauty and instances it only as commodity – what does Belinda look like? This context makes it possible to see in Pope's *Eloisa* and other poems not 'a voice for women in English poetry' but a circumscribed area in which female desire is localised as 'idea'. The later poems demonstrate that such desire can be actively embodied only as monstrosity. By the time of *The Dunciad* vocal confusion clarifies something. The Angel of Dullness is sent 'to scatter round/Her magic charms o'er all unclassic ground' (iii, 257–8). From the pervasiveness of corruption, from the inflation of print and of a pestilential paper-credit, it is clear that what you do not incorporate will incorporate you.

On this reading, of course, it is not the passionate Eloisa who figures the female voice but – absent and disfigured to a mere 'name' – Abelard. This returns us to the issues of what context and when. Pope transfers to Eloisa phrases which in Hughes's translation come from Abelard's side of the correspondence. Knowing this must at least complicate a notion of the poem as ventriloquism or wish-fulfilment. Knowing this also suggests the possibility that, rather than its being an afterthought, an appropriation of the female voice, or its supersession by spectacle, might have generated the poem. At any rate, in *Eloisa to Abelard* the male–female correspondence becomes a female monologue only for the male voice to re-emerge. The poem closes with a gesture of recovered potency: 'voice' is not what escapes but that which can be subsumed and therefore needs to be recovered. Of course the ending does not have to be read as a gesture of continuing mastery. By my count Lipking offers five plausible readings of it, all of which repeat the impossibility of completed desire. Such readings do not cancel each other out though they may contradict each other.[33] Voice is continually succeeded by spectacle. Synecdoches of person and place are functionally similar to the totalised views and voices of the later satires. The public view and the private voice co-exist; but the crucial question to be asked of Pope's text is how such antagonistic elements can be produced as a peaceful and hierarchical co-existence. We need to examine what I have called their rhetoric of incorporation.

Stephen Bygrave

Notes

1. Of course, this point has been made by other studies. After finishing the first version of this paper I read Ellen Pollak, *The Poetics of Sexual Myth*, Women in Culture and Society (Chicago and London, 1985), an impressive restatement of Pope's misogyny within a rather mono-lithically represented eighteenth-century patriarchy: Pollak's general case, and the reading of *Eloisa to Abelard* which closes her book, is distressingly similar to mine. I do not, however, see the need to establish a preference for Swift as some kind of countervailing 'progressive' alternative to Pope, and the notion of travestying the feminine will need extending (by me as well as by her) from those poems which explicitly represent women.
2. Lawrence Lipking, *Abandoned Women and Poetic Tradition* (Chicago and London, 1988), p. 68.
3. On the figure of synecdoche in *The Rape of the Lock* and *Windsor-Forest*, see some suggestive comments by Laura Brown in *Alexander Pope* (Oxford, 1985), pp. 28–30; also Pollak, *The Poetics of Sexual Myth*, pp. 95–7.
4. Rebecca Ferguson notes the similarity of this second line to two lines from the *Heroides*. *The Unbalanced Mind: Pope and the Rule of Passion* (Brighton, 1986), p. 15. It is also similar to a line from the 'Epistle to Mr. Jervas' (*TE*, vi, 156–8): 'The tender sister, daughter, friend and wife' (52).
5. Joseph Warton, *An Essay on the Writings and Genius of Pope* (London, 1756), p. 314.
6. See for example the fine essay by Murray Krieger, '*Eloisa to Abelard*: the escape from body or the embrace of body', *E-CS*, iii (1969–70), 28–47. Krieger describes the tension as a question of 'how to embrace the unembraceable, how to be intimate without sexuality, how to encompass the body of the disembodied. Of course, for sexual purposes, the emasculated is equivalent to the disembodied' (p. 47). I shall withhold comment on the assumptions that can generate the last sentence quoted. Krieger sees the poem as structured around Eloisa's shifting injunction to 'come' or 'come not', as does Gillian Beer, in an important article I discuss below, ' "Our unnatural No-voice": the heroic epistle, Pope, and women's Gothic', *The Yearbook of English Studies* 12 (1982), 125–51.
7. Compare Warton offering a run-through of the poem to bring out the way it speaks Eloisa's 'struggles and conflicts, between duty and pleasure, between penitence and passion', *Essay*, p. 305.
8. *Abandoned Women and Poetic Tradition*, p. 146.
9. Jean Hagstrum comments in *Sex and Sensibility: Ideal and Erotic Love from Milton to Mozart* (Chicago, 1980), p. 132, that Pope chose the story 'because . . . it was becoming archetypal. Of what? Not, surely, of religious conflict about love but of the sexual passion itself, which was increasingly regarded as the foundation of individual love and marriage'.
10. Ruffhead, p. 153.
11. W. B. Carnochan, *Confinement and Flight: An Essay on English Literature*

of the Eighteenth Century (Berkeley and Los Angeles, 1977), p. 81.

12. Sherburn, i, 338. (Sherburn conjectures a date in March 1716 for this letter.)
13. Sherburn, i, 407. Lady Mary Wortley Montagu marked lines 121-2, the lines quoted above, in her copy, putting a cross next to 'eye' and at the bottom of the page writing 'mine'. See Robert Halsband, *The Life of Lady Mary Wortley Montagu* (New York, 1960 edn), p. 76.
14. *Sex and Sensibility*, p. 126.
15. *Essay*, p. 333.
16. *Essay*, p. 321.
17. *An Essay on the Genius and Writings of Pope*, (2nd edn, London, 1762), p. 334.
18. *Essay* (both editions), p. 253.
19. Margaret Anne Doody, *The Daring Muse: Augustan Poetry Reconsidered* (Cambridge, 1985), p. 207.
20. Brean Hammond, *Pope* (Brighton, 1986), p. 175.
21. Beer, ' "Our unnatural No-voice" ', p. 127.
22. *Ibid.*, p. 140.
23. Compare the warning issued by Ruffhead that the poem might prove a source for seducers and sanction 'illicit deviations from the paths of virtue': in so doing Ruffhead is drawn into paradoxes similar to those in the poem, speaking of the 'unbounded freedom of [Eloisa's] attachment' pp. 171-2.
24. See Laura Brown, *Alexander Pope*, p. 107: '"Woman" is purely emblematic in *Epistle to a Lady*. A painting without a model, a sign without a referent, "woman" holds a place for male fantasy to fill'.
25. See Reuben A. Brower, *Alexander Pope: The Poetry of Allusion* (Oxford, 1959), pp. 66-74, for the way the characteristic dualism of the poem imitates its Ovidian models.
26. Compare the couplet which appeared in editions of *Eloisa to Abelard* up to 1720, at line 258:

    Cut from the root my perish'd joys I see,
    And love's warm tyde for ever stopt in thee.

27. Compare Pope's fragmentary inscription to Martha Blount in a copy of Lintot's *Miscellany* in 1712:

    Each pretty Caracter with pleasing Smart
    Deepens the dear Idea in my heart.

    (*TE*, vi, 231)

28. See Peter Stallybrass and Allon White, *The Politics and Poetics of Transgression* (Brighton, 1987), pp. 84ff. See also Mary E. Knapp, *Prologues and Epilogues of the Eighteenth Century*, Yale Studies in English, 149 (New Haven, 1961).
29. Compare Hagstrum: 'a full account would have to relate love madness and hate madness and perhaps see *The Dunciad*, with its scatology, its ugly but powerful regressiveness, its images of obscenity and frenzy, as the obverse of the passion so nobly and sympathetically treated in *Eloisa to Abelard*', *Sex and Sensibility*, p. 123.
30. Edward Said, 'Swift's Tory anarchy', in *The World, The Text and the*

Critic (Cambridge, Mass., 1983), pp. 54–71 (pp. 66–9).

31. An impressive example is Laura Brown's argument for Pope as celebrant of imperialism. She says, for example, that women function in Pope's poetry 'as the privileged locus for the display of the products of accumulation' (p. 103), the paradigm-case being Belinda. This leads her to a conclusion similar to the one I draw from 'Eloisa', namely that Pope 'uses' women 'as surrogates for male stability' (p. 106). What is more questionable is that she wants to save the appropriable versions of ideological fracture for *The Dunciad*. If *Windsor-Forest* is a panegyric of English imperialism, *The Dunciad* is a critique of capitalism and 'the legitimate celebratory pastoral scene to which *Windsor-Forest* only alludes' (p. 157).

32. The more famous version is the couplet from the *Epistle to Dr. Arbuthnot*: 'That not in Fancy's maze he wander'd long/But stoop'd to Truth, and moraliz'd his song' (340–1).

33. Lipking's readings are offered on pp. 150–2. On 'contradiction' I have in mind the argument by John Barrell and Harriet Guest, 'The uses of contradiction: Pope's "Epistle to Bathurst" ', in Barrell's *Poetry, Language and Politics* (Manchester, 1988), pp. 79–99, as to why the eighteenth-century long poem can contain not only disparate materials but also arguments that are demonstrably contradictory. In Pope's case, assertions of a *concordia discors* are versions of economic contradiction which the poems do not resolve because they do not have to. The conventions of their reading and publication suggest that individual 'beauties' (or portraits) need only be consistent in themselves.

8

'Intestine Wars'
Body and text in An Epistle to Dr. Arbuthnot and The Dunciad

Rebecca Ferguson

In a word, certainly he never had the least taste of Physiology, who conceiveth, that any thing which is generated can be eternal; for what Composition is there, which is not dissolveable? Or what is there, that hath a Beginning, and no End? Though there were no external Causes to destroy its Frame, yet wants there not an intestine motion, and, even within the most compact and durable Bodies, an unvanquishable inclination of Atoms downwards, whence their dissolution must necessarily follow.
Thomas Stanley, *The History of Philosophy* (2nd edn, 1687), p. 871

The above passage, taken from Stanley's exposition of the Epicurean school of philosophy, is a graphic statement of the vulnerability and the finite life of bodies. If they are generated and have a beginning, they must necessarily have an end; if not destroyed from without, they have a no less pressing tendency to destroy themselves from within. Immediately preceding this summary statement is a fascinating discussion in which the myriad potential combinations of the letters of the alphabet to form words (both comprehensible and incomprehensible) is compared with the sheer profusion of the processes of generation and corruption in bodies. Fortunately, the Epicurean atoms are selective in how they combine themselves to form compound beings and species, careful to 'associate with those which are agreeable to them' and to 'pass by, and, as it were, reject others'; hence they avoid creating 'Monsters'. Likewise, letters cannot be merely jumbled anyhow to produce words 'innumerable, inexpressible, and incomprehensible', but by selection

137

and combination we form 'words, accommodated to Pronunciation and Reason', suitable to be spoken or written. Words (properly defined) are selectively bred, and this is what makes them legitimate.[1]

The analogy being drawn here yields a potent and pervasive metaphor, that of writing as a physical body. Indeed, if the reader is willing, it is interesting to consider the passage first quoted as a poignant commentary on the immanent dissolution of texts, for once the text is conceived as a living being, it follows that it is equally subject to change and that its lifespan is limited.

Pope's poetry is replete with the imagery of the body, both in a state of ideal harmony and of disintegration. This essay looks at the specific links between Pope's metaphoric formulations of the body as writing, and writing as the body, and considers some of the consequences of these metaphors – what is expressed through the diversity of fates which can afflict the body, and the various subversions that the body can perform. Key concerns arising from these are, for example, the nature of literary engendering, creativity and organic growth, sexual and linguistic conjunctions, and also the genealogy and behaviour of offspring (which may be passively subject to defilement, mutilation and mortality, but may equally engage in wilful rebellion and deviance). As I hope to show, the predominant force of these metaphors is to probe the difficult issue of what is supposedly 'legitimate' and 'illegitimate' in the processes of writing and reading, and to emphasise the vulnerability of the written word and of authors themselves.

A distinction can be suggested between wit as an impregnator of the mind, producing the organically growing work itself, and the printed text as a product, a separate and autonomous body. Roland Barthes' observations on the metaphoric differences between work and text are helpful here:

> The author is reputed the father and the owner of his work . . . while society asserts the legality of the relation of author to work. . . . As for the Text, it reads without the inscription of the Father. Here again, the metaphor of the Text separates from that of the work: the latter refers to the image of an *organism* which grows by vital expansion, by 'development' (a word which is significantly ambiguous, at once biological and rhetorical); the metaphor of the Text is that of the *network* . . . the Text is that space . . . where languages circulate (keeping the circular sense of the term).[2]

These motifs emerge, significantly, within *An Essay on Criticism* and in parts of the *Imitations of Horace*. But perhaps the most striking permutations on the theme occur in *An Epistle to Dr. Arbuthnot* and *The Dunciad*, both of which are deeply concerned with writing as *process*, with the begetting of works, and with what will become of authors. In both, anxieties about authorship come into play, within and beyond the sophisticated play of satire. Pope's facility or fertility in punning is itself presented as a kind of multiple birth, yet within his own fictional and rhetorical terms the location of the beginnings and ends of literary creation, of origins and points of closure, proves elusive. In the famous line from the first of the *Imitations* (*Satire* II i), the image of writing is presented as the unmediated utterance of truth, a kind of spontaneous effluence of the body which overrides any distinction between intellect and emotion – 'My Head and Heart thus flowing thro' my Quill' – but this myth of physical and personal integrity is itself undermined by Pope's antagonist in the *Epilogue to the Satires*, *Dialogue One*, who accuses him instead of bodily decrepitude, 'Decay of Parts', and of plagiarising his text from Horace (5–10).

Other reassuring models are put forward in the *Essay on Criticism*, including the platonic one whereby literary 'Judgement' is attuned to 'Nature', a body of organic and spiritual perfection with nature as the *nous*, 'th'informing Soul',[3] in/forming in the *literal* sense of giving it shape, 'feeding' from within without taking visible form itself:

> In some fair Body thus th'informing Soul
> With Spirits feeds, with Vigour fills the whole,
> Each Motion guides, and ev'ry Nerve sustains;
> *It self unseen*, but in th'*Effects*, remains.
>
> (76–9)

Perfection as a principle here consists in a kind of incorporeality, interiority; its very nurturing role is insubstantial, so that this body has nothing to ingest. It is self-sufficient, and it is ungendered. But in a later and much more developed passage of the *Essay* (476–93), it is the most interior and originary faculty of literary creation, 'wit', which is ejected from the 'Golden Age', and in post-lapsarian degeneracy fails to emulate the '*Patriarch-Wits*' of those times, whose lifespan had extended beyond the dictates of nature to a thousand years. Instead, modern poets attain only a mortal 'bare Threescore'; they witness the collapse of their line and of their own literary forebears ('Our Sons their Fathers' *failing Language* see'),[4] and they find that their word as divine *logos*, the commanding power of their *fiat*, fails to bring any '*new World*' into being. Finally, instead of engendering according to this line of poet-creators, the faculty of wit shifts gender so as to evade control, self-regulation and the laws of sexual possession:

> What is this *Wit* which must our Cares employ?
> The *Owner's Wife*, that *other Men* enjoy.
>
> (500–1)

The final image presents us with a Wit that is bereft of its authority, integrity and longevity; its offspring, like those of a cuckolded husband, cannot be guaranteed as its own at all.

That authors aspire to be the undisputed fathers of their own texts is a commonplace of eighteenth-century rhetoric,[5] as it is in certain works of contemporary theory;[6] but the terms of this problematic authority, its uncertainties and liabilities, are explored by Pope in particularly suggestive ways.

Few texts seem to offer so many variants on the imagery of birth as *The Dunciad*, and it is a text in which the acts of generation too are widely diffused.[7] In the opening of the 1743 four-book version, where Dulness broods over her realm with 'mighty wings out-spread/To hatch a new Saturnian age of Lead' (i, 27–8), and in book III, where she brings that process to fruition and gathers the British Isles 'Dove-like . . . to her wings again', the goddess acts most clearly as the Holy Ghost or informing Soul of her universe. Significantly, Pope resolves the ambivalence of gender which persists in the invocation to *Paradise Lost* which he has closely parodied. There the Holy Spirit is both impregnator and incubator:

> . . . thou from the first
> Wast present, and with mighty wings outspread
> Dove-like sat'st brooding on the vast abyss,
> And madest it pregnant.
>
> (*Paradise Lost*, i, 19–22)

Dulness is much more clearly a 'Mighty *Mother*', a breeder of multitudinous offspring (iii, 129–38) like Milton's womb of Earth herself; she is a 'Nursing-mother' (i, 312) who suckles and fattens her offspring back into the sleep and stupor of infancy. As *anti-logos*, she finally consumes what is bred on earth, just as the North, the 'great Nurse' of tribes of vandals, pours forth her myriad sons to destroy 'infant letters'; the consuming of texts by fire, a metonym for the end of civilisation, is a prelude to the apocalypse of the poem's ending. As a female entity, her powers of generation are closely associated with her prostitution of herself: she grants her 'favours' to a host of male protégés, and when she is revealed to the gaze of her admirers at iv, 18, it is her nether regions that are presented.[8]

With her children, both the line and the process of generation are more complex. Cibber in effect has several parents, who supersede one another as the poem proceeds. First, we witness him in association with his 'literal', mortal father, the sculptor Caius Cibber, by whom he is provided with the statues of his 'brazen, brainless brothers' above Bedlam gates. He inhabits the emptiness of his cell, the cave of poverty and poetry, which turns out to be a bizarre womb, and from this, the aberrations of the dunces are conceived, aborted or brought to grotesque fruition:

> Hence Bards, like Proteus long in vain ty'd down,
> Escape in Monsters, and amaze the town.
>
> (i, 37–8)

These monsters are at once the burgeoning material products of the printing press – 'Miscellanies . . . Journals, Medleys, Merc'ries, Magazines' – and the semi-animated products of the mind, the 'nameless Somethings' which 'in their causes sleep'. The suggestiveness of this celebrated passage (i, 55–78) lies not only in Pope's evocation of the amorphous, seething forms of life (so redolent of the Epicurean image of incipient creation, where atoms commingle indiscriminately to try to *find* their form[9]), but in the way in which these forms spring from the conjunctions of language and of *literary* forms (a process which ironically Pope enacts himself by fertile punning). Poetic feet, 'similes unlike', genres that copulate and beget confused cross-breeds, puns – all of these finally lay down a new, inverted physical order, like the *logos* run amok.[10] It is a scene of 'equivocal generation' (*abiogenesis*), which as David Fairer has suggested[11] has affinities with the reference to the indeterminate writers in *An Essay on Criticism*:

> . . . half-form'd Insects on the Banks of *Nile*;
> Unfinish'd Things, one knows not what to call,
> Their Generation's so *equivocal*.
>
> (41–3)

The literal meaning of 'equivocal' (which Pope has italicised) is of interest here (OED: 'Having two or more significations equally appropriate; capable of double interpretation; ambiguous: 1601); as is the double meaning of 'Generation' (a way of breeding, or a line of

141

descent). The whole phrase refers not only to the bringing together of indeterminate forms, but also (as the reference in the *Essay* to the mud of Nile makes clear) to the idea of spontaneous *self*-generation, something that manages to beget itself without parents, proliferating by itself and from itself.[12] (Sporus might be considered such a creature of 'spontaneous generation', not only in the sense that Pope chiefly emphasises rhetorically, of being an 'Amphibious Thing', but in the manner in which he 'spits himself abroad' in the form of his libellous but profuse writings.) The *Dunciad* passage crucially involves breeding from the brain and from language itself, without 'authority', and this idea is rendered equally graphically in the succeeding image of the poet, surrounded by his 'embryo' and 'abortion', in the throes of a kind of fluid birth or logorrhoea: 'Nonsense precipitate, like running Lead,/That slip'd thro' Cracks and Zig-zags of the Head' (i, 123-4).[13]

These female and male places of birth achieve a conjunction at the opening of book III. Cibber lies with his head upon the lap of Dulness and his brain conceives and enters its own underworld, where the 'poetic souls' demanding their 'new bodies' (i.e. printed pages and bookbindings) are transposed by metempsychosis into the physical forms of texts and wing their way to the booksellers. What is striking here is the lightness, indeed 'impatience', of these texts in their urge to 'rush to the world', set against the heaviness of the skulls of their makers (or perhaps their readers?), 'Of solid proof, impenetrably dull'. This new generation, the books themselves, has a positively ethereal freedom, however short its lifespan. Another image for the lightness and profusion of mass-produced texts occurs in the closing of the games in book II (361-4), where printed papers descend like snow on the heads of the celebrants from what are punningly described as 'dark volumes' of clouds. Their freedom and new life are comically, even touchingly evoked in some parts of *The Dunciad*, but they carry their threats as well.

To return to the problem of birth and lines of descent: the concepts of origin and of the progress of time and generations may be expressed in two essentially contradictory figures. First, there is linearity, the genealogy of 'line' (which Pope equates at i, 103-4, through another pun, with the *written* line). Sons succeed fathers and live to complete their wills and prophecies: 'She saw, with joy, the line immortal run'. . . . 'She saw old Pryn in restless Daniel shine,/And Eusden eke out Blackmore's endless line'. Pope uses further puns to advance the idea of this heritage as a kind of written text or will, an imprinting of each progenitor upon the next: Dulness '*marks*' in each son 'her Image full exprest', each sire is '*imprest* and glaring in his son', and (in another bookish pun) 'She saw slow Philips creep like Tate's poor page' (i, 105).

The second network of imagery (taking up the motif of the transmigration of souls, or metempsychosis) is that of eternal recurrence, of circularity, which as many have noted has a central place in the poem. It evades the problems of locating points of origin and of finality, and this is why, as Stanley's account in the *History of Philosophy* expresses it, it is for Plato the appropriate figure for the divine. God is called 'Father',

> as being cause of all things, and adorning the mind of Heaven and Soul of the World after his own exemplar and notions . . . he is neither genus nor species, nor difference. . . . Moreover, if he were a body, it would follow that he must be generable, corruptible, mutable, which to affirm of God were intolerable. (*History*, p. 186)

Concerning the circle imagery, Stanley cites a neoplatonic discourse ('after Hieronimo Benivieni') which distinguishes the imagery of moving around the circumference of a circle from that of concentric circles. Of the first he states that,

> In one respect this agrees with God, in another not; the property of beginning from a point and returning to it, is repugnant to him; who hath no beginning, but is himself that indivisible point from which all Circles begin, and to which they return: And in this sence it is likewise inconsistent with material things, they have a beginning, but cannot return to it. (p. 202)

These two images of circularity are reserved by Pope both for the influence of Dulness as the originary Goddess herself, who precedes Chaos, literacy and intellectual generation ('E'er Pallas issu'd from the Thund'rer's head' (i, 10)), and for Cibber as her chosen inheritor and most privileged son (*the Son*, in fact). In the opening of book III Cibber discovers his spiritual father – his literary progenitor – in Settle, whose speech transforms his transmigrating soul to the still centre, the fixed principle of circulation:

> As man's Maeanders to the vital spring
> Roll all their tides, then back their circles bring;
> Or whirligigs, twirl'd round by skilful swain,
> Suck the thread in, then yield it out again:
> All nonsense thus, of old or modern date,

143

Shall in thee centre, from thee circulate.

(iii, 55-60)

The passage presents a happy ideal of self-sufficiency and self-regulation. The inner and the outer, the first and the last, no longer need distinction and are no longer subject to difference. Time itself becomes a conflated past, present and future through the power of the visionary and the authority of Dulness (i, 71). Likewise, with the advent of Dulness in book IV, 'none want a place, for all their Centre found,/Hung to the Goddess, and coher'd around' (77-8). The figure of concentric circles is used most memorably to close book II on the theme of the power of words to induce slumber, while the open books provide beds for the clerks who read.

However, perfect circularity and reabsorption is not the only model at work in the poem. At other points, more unsettling fates beset authors and their texts, both parents and offspring. In Cibber's library, for example, authors are literally embodied in the volumes of their works, and they suffer accordingly – notably from Cibber's parasitism as a plagiarist, 'an industrious bug', who leaves shreds of his half-digested literary meals and what remains of 'crucify'd Moliere' strewn about the floor (i, 127-54). The non-conformists suffer defilement or burning ('the martyrdom of jakes and fire'), while the venerable fathers and 'Dry Bodies of Divinity' are mummified corpses, preserved only in death. In being personified in this way (as in Boileau's *Le Lutrin* and Swift's *Battle of the Books*), books go through dramas of death at the moment when Cibber, abjuring the 'dead Letter', lights his sacrificial pyre and 'Great Caesar roars, and hisses in the fires;/King John in silence modestly expires' (i, 251-2).

All of the above are in effect the patriarchs who make up the foundation of the pyre. But the sacrificial victims forming the pinnacle have a special status, for they are Cibber's own begotten works – not all of these, it seems, are embryos or still-births, or even 'lame' (i, 190). Some are at least mature enough to get about, wander off and prostitute themselves in the act of dissemination. They are models of a subversiveness which Cibber hopes to forestall by cutting off the life of their infant sisters, born in original sin yet still uninitiated as sexual adults. These remain in 'maiden sheets', that is, uncut paper or an undefiled bed:[14]

> 'O born in sin, and forth in folly brought!
> Works damn'd, or to be damn'd! (your father's fault)
> Go, purify'd by flames ascend the sky,
> My better and more christian progeny!

144

Unstain'd, untouch'd, and yet in maiden sheets;
While all your smutty sisters walk the streets.
Ye shall not beg, like gratis-given Bland,
Sent with a Pass, and vagrant thro' the land;
Not sail, with Ward, to Ape-and-monkey climes,
Where vile Mundungus trucks for viler rhymes;
Not sulphur-tipt, emblaze an Ale-house fire;
Not wrap up Oranges, to pelt your sire!
O! pass more innocent, in infant state,
To the mild Limbo of our Father Tate:
Or peaceably forgot, at once be blest
In Shadwell's bosom with eternal Rest!
Soon to that mass of Nonsense to return,
Where things destroy'd are swept to things unborn.'

(i, 225-42)

Pope describes this speech in his footnote as 'a tender and passionate Apostrophe to his own Works which he is going to sacrifice, . . . reflecting like a parent, on the many miserable fates to which they would otherwise be subject'. Cibber here is an Agamemnon making his last valediction to Iphigenia, or an Othello addressing his Desdemona as a book defaced by the inscription of 'whore'.[15] He has resolved in tragic fashion upon perfect self-sufficiency, to maintain only his originary being with no offspring either to succeed or subvert him, to consign these works of his to another father, 'our Father Tate', or 'Shadwell's bosom'. There are *degrees* of sin, culpability and retribution entailed in the printing and dissemination process, which he averts as far as may be. The whole scenario closely resembles what Derrida has to say in *Dissemination* about the family drama of *logos*. Analysing the metaphors of Plato's *Phaedrus*, he explains that Plato is concerned with the role of the logographer, or 'ghost writer', who writes speeches for others, 'speeches which he himself does not pronounce, which he does not attend, so to speak, in person, and which produce their effects in his absence' (p. 68); in other words, he deals with 'the genealogical break and the estrangement from the origin' which is entailed in writing as opposed to speech (p. 74). Derrida comments on 'the permanence of a Platonic schema that assigns the origin and power of speech, precisely of *logos*, to the paternal position' (p. 76), and he notes the ways in which, in Plato's formulation, *logos* can as it were become divided from itself through writing. He explains it thus:

One could say anachronously that the 'speaking subject' is the *father* of his speech. . . . *Logos* is a son, then, a son that would be destroyed in his very *presence* without the present *attendance* of his father. . . .

145

Without his father, he would be nothing but, in fact, writing. . . . The specificity of writing would thus be intimately bound to the absence of the father. (p. 77)

Socrates, he notes, insists upon 'the misery, whether pitiful or arrogant, of a *logos* committed to writing: "It always needs its father to attend to it, being quite unable to defend itself or attend to its own needs" '. But Derrida goes on to observe,

This misery is ambiguous: It is the distress of the orphan, of course, . . . but in pitying the orphan, one also makes an accusation against him, along with writing, for claiming to do away with the father, for achieving emancipation with complacent self-sufficiency. From the position of the holder of the scepter, the desire of writing is . . . denounced as a desire for orphanhood and patricidal subversion. (p. 77)

The conception of *logos* as having a father is one which is of course contingent on the fact that it is spoken of as a living being: 'In describing *logos* as a *zōon*, Plato is following certain rhetors and sophists before him who, as a contrast to the cadaverous rigidity of writing, had held up the living spoken word' (p. 79).

An ambivalent fusion of pity and authoritarian anxiety is present in the comedy of Pope's passage, and the substitution of daughters for sons is especially cogent since the subversive 'sin' of orphanhood is compounded by the sins of prostitution and a potential for illegitimate breeding.[16] While Cibber attempts to protect his works from vagrancy and homelessness, he also tries to prevent them from being used to assault *him* on stage ('Not wrap up Oranges, to pelt your sire!'). Perhaps it is relevant, too, that an actor is pre-eminently a speaker. Having chosen to give up on the painful business of creation and labour, Cibber regresses to retrieve his old home in Dulness, as it were by instinctive recognition (i, 266).[17]

In *To Arbuthnot*, it is Pope who must become the surrogate parent for the works of others, the 'Virgin Tragedy' and 'Orphan Muse' which have been sent to him like an abandoned child by the stranger hack. As Ripley Hotch has shown, the whole subject of the dutifulness of offspring is deeply probed in this poem.[18] The suggestions raised about Pope's literal and literary birth, his baptismal immersion in ink, his own capacity to give birth ('to bear'), and his breaking away as a satirist from the mould of his innocuous parents, are all fraught with contradiction and difficulty. In particular, it is not clear what kind of 'baptism' the dipping in ink

146

may be – a purification, a defilement, or an act which makes of the poet merely a pen?[19] Sinfulness is certainly a deep preoccupation (with Sporus in the role of the arch-enemy Satan), and strikingly it is *writing* and *publishing* which are seen as mounting up the debt of sin. When Pope first asks rhetorically, 'Why did I write?', the answer given is that verses came spontaneously like *speech* ('lisp'd in numbers'). He follows it up with the more urgent and implicitly damning question: 'But why then *publish*?' The answer he supplies is that he was encouraged by his literary predecessors, or fathers, to do so. The act of publishing *The Dunciad* is also treated, interestingly, as an irrepressible *outburst*: Pope's act is like that of Midas' wife, who was 'forc'd to speak, or burst' (72), and such outbreaks of speech are comparatively redeeming. One would hardly imagine from the fable that *The Dunciad* was so elaborate a written text, subject to the most painstaking process of composition. Unlike his fictionalised father, Pope is well aware of the 'Schoolman's subtle art', and he goes well beyond the supposedly transparent 'Language of the Heart'. It should come as no surprise that this progenitor is laid to rest, however gently, at the close of the poem.

In the final stages of *The Dunciad* (iv, 119–24) there occurs a particularly graphic illustration of the influential text as a literal father, and a patricidal onslaught on the body of that father. The episode alludes to the story of Medea, and its wit and relevance could easily be lost without the full scope of the allusion. Dulness, like a true Eastern tyrant, issues orders to the dunces to plunder and decimate the 'most distinguished Writers' of the past:

> When Dulness, smiling – 'Thus revive the Wits!
> But murder first, and mince them all to bits;
> As erst Medea (cruel, so to save!)
> A new Edition of old Æson gave,
> Let standard-Authors, thus, like trophies born,
> Appear more glorious as more hack'd and torn.

Pope's reference to the 'new Edition of old Æson', looking back to Ovid's *Metamorphoses* (book VII),[20] is subject to complex irony. Here the old man is the old book. In Ovid's story, Medea is able to restore the youth of Jason's father Aeson, but the black arts by which she does so consist in the slitting of his throat, the letting of all his blood and the substitution of potions of her own brewing. It is questionable whether he remains the same person, or indeed fully a human being. The incident is effective as an analogy for the way in which the dunces have taken over the texts, or bodies, of their forefathers –

147

somehow inhabiting them, but thereby changing their substance. At the same time, Pope's formulation of Dulness's injunction draws attention to Medea's act as a precedent ('as *erst* Medea'). His meaning is not only that this is an allusion to a past story, but that *within* that story Medea's act sets a precedent for the daughters of Pelias, who having witnessed her revival of Aeson request her to do the same for their father. Hence Medea incites them (knowingly) to unintentional patricide of the most gruesome kind: they chop him to pieces with heads averted and are pitifully taken aback at his failure to rise again.[21] As elsewhere in *The Dunciad*, there is a kind of innocence in the dunces' delusions which casts them in both a comic and ironic light.

Dulness's incitement goes beyond holding up authors for such martyrdom, but embraces their burial and memorials too. The dunces will impose upon them beyond the very grave:

> 'Leave not a foot of verse, a foot of stone,
> A Page, a Grave, that they can call their own;
> But spread, my sons, your glory thin or thick,
> On passive paper, or on solid brick.'
>
> (iv, 127–30)

The terms are not truly separated here, because the verse *is* the memorial, the page *is* the grave (the place in which the author reposes after death). But paper is passive, and brick no more resistant.

If in the story of Aeson the metaphor for the life of the text is the blood in the body, for the dunces and plagiarists an obvious substitute is the dead matter of excrement. Closing the *Imitations of Horace*, the *Epilogue to the Satires, Dialogue Two*, makes much of the famous 'filthy simile' of coprophilia:

> Let Courtly Wits to Wits afford supply,
> As Hog to Hog in Huts of *Westphaly*;. . .
> From tail to mouth, they feed, and they carouse;
> The last, full fairly gives it to the *House*.
>
> (171–80)

Dependency, political nepotism and plagiarism are treated together as another cycle of eternal recurrence and sufficiency in the economy of writing. Nothing need be wasted, because all waste matter serves for food. The imbibing of another's wit as a changing of its substance arises in Pope's imitation of Donne's second satire: 'Sense, past thro' him, no longer is the same,/For food digested takes another name' (33–4). Likewise, what the dunces consume, produce and thrive in is excrement, and producing this substance is a labour akin to their efforts at giving birth, as in the *Essay on Criticism* where poets 'Strain out the last, dull droppings of their Sense' (608). The antiquary Mummius, having swallowed his golden coins, gives them forth again 'at their second birth' (*Dunciad*, iv, 386); it is significant here that the coins with their imprints are analogous to texts themselves – their imprinting represents their first birth.[22] The metaphors follow the same pattern in *To Arbuthnot*. The hack, like a parasite, chews over and sucks upon the living or dead bodies of authors, but fails because of the constipatory condition of his poetic conception, so that he 'Just writes to make his barrenness appear,/And strains from hard-bound brains eight lines a-year' (181–2).

These different cycles – the circulation of food through the body by ingestion and defecation, the cycle from birth to death through generations, and the circulation of texts through different authors and readers – are suggestively drawn together in varying ways and to different effects within the wider network of Pope's metaphors. While Pope at some points links the ideas of bodily integrity and 'legitimate' breeding with the integrity of the author and that of the work as his undisputed offspring, by his elaboration of such themes as spontaneous generation, prostitution, illegitimacy, plagiarism and the dissemination of printed texts, he effectively shows that the purity and immortality of the written work cannot be guaranteed. Indeed, it can scarcely be hoped for. As a great work of fantasy, *The Dunciad* deals constantly in such connections and revelations, but shows Dulness and her dunces in a paradoxical light throughout. Both she and they are at once *logos* and *anti-logos*, the enemies of writing and, in other guises, the embodiments of writing or writers themselves, expressing all the anxieties attendant on authorship. If Dulness brings to bear the full destructive power of her 'uncreating word' at the end of the poem, if she presides over the proliferation, dissemination, appropriation and final destruction of texts, she plays much the same tricks upon her own offspring in the games of book II.[23] Here the grasping booksellers are cheated of an elusive substance, the bodily form of an author they would appropriate, and his written papers are seized by the winds and dispersed back to their originary author – the essence is in a manner of speaking saved and the outer shell of the 'author', the mere suit of clothes, is all that is left for the dunces to seize upon. For once, the assumed integrity of authors wins the day – but not for long.

Rebecca Ferguson

Notes

1. The passage is from 'Epicurus', chapter 17 ('Of the Generation and Corruption of Compounds'), p. 871. Quoted more fully for the reader's interest:

    Here the former comparison of Letters will serve to make us understand two things. One, that the particular manners of generation, and their opposite corruptions, . . . are (if not infinite, at least) innumerable, inexpressible, and incomprehensible, since of Four and twenty Letters only, which are in the Alphabet, there may be produced a multitude of words almost incomprehensible.

    The other is, that as words, accommodated to Pronunciation and Reason, are not made of every combination of Letters; so in natural things, all things are not made of all things; nor are all Atoms fit, by being joined together, to constitute any *Species* of compound things. For every thing requires such a disposition, as that the Atoms constituting it match, and, as it were, associate themselves with those which are agreeable to them, but pass by, and, as it were, reject others . . . otherwise Monsters would be ordinarily generated, as Half-men, Half-beasts; Chimera's, and Zoophyts.

2. Roland Barthes, 'From work to text' (1971), in *Image–Music–Text*, translated by Stephen Heath (New York, 1977), pp. 155–64 (pp. 160–1, 164).

3. G. Douglas Atkins opposes this image to others in the *Essay on Criticism* which present language on the one hand as dress, and on the other as the colours which are the very medium of painting (*Quests of Difference: Reading Pope's Poems* (Lexington, Kentucky, 1986), p. 24).

4. It is interesting to relate this particular passage to Edward Said's comments in *Beginnings: Intention and Method* (New York, 1975), p. 162:

    The unity or integrity of the text is maintained by a series of genealogical connections: author–text, beginning–middle–end, text–meaning, reader–interpretation, and so on. Underneath all these is the imagery of succession, of paternity, or hierarchy.

5. As one would expect, the motif appears repeatedly in dedications and prefaces, as in the preface to Lewis Theobald's *The Cave of Poverty* (London, 1714). Two major works rich in such reflections are Swift's *Tale of a Tub* and Fielding's *Tom Jones*. I am indebted to the discussion of the latter work (and of its affinities with Derrida) in David D. Hughes, 'Crises of authority in *Tom Jones, Clarissa*, and *Tristram Shandy*' (doctoral dissertation, University of Manchester, 1986); Michael Seidel gives an excellent account of Swift's *Tale* in his *Satiric Inheritance: Rabelais to Sterne* (Princeton, 1979) pointing out its concern with 'satirically weakened lines of descent: fathers to sons, ancients to moderns' (p. 169).

6. In particular, see Barthes (op. cit.); Jacques Derrida, *Dissemination* (1972; translated by Barbara Johnson (London, 1981)); Michel Foucault, 'What is an author?', in *Textual Strategies: Perspectives in Post-structuralist Criticism*, edited by Josue V. Harrari (London, 1980); and Edward Said (see n. 4 above). A good general account of the issue is given in Sandra

150

M. Gilbert and Susan Gubar, *The Madwoman in the Attic: The Woman Writer and the Nineteenth-century Literary Imagination* (New Haven and London, 1979); they observe: 'the patriarchal notion that the author "fathers" his text just as God fathered the world is and has been all-pervasive in Western literary civilisation' (p. 4).

7. Seidel (p. 232) remarks that 'much of the content of *The Dunciad* is generation's dirty dance'. Two other important and wide-ranging discussions, though with a different emphasis from mine, are Thomas E. Maresca, 'Language and body in Augustan poetic', *ELH*, 37 (1970), 374–88, and Philip Brockbank, 'The Book of Genesis and the genesis of books: the creation of Pope's *Dunciad*', in *The Art of Alexander Pope*, edited by Howard Erskine-Hill and Anne Smith (London, 1979), pp. 192–211.

8. See also Susan Gubar, 'The female monster in Augustan satire', *Signs*, 3.2 (1977), 380–94.

9. See Thomas Stanley, *The History of Philosophy* (2nd edn, 1687), p. 874: 'After many Convolutions, Evolutions, and making several Efforts, and as it were Attempts, trying all kinds of Motions and Conjunctions, they came at last into that Form'.

10. Derrida observes that, according to the account in Plato's *Phaedrus*, 'logographical necessity . . . ought to be analogous to biological, or rather zoological, necessity. Otherwise, obviously, it [logos] would have neither head nor tail' (*Dissemination*, p. 79). He is paraphrasing Socrates' very words; see *Phaedrus and Letters VII and VIII*, translated by Walter Hamilton (London, 1973), p. 79.

11. Fairer, *Pope's Imagination* (Manchester, 1984), pp. 23–4.

12. 'Equivocal generation' is thus defined by the OED: 'the (supposed) production of plants or animals without parents: spontaneous generation'. See also Dirk F. Passmann, 'Mud and slime: some implications of the Yahoos' genealogy and the history of an idea', *BJECS*, 11 (1988), 1–17. It is clear from many accounts of the idea that such creatures were often presumed to be, as Pope describes them, 'half-form'd', and Stanley describes them in that way: 'as when *Nilus* forsakes the Fields, and the Earth beginneth to grow dry, through heat of the Sun, the Husbandman, turning up the Glebe, finds several living Creatures, part begun, part imperfect, and maimed; . . . In like manner, amongst those first efforts of the Earth, besides the living Creatures perfectly formed, there were some produced, wanting Hands, Feet, Mouth, and other parts; without which, there is no way to take nourishment, or to live long, or to propagate their Kind' (*History of Philosophy*, p. 875).

13. This 'fluid birth' contains a strong reference to alchemy, with the head as a cracked retort.

14. The association of the female with the *blank* sheet, awaiting inscription by the male, is interestingly discussed by Susan Gubar, ' "The blank page" and the issue of female creativity', *Critical Enquiry*, 8.2 (1981), 243–63: 'when the metaphors of literary creativity are filtered through a sexual lens, female sexuality is often identified with textuality' (p. 245).

15. *Othello*, Act IV. 2. 71–2:

> Was this fair paper, this most goodly book,
> Made to write 'whore' upon?

16. Lewis Theobald has a similar point to make about the proliferation of errors in successive printed editions of Shakespeare's plays, specifically caused by the absence of manuscripts: 'The Press is set to work from a *printed* Precedent, and so the more the Editions of any Book multiply, the more the Errors multiply too, and propagate out of their own Species' (*Shakespeare Restored: Or, a Specimen of the Many Errors as Well Committed, as Unamended, by Mr. Pope in his late Edition of this Poet* (London, 1726) pp. ii–iii).

17. This is also a reference to Plato, as Pope's footnote points out (*Dunciad Variorum*, i, 221n.); he even cites Theobald's own translation of the *Phaedo*.

18. Ripley Hotch, 'The dilemma of an obedient son: Pope's *Epistle to Dr. Arbuthnot*', *Essays in Literature*, i (1974), 37–45; reprinted in *Pope: Recent Essays by Several Hands*, edited by Maynard Mack and James A. Winn (Hamden, Conn., 1980), pp. 428–43.

19. All of these are points raised in Hotch's discussion.

20. The episode is graphically rendered in *Ovid's Metamorphosis Englished by George Sandys* (8th edn, 1690), p. 133.

21. The title page of Theobald's *Shakespeare Restored* takes as epigraph a passage from Virgil's Aeneid (vi, 495), in which Aeneas has entered the underworld:

> — Laniatum Corpore toto
> DEIPHOBUM vidi & lacerum crudeliter Ora,
> Ora, manusque ambas —

In Dryden's translation, the passage is rendered:

> Here *Priam*'s Son, *Deiphobus*, he found:
> Whose Face and Limbs were one continu'd Wound.
> Dishonest, with lop'd Arms, the Youth appears:
> Spoil'd of his Nose, and shorten'd of his Ears.
> He scarcely knew him, striving to disown
> His blotted Form, and blushing to be known.

(See Dryden, *Poems*, iii, 1218.)

The image of the mutilated and outraged body is of course being used by Theobald to express the outrages committed by Pope on Shakespeare's text.

22. On the significance of imprinting coins and making them currency, see Ellen Pollak, *The Poetics of Sexual Myth: Gender and Ideology in the Verse of Swift and Pope* (Chicago, 1985), p. 124. The coins swallowed by Annius are, of course, no longer currency due to their antiquity, and have become as irrelevant as himself. The episode also represents a parody of the Incarnation, but with the stomach as the divinely-impregnated womb, and defecation as the 'second birth'.

23. These games are based on the *parentalia* (commemorative games to honour the father) of Aeneid V.

9

Romantic attacks
Pope and the spirit of language

John Whale

Epithets such as 'artificial', 'insincere', 'debased', 'tainted', 'vicious', and 'vile' suggest that Pope is a disturbing presence for Romantic writers. For them Pope's kind of poetry is much more than a matter of calm academic reflection. In the distinct cases of Wordsworth, Coleridge, Hazlitt and De Quincey we witness the Romantic ideology's struggle to promote genius and transcendence over social relevance and 'mechanical' production. While Hazlitt's empiricism moderates his view of Pope, the Tory organicism evident in Wordsworth, Coleridge and De Quincey intensifies their critiques because of a supposed threat to social cohesion. Romantic attacks on Pope are motivated by the threat of his influence, new reading audiences and the availability of literature. In the post-revolutionary and Napoleonic period fierce debates about Pope's style are automatically caught up in the fury of anti-Gallic sentiment and the fear of 'Jacobin' sympathies sweeping through popular audiences. Even later in the century – to judge by De Quincey's example – there is some concern that such a sceptical and ambivalent writer is not fit for the rapidly increasing number of working-class and artisan readers. Romantic criticism's idealised claims for a language of the spirit often turn out to be based on the bitter politics of organicism.

The assurance of Arnold's damning dismissal – 'Dryden and Pope are not classics of our poetry, they are classics of our prose' – depends on an assured Romantic inheritance. By 1872 a contributor to the *British Quarterly Review* could speak confidently on behalf of the 'Romantic doctrine'. It was a view, he argued, that 'made imagination the test of poetry' and by which 'the whole of English poetry from the Restoration . . . was pronounced a mistake. It was declared to be mere versification; the name of poetry was denied it. It wanted soul. It wanted nature. It did not touch the heart.'[1] What follows is an attempt to expose the darker side of such aesthetic criteria; especially 'soul'.

I

According to Wordsworth, Coleridge, Hazlitt and De Quincey, the 'Augustan Age' or the 'Restoration' can seem peculiarly resistant to transcendence, unlike the 'Age of Elizabeth' or the 'Age of Spenser, Shakespeare, and Milton' (as variously formulated) which was being increasingly colonised by Romantic writers – notably Coleridge and Lamb. This process is particularly associated with Shakespearean drama where, in the Romantic reception, public theatre gives way to private reading; play to poem, community to imagination. In many ways Pope stands in contradistinction to Shakespeare as regards correctness and French neoclassical values, and thus also in terms of nature and artifice. He is seen as working to rationalist prescription, not under the inspiration of unpremeditated genius.

The very nature of Pope's linguistic excellence was thought to cut him off from the capacities of a truly poetic language. Despite Arnold's much repeated dictum, a distinction was often made between the versification of Dryden and that of Pope which sees the former as more manly, vigorous and incorrect; qualities which were largely conceived of as having more potentiality. By comparison, Pope's smoothness and correctness, it is thought, seals his language in its own perfection. Latent in this distinction is the idea of faults letting in (or out) the genius, the idea that an impaired language can actually give rise to sublimity. Pope's language for them remains all surface, impenetrable, reflecting only itself; it is continuous, seamless – the perfect finished product. Significantly, though, the terms that they use to describe its supposed materiality are also those which determine their characterisation of its age. An artificial poetry comes from an artificial society; the language of poetry is itself as smooth and polished as the manners it depicts. Its very material excellence is preserved by and in the ethos of its age. All is dazzling. There is no depth for the Romantic reader to penetrate by an act of internalisation which would transcend historical difference in order to locate eternal human values.

This peculiarly contemporaneous language of the surface is also seen as a false effect in itself. The polish is the product of unnecessary labour on too solid and inert a substance. Its materiality is intrinsically suspect – manufactured and therefore reproduceable. In *Table Talk* (1782) Cowper had defined Pope's language in terms which both Coleridge and De Quincey would later see as dangerous mechanical reproduction:

> But he (his musical finesse was such,
> So nice his ear, so delicate his touch)
> Made poetry a mere mechanic art,
> And every warbler had his tune by heart.[2]

In Pope's case, musicality is clearly equated not with the organic but the mechanical, the measure of an effete society. Pope's excellence in this respect is considered exclusive, a perverse concentration on only one aspect of poetry. To judge of some adverse reactions, it is as if he has turned poetry inside out. What should be its internal pulse, scarcely heard but ever present, is now paraded with an ostentatious brilliance. For Coleridge, Pope in this respect threatens meaning: arbitrariness of sound dominates the sense. In his lectures Coleridge claims that: 'to read Dryden, Pope, and C[o]., you need only count syllables'; 'mechanical metre determines the sense'.[3] In Lecture XIV he comes to the conclusion that, 'in Pope, the use of words is for the most part purely arbitrary so that the context will rarely show the true specific sense, but only that something of the sort is designed'.[4] (This has close parallels also in Wordsworth and De Quincey, both of whom criticise the 'indirectness' of meaning in Pope's poetry almost as if they see an anarchy in ambivalence.)

Exactly what Pope's verse is thought to omit can be judged from Hazlitt's *Lectures on the English Poets*. His evaluation of Pope here is the most consistently generous of the four writers dealt with in this essay, and it represents his characteristic tendency to wage war on limited notions of taste, that narrow exclusiveness of view which he so frequently equates with egotism. (Elsewhere he particularly attacks Wordsworth's incapacity to appreciate Pope.) Allowing for the fact that Pope is not a poet of 'strong imagination', Hazlitt offers him to his reader as:

> a wit, and a critic, a man of sense, of observation and the world, with a relish for the elegances of art, or of nature when embellished by art, a quick tact for propriety of thought and manners as established by the forms and customs of society and a refined sympathy with the sentiments and habitudes of human life, as he has felt them within the little circle of his family and friends.[5]

This prepares the way for a definition of the 'poet of nature'. Just how limiting the scope of Pope's 'passion' is ('the little circle of his family and friends') can be gauged by the expansive sensibility of Hazlitt's contrasting figure who 'may be said to hold communion with the very soul of nature; to be identified with and to foreknow and to record the feelings of all men at all times and places, as they are liable to the same impressions.'[6] Not surprisingly, nature here is equated with historical transcendence on social, aesthetic and psychological levels, whereas the poet of artifice is only of his age. Hazlitt's poet of nature deals in 'eternal beauty' and shows us 'the first principles of his and our common nature'.[7] Typically, Hazlitt confirms Pope's limitations by reference to Shakespeare and Milton:

> The capacious soul of Shakespeare had an intuitive and mighty sympathy with whatever could enter into the heart of men in all possible circumstances: Pope had an exact knowledge of all that he himself loved or hated, wished or wanted. Milton has winged his daring flight from heaven to earth, through Chaos and Night. Pope's muse never wandered with safety, but from his library to his grotto, and from his grotto into his library back again.[8]

For Hazlitt, Pope's 'smooth and polished verse' will not admit soul. Pope's offence against the spirit of this poetic religion is confirmed by Hazlitt's statement that: 'He had none of the enthusiasm of poetry; he was in poetry what the sceptic is in religion.'[9]

In his three *Essays on Epitaphs* Wordsworth argues for a kind of writing that will allow the universal principles of the mind to shine through. In his ideal formulation the particular is able to give rise to the general, the present to the eternal. According to Wordsworth, 'what is most needful and most difficult' to achieve in an epitaph is to 'give to universally received truths a pathos and spirit which shall re-admit them into the soul like revelations of the moment'.[10] In his consideration of epitaph Wordsworth cuts against literary boundaries: inscriptions in a country churchyard are to be weighed against more literary productions. The test is extra-literary – ostensibly psychological, implicitly religious, ultimately social. Judged by the standards of 'humanity' – the rude forefathers of the hamlet – Pope is found wanting. In a poetic form which, for Wordsworth, goes beyond merely literary taste by calling for an appreciation of spirit within the language, Pope is a dangerous intruder. To be a 'sceptic' (to use Hazlitt's word) in this context is to commit an act of bad faith.

Not surprisingly, therefore, Wordsworth's *Essays on Epitaphs* contain some of the most scathing attacks on Pope in the Romantic period – though their target is highly specialised. According to the principles that Wordsworth adumbrates in these essays, Pope offends against 'human nature', and his censure is accordingly severe:

> If my notions are right, the Epitaphs of Pope cannot well be too severely condemned: for not only are they almost wholly destitute of those universal feelings and simple movements of the mind which we have called for as indispensable, but they are little better than a tissue of false thoughts, languid and vague expression, unmeaning antithesis and laborious attempts at discrimination. Pope's mind had been employed chiefly in observation upon the vice and follies of men. Now, vice and folly are in contradiction with the moral principle which can never be extinguished in the mind: and, therefore, wanting this control, are irregular, capacious and inconsistent with themselves.[11]

Here Wordsworth uses Johnsonian terms to undermine Pope's epitaphs, and more generally Johnson's evaluation of Pope, by attacking on two fronts. Either they fail as generalisations because it is 'feelings' which are 'universal', or they fail as particular distinctions because they are ultimately vague. Either way Pope cannot win.

In other words, this is no place for the discriminating satirist to display a critical intelligence. To be a satirist is to be tainted with the spirit of negative thinking. (Like De Quincey, Wordsworth seems to subscribe to the popular idea that the satirical view is contagious.) This is also no place for correctness or the niceties of taste. Only the simple grandeur of human nature will do. According to Wordsworth, the 'charm of sincerity lurks in the language of the Tombstone and secretly pervades it. There are no errors in style or manner for which it will not be, in some degree, compensated.' To a considerable extent the bad faith consists in the use of poetic language. Critical intelligence and polished verse together justify, for Wordsworth, his referring to Pope's 'vicious expression'.[12] Poetry is, not surprisingly, being subsumed under an idea of plain 'humanity' in line with a levelling simplicity: 'In a far greater degree are Pope's Epitaphs debased by faults which he could not I think have fallen into if he had written in prose as a plain Man, and not as a metrical Wit.'[13] Just how far 'poetry' is being shifted can be gauged when Wordsworth makes another plea for the power of simplicity:

> Why was this not simply expressed; without playing with the Reader's fancy to the delusion and dishonour of his Understanding, by a trifling epigrammatic point? But alas! ages must pass away before men will have their eyes open to the beauty and the majesty of Truth and will be taught to venerate Poetry no further than as She is a Handmaid pure as her Mistress – the noblest handmaid in her train![14]

157

Before 'poetry' disappears altogether, the last clause must be inserted. It is precisely the truth of poetry which is, in Wordsworth's view, travestied by Pope's inversion/perversion of language. In an example written, as Wordsworth carefully informs us, 'at a time when vicious writings of this kind accorded with the public taste' there is exhibited the common mistake of assuming that, 'What was natural in prose would be out of place in verse:- that it is not the Muse which puts on the garb but the Garb which makes the Muse.'[15]

When, in the preface to *Lyrical Ballads*, Wordsworth wants to do away with the distinction between prose and poetry, he describes them as sharing the same garb: 'They both speak by and to the same organs; the bodies in which both of them are clothed may be said to be of the same substance . . . the same human blood circulates through the veins of them both.'[16] This characteristically 'grounded', corporeal Wordsworth provides at the same time a shift from substance to spirit which is so typical of organicism, and the essays on epitaphs deal in the same combination: writing as physical inscription doubles as a writing of the spirit. The flowing of human blood gives rise to soul. Rather than dealing with clothes and bodies, we are dealing with, respectively, bodies and souls. According to this idea, the language of Pope's poetry holds out a false promise. What should be aids to internalisation turn out to be false vestments. Pope is damned by his own singular excellence: 'We see that Pope by the power of verse alone, has contrived to render the plainest common sense interesting, and even frequently to invest it with the appearance of passion.'[17]

This movement away from material substance and corporeality is at its most extreme when Wordsworth, in the third of the *Essays on Epitaphs*, outlines those qualities which have been threatened by the tainted example of Dryden and Pope:

> Energy, stillness, grandeur, tenderness, those feelings which are the pure emanations of nature, those thoughts which have the infinitude of truth, and those expressions which are not what the garb is to the body but what the body is to the soul, themselves a constituent part and power or function in the thought – all these are abandoned for their opposites . . .[18]

When Wordsworth returns in this paragraph to his clothing analogy, it becomes clear that the bad influence of Pope is not just incapacity or weakness: it is a threat. Since words are in touch with power, to play with them is not to waste them: it is to play with fire. The bad faith of a Pope has its own wasting energy. In this immoral incarnation the dress of thought turns out to be a Nessus' shirt of the soul. Wordsworth's expression of this negative power of language has not surprisingly provided deconstructionist critics with an exciting base:[19]

> Words are too awful an instrument for good and evil to be trifled with: they hold above all other external powers a dominion over thoughts. If words be not (recurring to a metaphor before used) an incarnation of the thought but only a clothing for it, then surely will they prove an ill gift: such an one as those poisoned vestments, read of in the stories of superstitious times, which had power to consume and to alienate from his right mind the victim who put them on. Language, if it do not uphold, and feed, and leave in quiet, like the power of gravitation or the air we breathe, is a counter-spirit, unremittingly and noiselessly at work to derange, to subvert, to lay waste, to vitiate, and to dissolve.[20]

In order to provide a healthy writing of the spirit, language must be made flesh. It has the dangerous potential to be too powerful in its own right. Only by being harnessed to thought can language become invisible and keep faith with reality.

One can appreciate now that the severe moral condemnation of Pope referred to earlier is produced by an abuse of linguistic power. Far from the satirist being a malevolent manipulator of words, it can be seen that he is a 'victim' 'alienated from his right mind'. To express the theoretical commonplace: he does not use language, language uses him. The positive power of language Wordsworth expresses here – its ability to 'uphold, and feed, and leave in quiet' – highlights the unobtrusive nature of its action, almost belying the source of power, especially in that peculiarly haunting phrase, 'to leave in quiet'. Typically power and stillness go together, as in Wordsworth's earlier list: 'Energy, stillness, grandeur, tenderness'.

Clearly, Pope's troubling, negative and ostentatious satirical intelligence is antithetical to Wordsworth's silent and 'natural' memorials. Satire's characteristic structure of thought, it is assumed, is disruptive of the solemn stillness required by epitaph. It constantly seeks to disturb us into thought, and proclaim itself. By rights it should lose itself in its object, but instead it is busy with nice distinctions, 'worrying the reader's fancy with an epigrammatic point'.[21] In the third essay Wordsworth refers to a 'mode of thought which is only natural while we are delineating vice under certain relations' but is misapplied in epitaph writing. Such a 'mode of thought' is a sure sign that the writer has no 'clear insight into the internal constitution of virtue' and that he has not been touched by the effects of 'the invisible deity'.[22] Stylistically, this implies a disruptive self-consciousness which Wordsworth, De Quincey and Coleridge seem to associate with the couplet.

In *Biographia Literaria* Colderidge provides an extended commentary on this antithetical mode of thought. Once again the context is Pope's negative influence. Coleridge offers a retrospective view of his reasons for demoting a certain school of poetry (not least among these reasons, of course, is the influence of William Lisle Bowles):

> I saw, that the excellence of this kind consisted in just and acute observations on men and manners in an artificial state of society, as its matter and substance: and in the logic of wit, conveyed in smooth and strong epigrammatic couplets, as its form. Even when the subject was addressed to the fancy, or the intellect, as in the Rape of the Lock, or the Essay on Man; nay, when it was a consecutive narration, as in that astonishing product of matchless talent and ingenuity, Pope's Translation of the Iliad; still a point was looked for at the end of each second line, and the whole was as it were a sorites, or, if I may exchange a logical for a grammatical metaphor, a conjunction disjunctive, of epigrams. Meantime the matter and diction seemed to me characterized not so much by poetic thoughts, as by thoughts translated into the ordinary language of poetry.[23]

Paradoxically this 'conjunction disjunctive' mode of thought is at one with the smooth and polished style. The whole of this passage is forced to separate form and content – or in Coleridge's terms 'form' and 'matter'. The 'conjunction disjunctive of epigrams' is, as it were, an artificial stimulant to thought and an arbitrary accession to the fashionable literary language. In the very awkwardness of Coleridge's grammatical phrase lurks the suggestion of self-defeating paradox.

In 'Lord Carlisle on Pope' De Quincey follows in Coleridge's shadow, but he makes his own distinctive contribution to the description of the structure of Pope's thought. His imagery once again suggests artificiality and superficiality; more importantly, as in Hazlitt's *Lecture on the English Poets*, the temporary nature of such productions is stressed. In making a distinction between Dryden and Pope he goes one better than a masculine/feminine distinction by offering a healthy/sick one. This is characteristic of his writing, in which illness is pervasive and an aberrant organicism can take the form of a blighting disease. In the following passage Dryden's diseased organicism has more power, according to De Quincey, than Pope's artificial fireworks:

> I admire Pope in the highest degree; but I admire him as a pyrotechnic

160

artist for producing brilliant and evanescent effects out of elements that
have hardly a moment's life within them. There is a flourish and a
startling explosion, then there is a dazzling coruscation, all purple and
gold; the eye aches under the suddenness of a display that, springing
like a burning arrow out of darkness, rushes back into darkness with
arrowy speed, and in a moment all is over. Like festal shows, or the
hurrying music of such shows

'It WAS, and it is not.'

Untruly therefore, was it ever fancied of Pope that he belonged by
classification to the family of Drydens. Dryden had within him a
principle of continuity which was not satisfied without lingering upon
his own thoughts, brooding over them and oftentimes pursuing them
through their unlinking, with the SEQUACIOUSNESS (pardon a Coleridgean word) that belongs to some process of creative nature, such as
the unfolding of a flower. But Pope was all jets and tongues of flame;
all showers of scintillation and sparkle. Dryden followed, genially, an
impulse of his healthy nature. Pope obeyed, spasmodically, an
overmastering febrile paroxysm.[24]

Although Dryden's 'sequaciousness' is linked to self-consciousness, it
is precisely this which provides evidence of the genial power of
organic revelation, evident in the 'unfolding of a flower'. Clearly
there is a kind of self-consciousness that can hold communion with
the internal spirit of things and thus allow a role for intellect as well as
passion in the process of creativity.

II

That the structure of Pope's poetry is thought to militate against a
writing of the spirit has wider implications. If, on a local level, Pope's
couplets are troubling because of their correctness and consequent
inflexibility, on a more general level they are symptomatic of the
society in which they are situated. Not surprisingly, therefore, for
these Romantic writers the issue extends beyond poetry. (We have
already seen Wordsworth breaking down the distinction between
poetry and prose as a consequence of evaluating Pope.) When these
writers assess achievement of creative excellence in the field of
discursive prose their criteria are strikingly similar and just as
sociological as those employed on Pope's poetry. In a way, the
very discursivity of non-fictional prose provides a more obvious
manifestation of this structure of thought and its relation to self-
consciousness.

Both Hazlitt and De Quincey, despite their very different political
affiliations, single out Burke for excellence of prose style. The

161

difference between their views is a measure of De Quincey's Tory
organicism and Hazlitt's liberal empiricism. Hazlitt's account is based
on the almost physical reality of events, the extent to which prose
unlike poetry must of necessity be embedded in its subject. Burke's
'dazzling' and 'daring' prose 'still has an actual resting-place and
tangible support under it'.[25] De Quincey, on the other hand, concen-
trates on the act of revelation possible in what is for him an extempore
medium. His comparison is the frequently-used one between Burke
and Johnson. The difference between the 'sequaciousness' of a
Dryden and the 'conjunction disjunctive' of Pope is again unspoken
but apparent:

> For one moment reader, pause upon the spectacle of two contrasted
> intellects, Burke's and Johnson's: one an intellect essentially going
> forward, governed by the very necessity of growth – by the law of
> motion in advance; the latter, essentially an intellect retrogressive,
> retrospective, and throwing itself back on its own steps. . . . Dr
> Johnson never, in any instance, GROWS a truth before your eyes,
> whilst in the act of delivering it, or moving towards it. . . . But to
> Burke, such is the prodigious elasticity of his thinking. . . the mere act
> of movement became the principle or cause of movement. Motion
> propagated motion. . . . In this power . . . is seen something allied to
> the powers of a prophetic seer, who is compelled oftentimes into seeing
> things, as unexpected by himself as others.[26]

This parallels the comparisons between Pope and Dryden that we
have already encountered, in which it is claimed that Dryden's
greater irregularity is preferable to Pope's correctness. De Quincey
elsewhere repeats this distinction in more extravagant philosophical
terms, and provides further clarification of the connection between
revelation and his brand of organicism:

> Burke's motion, therefore, was all a going forward. Johnson's, on the
> other hand, was purely regressive and analytic. That thought which he
> began with, contained, by involution, the whole of what he afterwards
> put forth. The two styles of conversation corresponded to the two
> theories of generation – one (Johnson's) to the theory of Preformation
> (or Evolution), where all the future products, down to the very last, lie
> secretly wrapped up in the original germ; consequently nothing is
> positively added, everything is simply unveiled – the other (Burke's)
> to the theory of Epigenesis, where each stage of the growth becomes a
> causative impulse to a new stage – every separate element in the
> mysterious process of generation being, on this hypothesis, an absolute
> supervention of new matter, and not a mere uncovering of old, already
> involved at starting in the primary germ.[27]

162

De Quincey's celebration of the organic quality of Burke's prose style ('secretly wrapped up in the original germ') in scientific terms of creativity and matter echoes *The Dunciad* where Pope watches in troubled fascination the first stirrings of dunce-creativity ('Where nameless Somethings in their causes sleep'[28]).

When Coleridge attempts to define the style which arose after the 1688 revolution, he specifically links it with the commercialisation of society and the disappearance of the 'clerisy'. Coleridge's history of style is reminiscent of Eliot's idea of the setting in during this period of a dissociation of sensibility, but it is more overtly sociological in its focus. The terms in which he writes of this style, and in particular of Johnson's, cast a revealing light on the reaction against Pope:

> The thought was carefully kept down to the immediate apprehension of the commonest understanding, and the dress was as anxiously arranged for the purpose of making the thought appear something very profound. The essence of this style consisted in a mock antithesis, that is, an opposition of mere sounds, in a rage for personification, the abstract made animate, far-fetched metaphors, strange phrases, metrical scraps, in everything, in short, but genuine prose. Style is, of course, nothing else but the art of conveying meaning appropriately and with perspicuity, whatever the meaning may be, and one criterion of a style is that it shall not be translatable without injury to the meaning. Johnson's style has pleased many from the very fault of being perfectly translatable; he creates an impression of cleverness by never saying any thing in a common way.[29]

Translatability is peculiarly associated with Pope – somewhat ironically – due to the success of his Homeric works. In Coleridge's generalisation about the writing of a whole age, translatability provides the proof of the hollowness of its preoccupation with style. The antithetical mode of thought has no substance: it is no more than 'mock antithesis'. By way of confirming the ephemeral nature of such a style and the society that produces it, Coleridge offers his own comparison between the styles of Johnson and Burke. In *Table Talk* he presumes that 'no one will . . . set Johnson before Burke', and he draws attention to Burke's 'discursive and continuous' qualities. Johnson, on the other hand, writes in a style that creates 'short sharp things . . . which produce a more decided effect at the moment, and which are so much more easy to carry off'.[30] Flashy style and commonplace thought make for a proliferation of writing in a commercial society based on vanity and ignorance. Such proliferation will never produce a writing in touch with eternal spirit.

III

Many of these attacks on Pope are also critiques of an 'artificial society'. In putting forward the view that Pope's work cannot transcend its own age, these Romantic writers are able to promote their own aesthetic in terms of eternal human values. By decrying Pope's writing for its failure to manifest imagination (as Coleridge defines it) and the passion of genial feelings, and most of all for its failure to reveal a sublime communion of the spirit, they release themselves from historical specificity. But by focusing on the context for these attacks it can be seen that its critique of an artificial society, and the absence of spirit which accompanies it, reflects back on the contemporary scene. The eternal human values produced by sublime transcendence turn out, not surprisingly, to be directed at specific forms of social and political power.

It has already been claimed that the Pope controversy is heavily loaded with the politics of literary canon formation;[31] especially in the contest between French and English cultural values in the Napoleonic era, and elements of this are certainly present in some of the attacks we have considered. Both Wordsworth and Coleridge in the 'joint' record of their meeting with Klopstock, for example, raise the issue of the contest between French and English cultures by specific reference to Pope, and they each react rather xenophobically to cultural mixing. Their idea of the purity of the English language in the late 1790s is a stark indicator of relations with France:

> He asked whether it was not allowed, that Pope had written rhyme poetry with more skill than any of our writers – I said, I preferred Dryden, because his couplets had greater variety in their movement. He thought my reason a good one; but asked whether the rhymes of Pope were not more exact . . . I told him that we were not so exact with regard to the final endings of lines as the French. . . . He seemed to think, that no language could ever be so far formed as that it might not be enriched by idioms borrowed from another tongue. I said this was a very dangerous practice; and added that I thought Milton had often injured both his prose and verse by taking this liberty too frequently. I recommended to him the prose works of Dryden as models of pure and native English.[32]

Wordsworth's statements in *Essays on Epitaphs* possess less obvious social justification for their literary claims than do those of Coleridge and De Quincey, yet for all their levelling simplicity, their very attempt to engage with the universal principles of the mind brings them close to the Burkean ethos of the earlier essay on 'Morals'.

Wordsworth's statement in the third *Essay on Epitaphs* that an epitaph should "give universally received truths a pathos and spirit which shall re-admit them into the soul like revelations of the moment'[33] has to be read against his admission that 'such a frail memorial then is not without its tendency to keep families together; it feeds also local attachment which is the tap-root of the tree of patriotism'.[34] Social cohesion combined with the customary power of the mind – the strength of 'habit' – tends to fall in with a reactionary ideology. The power of such a pastoralism is ripe for a Burkean ideology that finds its base in the 'smallest platoon of social life'.

If Wordsworth's *Essays on Epitaphs* only hint at the challenge to social cohesion provided by Pope's bad example of disruptive rationalism, then both the statements of Coleridge and De Quincey we have considered are surrounded by overt social commentaries directly related to the threat of an expanding reading public. Coleridge's brief handling of Pope's language in the *Biographia* is side by side with a patriotic appeal to English culture. The passage that peaks with the description of a 'conjunction disjunctive of epigrams' moves with ease from the 'writings of Mr Pope' to 'that school of French poetry'.[35] The association of the couplet, or more particularly the epigrammatic, with this foreign culture, is made even more explicit, and is given starker sociological terms, a little later in the *Biographia*:

> I have attempted to illustrate the present state of our language, in its relation to literature, by a press-room of larger and smaller stereotype pieces, which, in the present anglo-gallican fashion of unconnected, epigrammatic periods, it requires but an ordinary portion of ingenuity to vary indefinitely, and yet still produce something, which, if not sense, will be so like it, as to do as well. Perhaps better: for it spares the reader the trouble of thinking; prevents vacancy, while it indulges indolence; and secures the memory from all danger of an intellectual plethora. Hence of all trades, literature at present demands the least talent or information; and, of all modes of literature, the manufacturing of poems.[36]

Likewise, De Quincey's commentaries on Pope are strongly determined by their contexts and in particular by consideration of the idea of an expanding audience. 'Alexander Pope', by being a commissioned entry for the *Encyclopaedia Britannica*, is a largely biographical account freed from overt social polemic. 'The Poetry of Pope' contains his relatively famous distinction between the 'literature of knowledge' and the 'literature of power'; a distinction which arises not just out of a dilettante response to Wordsworth's imagination, but out of the revolution in printing. The problem for De Quincey is that his idea of an implicit 'natural' teaching in literature is at odds with increasingly popular consumption. This problem is even more apparent in the article dealing with Lord Carlisle's lectures to artisans and mechanics in 1851. De Quincey's attack on Pope here is extreme. The dangerous trait of Pope's writings, he argues, is a deep-seated falsehood which takes place at a philosophical rather than a personal level. Since Pope's works are caught up in a 'ruinous self-contradiction' De Quincey is led to ask: 'Is that the sort of writer to furnish an advantageous study for the precious leisure, precious as rubies, of the toil-worn artisan?'[37]

Exactly how dangerous a social force Pope can be for an ill educated, artisanal audience can be judged by De Quincey's assessment of *An Essay on Man*. The danger lies in the rich hermeneutic possibilities of such a text. Here ambiguity, De Quincey suggests, could result in anarchy:

> Beyond a doubt the 'Essay on Man' would, in virtue of its subject, prove the most attractive to a labouring man of all Pope's writings, as most of all promising a glimpse into a world of permanence and of mysterious grandeur, and having an interest, therefore, transcendent to any that could be derived from the fleeting aspects of manners or social conventionalisms . . .

At the very point where permanence and transcendence could meet, however, *An Essay on Man* offers a dangerous relativism. What had been thought to be safe and central turns out to possess all the threat of a cultural 'other':

> The 'Essay on Man' in one point resembles some doubtful inscriptions in ancient forms of Oriental language, which, being made up elliptically of mere consonants, can be read into very different senses according to the different sets of vowels which the particular reader may choose to interpolate. According to the choice of the interpreter, it may be read into a loyal or a treasonable meaning.[38]

Hazlitt's optimistic belief in the effect of the printing revolution and a growth of the reading public clearly distinguishes him from Coleridge and De Quincey. For Wordsworth, Coleridge and De Quincey Pope's work possesses qualities that threaten the stability of post-revolutionary British society in the face of an expanding reading public. Pope poses a threat because his poetic mode has already proved to be popular and imitable. Their principle of the organic might understandably have trouble competing with a view of poetry which sees itself as being at one with the conventions of society and which seems to lend itself so appropriately to the expanding com-

166

modity market of literature. Cowper's idea that Pope could 'make Poetry a mere mechanic art' might well haunt Wordsworth in 1810, Coleridge in 1817 and De Quincey in 1851. Pope's offence against the 'spirit' of language clearly articulates for them the threat posed to society in the early nineteenth century. Theirs is no easy containment. Paradoxically, an 'aristocratical' poet from an artificial society could threaten subversive activities in the realm of culture.

Notes

1. Mark Pattison, 'Pope and his editors', *The British Quarterly Review* (1872); reprinted in *Essays*, edited by H. Nettleship (London, 1889), ii, 335. For an account of the Romantic period's complex reaction to Pope and, consequently, a qualification of Pattison's oversimplification see: Upali Amarasinghe, *Dryden and Pope in the Early Nineteenth Century: A Study of Changing Literary Taste 1800–1830* (Cambridge, 1962), and James Chandler, 'The Pope controversy: Romantic poetics and the English canon', *Critical Enquiry*, 10 (1983), 481–511.
2. *Table Talk*, 652–5, in *The Poems of William Cowper*, edited by John D. Baird and Charles Ryskamp (Oxford, 1980), i, 258.
3. *Coleridge's Miscellaneous Criticism*, edited by Thomas Middleton Raysor (London, 1936), p. 133.
4. Ibid, p. 218.
5. *The Complete Works of William Hazlitt*, edited by P. P. Howe (London, 1918), ix, 299.
6. Ibid.
7. Ibid, ix, 300.
8. Ibid.
9. Ibid.
10. *The Prose Works of William Wordsworth*, edited by W. J. B. Owen and J. W. Smyser (Oxford, 1974), ii, 83.
11. Ibid, ii, 80.
12. Ibid, ii, 77.
13. Ibid, ii, 76.
14. Ibid, ii, 79.
15. Ibid, ii, 74.
16. Ibid, i, 134.
17. Ibid, i, 150.
18. Ibid, ii, 84.
19. For example see: Frances Ferguson, *Wordsworth: Language as Counterspirit* (New Haven and London, 1977); Cynthia Chase, 'The Ring of Gyges and the Coat of Darkness: reading Rousseau with Wordsworth', and Mary Jacobus, 'The art of managing books: romantic prose and the writing of the past', both in *Romanticism and Language*, edited by Arden Reed (London, 1984), pp. 50–85, 215–46.
20. *Prose Works*, ii, 84–5.
21. Ibid, ii, 79.

22. Ibid, ii, 8.
23. *Biographia Literaria*, edited by James Engell and Walter Jackson Bate (Princeton, 1983), i, 18–19.
24. *The Collected Writings of Thomas De Quincey*, edited by David Masson (Edinburgh, 1889–90), xii, 26–7.
25. Hazlitt, *Complete Works*, xii, 10.
26. Masson, x, 269–70.
27. Ibid.
28. *The Dunciad*, i, 56.
29. *Miscellaneous Criticism*, p. 220.
30. Ibid, p. 423.
31. See James Chandler, 'The Pope controversy: Romantic poetics and the English canon'.
32. Satyrane's Letters, no. 3, in *Biographia Literaria*, edited by Engell and Bate, ii, 203–4. See also William Wordsworth, 'Conversations with Klopstock', in *Prose Works*, edited by Owen and Smyser, i, 94–5.
33. Ibid, ii, 93.
34. Ibid.
35. *Biographia Literaria*, i, 18.
36. Ibid, i, 39.
37. Masson, xii, 27.
38. Ibid, xii, 33.

10

Pope, Blake, Heraclitus and oppositional thinking

David Fairer

I

In the canon of English literature as it has developed during this century, Pope and Blake have regularly been used to signify opposing forces. The mighty opposites which they represent – those ignorant armies of Augustan and Romantic – continue to clash by night in innumerable survey courses: the poetry of 'Whatever is, is right' and the poetry of 'What is now proved was once only imagined'; the celebrator of Newton set neatly against the enemy of Newton;[1] cultural consensus giving ground inevitably to cultural revolution. In Blake criticism, Pope often has a brief role as the heroic-couplet-writing, classical, consensus-seeking 'Augustan' who can embody all that Blake detested in the poetry of the preceding age. Of such critics, Hazard Adams and Robert Gleckner are perhaps the most dismissive,[2] Northrop Frye the most cunning and playful. Frye's presentation in *Fearful Symmetry* (1947) is self-consciously prototypical: he admits that his discussion of Pope 'calls for the isolation of the anti-Blakean aspects of the Age of Reason; in short, for caricature', and so Pope moves easily into place as an anti-Blake. In the succeeding war of contraries we encounter in turn the Pope-Augustan's 'repression of creative power', his 'tactful and communicable mediocrity', his appeal to 'the minimum of imaginative response', his 'expression of generalized platitudes' – and many more.[3]

For all Frye's wit and generalising brio there is something wrong with a view of Blake which has to create a caricature opponent in order to define itself, and there is certainly something wrong with

169

such an inert view of Pope. But should they be left in static opposition, merely confirming each other's identity as two building-blocks in the structure of literary history? Or is it possible to be truer in the end to the Blake who wrote 'Opposition is true friendship'[4] and to explore briefly some ways in which the two poets might illuminate rather than define each other? I want to set the barrier aside and place Pope and Blake within the same discourse, and pose the question: if the two poets can be conveniently related, is it because they are disturbingly akin? Rather than polarise them, I want to view them as sharing a fascination for polarity; rather than leave them in fruitless opposition, I want to see them as having in common a single oppositional discourse.

The term 'oppositional' in this context is intended to express partly a certain cast of mind or process of thought, but also a wider imaginative procedure and more deep-seated ethical conviction.[5] Rather than employing organicised pairings of rootedness–growth, contemplation–memory, or stasis–homecoming, and working through them to locate a truth or discover and validate a unifying voice (a procedure characteristic, for example, of Wordsworth),[6] an oppositional discourse – essentially inorganic in nature – prioritises the engagement of opposites with each other; it keeps conflicting ideas in play, so as to sustain a field of force within which the mind can work. Oppositional thinking in this sense thrives on paradox (a term that Pope critics are happy to use); but I would argue that it widens this into the more far-reaching conviction that polarities reaffirm through their mutual contradiction the validity of the system which sets them in opposition, just as love and hate reinforce a single shared discourse of passion in a way that love and indifference can never do. One pair is a confirmation through reversal, the other a denial through disengagement. Oppositional thinking offers the insight that 'A' and 'not A' presuppose rather than deny each other, and it is therefore alert for the moment of *enantiodromia,* when an idea turns instantaneously into its opposite.[7] But the opposing terms, by remaining in conflict, do not prevent unity. On the contrary, their sustained antagonism guarantees a unity that articulates the conflict itself. This principle underlies Blake's best-known and most direct assertion of the creative potential of opposites, plate 3 of *The Marriage of Heaven and Hell*:

> Without contraries is no progression. Attraction and repulsion, reason and energy, love and hate, are necessary to human existence.

Blake's contraries,[8] through a language of antagonism, set up a force-field between their two terms, an energy which is mutually creative and sustaining. It is threatened by two things: the kind of abstract reasoning which affirms one term to deny the other (Blake's *negation* or *spectre*), and the state of equilibrium, in which the two terms become equally true and leave each other undisturbed – such is to be found in Beulah, Blake's world of loving sojourn, a place of sleep, not energy:

> There is a place where contrarieties are equally true.
> This place is called *Beulah*; it is a pleasant lovely shadow
> Where no dispute can come[9]

Blakean contraries do not deny or destroy one another, since they interdepend within a single greater term, just as attraction and repulsion create each other in magnetism. Nor do they settle into equilibrium, since a balanced, static state creates no energy. Blake's conception of contraries and of the oppositional nature of their energy offers some useful lines of thought. My concern is to focus on Pope in these terms, some of whose finest poetry works to preserve the force-field between polarities in ways that a related oppositional discourse such as Blake's can alert us to. Rather than desiring an equilibrium, or the compromise of a mediating term or middle ground, or a damping down of energies by the moderation of extremes, or the victory of one term over the other, Pope's oppositional thought, like Blake's, works to sustain notions of polarity.

Romantic criticism has long recognised the generating force of this idea in Blake's writing, but criticism of eighteenth-century poetry remains hindered by a vocabulary which has ceased to be a sharp and enabling instrument. Certain crucial terms which span aesthetic, social/ethical, religious and political categories, and which tend to recur in discussions of eighteenth-century poetry, have gathered round themselves a predictable set of ideas so as to form a concordant and satisfying pattern which can be projected onto the eighteenth century. In Pope criticism, especially, certain terms tend to be moved around like labelled counters, and as each falls into place an all too familiar picture begins to form. Words such as *order, harmony* and *concordia discors* – vital concepts in Pope's writing – can never seem to drag themselves free of other words with which they are simplistically equated: *stasis, balance/equilibrium,* and *compromise.* It is the purpose of this paper to initiate, with the help of Blake and Heraclitus, a reassessment of *order, harmony* and *concordia discors* in dynamic

171

terms, a project which might be useful in refreshing critical vocabulary. I wish to argue that any investigation of Pope's poetry needs to problematise these words by acknowledging that within an oppositional discourse such as I have outlined they are made to mean differently and take on certain specific complexities.

II

Pope critics have not entirely ignored parallels between Pope and Blake. Martin Price has forged some fascinating links between Urizenic selfhood and the self-absorption of Pope's dunces, and in seeing *An Essay on Man* as 'an implicit dialogue, working between the extremes of selfhood and harmonious love' Price draws a parallel with *The Marriage of Heaven and Hell,* in which 'the true order lies in the constant reciprocal action of reason and energy'.[10] More recently, Wallace Jackson has suggested that we should 'read Pope in much the same way we read Blake',[11] and he uncovers an impressive personal myth within which Pope is continually rewriting himself. A few critics to different degrees have recognised a dialectical element in Pope's poetry: Jackson's perception of the 'contrary fictions, the opposed progresses of good and evil'[12] in *The Dunciad* takes further Ronald Paulson's remarks on the 'enveloping fiction of provocation and response'[13] in Pope's later satires, and Ralph Cohen has set the 'relational' procedure of Pope's poetry against the organic premisses of his critics.[14] But these are minority voices as yet, and the tendency persists, even among Pope's shrewder critics, to assert that whenever Pope juxtaposes extremes he does so in order to work out a compromise or equilibrium between them. The remark of a noted Blake scholar that in *An Essay on Man* reason and self-love achieve 'merely a compromise through opposition'[15] has been echoed by Leopold Damrosch, who speaks of *concordia discors* as a 'complacent Augustan notion', adding that 'in the Augustan tradition the strife of opposites always implies a damping down of energy in mutual accommodation'.[16] Maynard Mack, in his influential introduction to the Twickenham volume of the *Essay,* has appropriately cited the ideas of Heraclitus in his discussion of Pope's thought, but only to interpret both of them in terms of an achievement of equilibrium. He cites

the Heraclitean *concors discordia,* where every member of the universal orchestra contributes something and all are reconciled by a Providence

172

that both composes and conducts. Thus the equilibrium of opposites by which God established a cosmos out of the chaos of the elements must be matched in the individual's life by an equilibrium of passions.[17]

The core of my argument is that this is a misreading of Heraclitus, and of Pope.

The term *concordia discors* (alternatively *discordia concors*)[18] occurs regularly in Pope criticism, where it is mistakenly equated with the concept of 'order in variety' and is allowed to lose the essential contradictory, oppositional element. In the above quotation, for example, Mack's 'universal orchestra' draws together a whole range of notes, rhythms, timbres, soft and loud, solo and tutti, and articulates them symphonically – but contradiction is thereby transcended, not sustained. The crucial point is that Heraclitean *concordia discors* is not 'concord *out of* discord', but '*simultaneously* concordant and discordant'. The difference is vital. The concept of a providential reconciliation of disparate elements, the assertion of a grand design which results in an 'equilibrium' of astonishing variety and intricacy is certainly traditional, but it is not Heraclitean. The key idea of Heraclitus' fragments is a quite different and more Blakean one: a notion of polarity which asserts not only the generating power of contradiction but the fact that creation continues to articulate the strife that gave it birth. It does not achieve a mutual accommodation or a unifying that fits the disparate parts into a whole. The suggestive links with Blake are implied by the following passage, from Alan Watts's *The Two Hands of God. The Myths of Polarity* (1963), which introduces a discussion, not of Blake, but of Heraclitus:

> To say that opposites are *polar* is to say much more than that they are far apart: it is to say that they are related and joined – that they are the terms, ends, or extremities of a single whole. Polar opposites are therefore *inseparable* opposites, like the poles of the earth or of a magnet.[19]

And Andrew Benjamin, in a post-structuralist reading of Heraclitus, has spoken of 'the belonging-together of the different in which difference is not effaced.'[20] In the surviving fragments of this pre-Socratic philosopher we find an oppositional discourse articulated most memorably, and so it will be appropriate to use the thought of Heraclitus as a catalyst in the following reaction between Pope and Blake. He will help to make my reading of Pope a less specifically 'Blakean' one by placing both Pope and Blake within a Heraclitean 'strife of opposites'.

Immediately, however, an issue of terminology raises itself: *paradox* and *antithesis* continue to find favour with Pope critics, while *contraries* and *dialectic* serve for those who write on Blake. The relationship between these two vocabularies of opposites – the one implying miniaturised contradiction, the other mightily clashing forces – is symptomatic of the way Pope and Blake are held apart by critical language. It is perhaps necessary to remind ourselves that the principles of any system function irrespective of scale, and that in any case Pope is as much the poet of the cosmos as Blake is of the cornea.

III

My argument that Pope's poetry does not achieve a 'mutual accommodation' or equilibrium of opposites appears to be refuted at the outset by a phrase in *Epistle to Bathurst,* and it is best to confront it at once. In line 168, in a positive context, we encounter the term 'reconcil'd extremes'. The whole paragraph reads as follows:

> Hear then the truth: ' 'Tis Heav'n each Passion sends,
> And diff'rent men directs to diff'rent ends.
> Extremes in Nature equal good produce,
> Extremes in Man concur to gen'ral use.'
> Ask we what makes one keep, and one bestow?
> That POW'R who bids the Ocean ebb and flow,
> Bids seed-time, harvest, equal course maintain,
> Thro' reconcil'd extremes of drought and rain,
> Builds Life on Death, on Change Duration founds,
> And gives th'eternal wheels to know their rounds.
>
> (161–70)

The word 'reconcile' is rare in Pope's verse (including the Homer translations, it occurs only four times) so its use here needs attention. In this passage Pope is establishing opposite forces in directional terms (the ebb and flow of the sea in the natural world, hoarding and giving in the human economy); and, Pope implies, just as life and death admit no intermediary, neither do these forces, which create an order through their opposition. The reconciliation is not an equilibrium: the sea does not ebb and flow with the purpose of achieving a perfect moment of poise at the turning of the tide; the extremes of drought and rain are not compromised in an everlasting gentle shower. Meaning, in other words, is not to be found at some point between the terms – oppositional discourse does not centre meaning, or provide for meaning-as-resolution, in this kind of way. Opposing identities, as in the above passage, are retained and stressed. The phrase 'reconcil'd extremes' here does not signal a coming-to-terms (as in 'Pleasure reconciled to Virtue') but the assertion of a wider perspective of meaning, just as 'harvest' is not a mediating concept between drought and rain, but a larger meaning expressed in the opposition of forces. Typically Popeian is the *chiasmus* of line 169, where the *building* and *founding* do not stabilise the terms they embrace, but achieve an interdependence of opposites (*Life/Death, Change/Duration*).

These are fine but vital distinctions; we need to be aware that there are various distinct ways of 'reconciling' – none of which is the case in the above passage. It might be helpful to differentiate, for example, between opposites that fuse together, opposites that remain distinct but settle into equilibrium, and opposites which are reconciled through a mediating term; or to follow Aristotle's early and very influential distinctions in chapter ten of his *Categories* between correlatives, privatives, negations and contraries (his subcategory of 'unmediated opposites' has particular bearing on this discussion).[21] In any event, the concept of 'reconciling' itself needs further thought. We should try to see, for example, that the element of compromise is not essential to it, and that reconciliation can occur through finding a single discourse within which two ideas interrelate. In these terms, to reconcile love and hate would be to articulate the discourse within which they create meaning together. This reconciliation-through-opposition is at first sight a nonsensical notion in that it says that contradictory ideas are true. This, however, is exactly the point of Heraclitean thinking – that 'truth' is not the single term on the '$x =$' side of the equation, but is in the equation itself and the complex relationships it expresses.

I want therefore to suggest that reconciliation need not always be viewed as expressing compromise, and that a discussion of Pope's work can gain from an awareness of some of the complications available in the term. Pope, rather than exploiting opportunities for compromise, often raises compromising possibilities before shying away from or disrupting them and achieving far more complex kinds of reconciliation.

This disruptive element in Pope's work has been seen by some critics as conceptual inconsistency or confusion. A. D. Nuttall acutely assesses the lines of thought of *An Essay on Man*, pouncing on Pope at moments when disruptions occur,[22] and in a stimulating article John Barrell and Harriet Guest[23] have recently isolated a characteristic

175

'contradiction' in the eighteenth-century long poem. Their reading of *Epistle to Bathurst* aims 'to analyse how the different discourses of the poem can be read as contradicting each other'. As part of this project they see lines 155–78 (which includes the passage discussed above) as exemplifying *concordia discors*, which they take to mean a providential 'harmonious reconciliation of extremes, of contraries', and underlying their critical procedure is the notion of the poet's failure, through conceptual confusion, to 'harmonise' contradictory discourses. In place of these scenarios of Pope's inability to achieve consistency or harmony between the perceived contradictions of his poetry, I want to project a Pope who is pursuing a more complex discourse of contradiction.

IV

Clearly, a crucial element to this analysis is the nature of 'harmony' itself – a term that literary criticism often uses innocently without acknowledging its problematic nature or recognising that competing notions of harmony are available. For my own purposes, for example, it is important to distinguish between Heraclitean and Augustinian concepts along the lines offered by Leo Spitzer: 'Whereas the Stoics (like Heraclitus) had thought of Harmony as forcing together the inimical, Augustine has in mind the ability of harmony to smooth out apparent discord.'[24]

Heraclitus' fragment 10 makes an assertion of *concordia discors* which is entirely uncompromising:[25]

> Things grasped together:- things whole, things not whole; being brought together, being separated; *consonant, dissonant*. Out of all things one thing, and out of one thing all things. [My emphasis]

Nothing could be further from a reassuring 'order in variety' than this 'forcing together' of Heraclitean *concordia discors*. The dynamic order expressed in the grasping hand exemplifies the conception of harmony as sustaining rather than denying opposing elements. We can hear Pope echoing Heraclitus in his declaration in *An Essay on Man*: 'ALL subsists by elemental strife' (i, 169), an idea whose essential statement is contained in Heraclitus' fragment 8:

> What opposes unites; the finest attunement [*harmonia*] stems from things bearing in opposite directions, and all things come about by strife.

Pope, Blake, Heraclitus

Heraclitus' Blakean phrase, 'what opposes unites' (a more exact translation is 'the counter-thrust brings together') defines a creation-by-strife in terms of opposing forces, counter-thrusts. Heraclitus' *harmonia* (here translated as *finest attunement*) is not a concord of sounds or a balancing, but a complex principle of continuous adjustment.[26] His fragment 51, for example, reads:

> They do not understand how, while differing from, it is in agreement with itself. There is a back-turning connection, like that of a bow or lyre.

This back-turning connection (*palintropos harmonia*) resists stasis or equilibrium: for Homer's *palintopos,* the more static tension or tuning of the string, Heraclitus substitutes the unusual dynamic word *palintropos,* the string turning back on itself.[27]

Leo Spitzer, in *Classical and Christian Ideas of World Harmony,* discusses this Heraclitean fragment in terms which suggest that Pope criticism often takes too simplistic a view of the notion of harmony:

> Harmony dominates, but a harmony which comprehends strife and antagonism . . . 'the making concordant of the discordant' confronts us with the two antagonistic forces of harmonious unification and discordant manifoldness, but the *symphronesis,* the 'thinking-together', is triumphant[28]

The creative act is one of *comprehension* – not merely recognising an intriguing paradox (which leads nowhere), not choosing one term and rejecting the other, not seeking a means of balancing out the opposites, or winning a middle ground on which to mediate between them, but a Heraclitean *harmonia.* When, for instance, Pope talks of 'All Discord, Harmony, not understood' (*Essay on Man,* i, 291), we should avoid taking this as a glib reassurance that if we could only understand the universe properly, we should all recognise it as harmoniously ordered;[29] rather, the line says that *all* discord becomes harmonious *in comprehension,* when subjected to *symphronesis,* a thinking-together. It does not cease to be at strife with itself, it merely begins to exist in a new relationship to *us.*

Heraclitus obsessively asserts and sustains polarities, but at the same time he insists everything is one. Such a unity, however, is more complex than the *concordia discors* of literary critics; in the words of Philip Wheelwright:

> The unity of things as Heraclitus understands it is a subtle and hidden

177

sort of unity . . . The oneness of things, or rather their mutual
attunement, cannot exist or even be conceived apart from their
manyness and discord . . .[30]

And in T. M. Robinson's summary of Heraclitean 'law' we find
Blakean and Popeian terms coming together:

> The justice that is cosmic law is the justice of disruption and
> revolution, of war and violence, not that of balm and healing . . . If this
> strikes us as paradoxical, it is because of our failure to recognize the
> different perspective that a God's-eye-view necessarily has of the real:
> [as Heraclitus said:] 'to God all things are fair and just, whereas
> humans have supposed that some things are unjust, other things just'
> (fragment 102). According to such a God's-eye-view all change,
> however violent, be it the macrochanges of nature and the outer
> cosmos or war among states, or civic strife, or the battles that rage in
> the human heart, can be seen as integral parts of the law or 'plan' that
> 'steers all things' (fragment 41).[31]

A 'justice' of disruption and revolution that is at the same time a
divine *symphronesis* in which 'all things are fair and just' and which
does not yield to human comprehension – indeed seems to affront our
human craving for benevolence and fair play – offers a way of
complicating our reading of book I of *An Essay on Man,* putting a
more discomfiting emphasis on statements which can in isolation
sound complacent and optimistic ('All Discord, Harmony, not
understood;/All partial Evil, universal Good'). Likewise, the disturbing *co-ordination* of law and war, justice and revolution, can
suggest links with a dynamic Blakean order within which energy is
expressed through, rather than suppressed by, its engagement with its
contrary. In *The Marriage of Heaven and Hell* the latter (reason) exerts
its pressure as the 'bounds or outward circumference' and thereby
works to prevent energy spending itself in an unresisting void.

V

With the Heraclitean model before us, we can begin to recognise
ways in which Pope, like Blake, continually exploits the bracing push
and pull of conflicting forces. It is more than a mere fascination for
the paradoxical, rather an encounter within a gravitational field where
polarities refuse to disengage. A text which exemplifies this is Pope's
letter to John Caryll, 14 August 1713:

> You can't wonder my thoughts are scarce consistent, when I tell you

how they are distracted! Every hour of my life, my mind is strangely divided. This minute, perhaps, I am above the stars, with a thousand systems round about me, looking forward into the vast abyss of eternity, and losing my whole comprehension in the boundless spaces of the extended Creation, in dialogues with Whiston and the astronomers; the next moment I am below all trifles, even grovelling with Tidcombe in the very centre of nonsense . . . Good God! what an Incongruous Animal is Man? how unsettled in his best part, his soul; and how changing and variable in his frame of body? The constancy of the one, shook by every notion, the temperament of the other, affected by every blast of wind. What an April weather in the mind! In a word, what is Man altogether, but one mighty inconsistency.

(Sherburn, i, 185–6)

What seems to catch an essential Popeian flavour here is the way he juxtaposes centrifugal and centripetal forces, presenting his relapse into nonsense not as a descent, but as an implosion into 'the very centre'. (This is caught in the phrase 'Then drop into thyself, and be a fool!' *Essay on Man,* ii, 30.) In this letter Pope does not move from a positive soaring to a negative sinking – in fact his outward astral path is a journey into incomprehension, merely a different kind of nonsense: the boundless spaces are directionless (he looks at the same time 'round about', 'forward' and into the abyss) and they are no more enlightening than the solid core. Pope's poetry, in similar ways to Blake's, tends to present negatively both a flight outwards that misses its direction and dissipates the energy expanded, and a collapse into a static centre. In both cases the energy is lost.

But Pope concedes that there can also be a virtuous contraction to a still point of integrity, that 'point where human bliss stands still' (*Essay on Man,* iv, 311). Martin Price comments: 'the contraction to a point is like the inward-turning spiral of a vortex; once man reaches the center, his mind can open out again into selfless love',[32] and he quotes the passage from Pope's *Essay* where a pebble stirs the peaceful lake:

> The centre mov'd, a circle strait succeeds,
> Another still, and still another spreads,
> Friend, parent, neighbour, first it will embrace,
> His country next, and next all human race,
> Wide and more wide, th'o'erflowings of the mind
> Take ev'ry creature in

(iv, 365–9)

In Blake's *Jerusalem* Los asserts a similarly benign contraction/ expansion as he attempts to prevent Albion from solidifying into a Blakean death of the spirit:

179

We live as one man; for contracting our infinite senses We behold multitude; or expanding, we behold as one, As one man all the universal family . . . (34, 17–19)

Contraction opens out into 'multitude' and *expansion* conjoins into 'one'. In this passage Blake's 'limit of contraction' has become a preparatory coiling of a spring. Both Pope and Blake, then, are capable of locating positive *and* negative within the same terms of contraction/expansion. But this comparison also suggests how important it is for each poet to preserve the pull of opposing forces and to exploit their alternation, to move from many to one and from one to many.

VI

'Expect poison from the standing water' reads the forty-fifth of Blake's *Proverbs of Hell*. Perhaps Pope's most memorable lines linking stasis and stagnation are from *An Essay on Man*, book II:

> Fix'd like a plant on his peculiar spot,
> To draw nutrition, propagate, and rot
>
> (ii, 63–4)

This kind of fixity in which fertility is part of a vegetable cycle is the negative form of selfhood; it draws things into itself and recycles them in an existence that parodies a positive contraction/expansion. Here the turning-back on itself is a profitless ebb and flow with no driving current, no energy to give direction, like the endless recycling of Dulness ('Suck the thread in, then yield it out again', *Dunciad*, iii, 58). It lacks a positive 'Self-love, the spring of motion' to impel it to action. However, mere impulse, though it may have a spurious appearance of energy, is not enough either, as Pope's alternative points out:

> Or, meteor-like, flame lawless thro' the void,
> Destroying others, by himself destroy'd.
>
> (ii, 65–6)

Here self-love as total self-interest burns itself up, the energy of its original impulse finally dissipated in the void. Both images of destruction – the decay of a static system and the spent combustion of a lawless one – are betrayals of creative energy.

In the Popeian text both constriction and dispersal, those negative aspects of a creative contraction and expansion, threaten directional, oppositional energy. The two teachers in book IV of *The Dunciad* (Dr Busby and the lac'd Governor) exemplify this contrast. Dr Busby of Westminster School is the enemy of oppositional thinking:

> When Reason doubtful, like the Samian letter,
> Points him two ways, the narrower is the better.
>
> (iv, 151–2)

Busby's brusque singleness of mind, which refuses to sustain two terms or confront a paradox, pursues its narrow path. Any openings must be closed down as far as possible, and the chains of schoolmasterly authority confine his students in a world of words without images, discipline without vision:

> Plac'd at the door of Learning, youth to guide,
> We never suffer it to stand too wide.
> To ask, to guess, to know, as they commence,
> As Fancy opens the quick springs of Sense,
> We ply the Memory, we load the brain,
> Bind rebel Wit, and double chain on chain,
> Confine the thought, to exercise the breath;
> And keep them in the pale of Words till death.
>
> (iv, 153–60)

A generous sense of the hesitancy of youthful knowledge (*to ask, to guess, to know*), of beginnings, openings and quickenings, meets the headmaster's relentless closing down of possibilities, a singleness of mind which denies multiplicity or contradiction. (No 'One thought fills immensity' for him!) But *rebel Wit* takes a quiet revenge at Busby's moment of triumph: the *quick springs* of Sense register themselves not just as the mechanical springs of a door or lid that must be kept closed, but as those traditional 'living waters' of nature, grace and creativity which the Busby-principle denies. *Sense* can be viewed, in other words, as mere mechanism, or as a quasi-divine motion. The text, as Busby speaks, opens out a philosophical debate and unblocks the very line of thought that the speaker wants to seal off. These may not be specifically Blake's 'mind-forged manacles' ('London', 8), but when the spectre boasts 'We hang one jingling padlock on the mind' we feel that Pope has caught at least some of the intellectual and spiritual implications of the Urizenic principle, limiter of energy, lawmaker, represser and builder of the enclosing Mundane Shell.

But there is another teacher in book IV who also betrays energy;

but here it is dissipation, rather than constriction, which is the key idea. The 'lac'd Governor' enters with his student, fresh from the Grand Tour, and his travelogue becomes a parable of wasted energies and loss of momentum. The wider his pupil's travels, the more exquisite the experiences, the more it is a story of waste and loss. The original impulse is a sublime outburst, but he soon begins to lose direction:

> Thence bursting glorious, all at once let down,
> Stunn'd with his giddy Larum half the town.
> Intrepid then, o'er seas and lands he flew:
> Europe he saw, and Europe saw him too.
>
> (iv, 291-4)

The energy of his flight is undermined by duncely giddiness, and after a river that 'runs', then one that 'rolls', he is soon succumbing to the languorous movement of the Italian air and its disembodied echoes:

> To Isles of fragrance, lilly-silver'd vales,
> Diffusing languor in the panting gales:
> To lands of singing, or of dancing slaves,
> Love-whisp'ring woods, and lute-resounding waves.
>
> (iv, 303-6)

And as he spreads himself abroad, his activities spend his energies. He begins to 'saunter' and all his indulgences draw his spirit into perverse directions. By line 319 we have dropping, spoiling and losing, and we move from the 'half' of line 323 to the 'nothing' of line 324 as the youth turns into the languidly-diffused Italian air itself: 'And last turn'd *Air,* the Echo of a Sound!' (322). In Pope's language, the young man is relentlessly dispersed and disembodied; a glorious burst of energy has completely dissipated itself.

Dr Busby and the governor's pupil exemplify the negative aspects of Popeian contraction/expansion, seen as constriction/dispersal, but those opposites, as if in parody of my earlier discussion of Heraclitean strife, are part of a wider order embodied in the universal principle of Dulness. After all, her own cosmic law needs, we might think, a system of opposites. But the discourse of Dulness is not an oppositional one, and as the dunces submit to her influence, their individual forces, centrifugal and centripetal alike, become subsumed in the universal Cartesian vortex[33] that swirls around the goddess. She becomes, in Pope's earlier words, 'the very centre of nonsense':

> The gath'ring number, as it moves along,

Involves a vast involuntary throng,
Who gently drawn, and struggling less and less,
Roll in her Vortex, and her pow'r confess.

(iv, 81-4)

It is characteristic of Dulness that she has within the poem no opposite force to counter hers.[34] Amid the endless circling, slipping, sliding and sinking motions that surround her, all individual directions seem subsumed in one. And yet, before collapsing into nonbeing the performing troupe of dunces evinces considerable individual parodic energy, from moments of ecstatic vision to sudden surging convictions of their physical prowess.

In his *Principia* Newton showed that unlike his own dynamic system, the Cartesian system of vortices would eventually run down and lose all its energy.[35] This is the threat which the whirling misdirections of Dulness poses, and it can be glossed by Heraclitus' fragment 125: 'Even the sacred barley-drink separates if it is not stirred'. The *kukeon* (a ceremonial drink of ground barley, grated cheese and wine) separated out into its individual ingredients if it was allowed to stand, so that the *kukeon* itself no longer existed, only its discrete parts. The image highlights the frantic busy-ness of *The Dunciad* which lurches between a mock-sublime merging of elements and a petty fragmentation into disconnected physical detail. For all the monomania of the Dulness-principle, there is a deep division within it between visionary aspirations and intractable physicality. Philip Wheelwright, in explicating the barley-drink fragment, makes a distinction between a positive *stirring* of the self through new experiences, and a mere stubborn, unchecked motion. His words can help us see that the activities of the dunces, by lacking the challenge of opposition, betray the idea of genuine change. Wheelwright could almost be speaking of them when he writes:

To hold on stubbornly to one's way of life is to lose it. . . . An unstirred self, like an unstirred barley-drink, tends to decompose, breaking up into dregs of material impulse on the one hand and ghostly ideal aspirations on the other.[36]

This division between *ghostly ideal aspirations* and *dregs of material impulse* is startlingly manifested throughout in the activities of the dunces; but it is also present in the splitting of the text itself: each page is separated out into verse which rises to the top and the dregs of the footnotes, fragmented, literal and material, pulling the eye down the page.

183

Dulness herself is also split apart: she is at the same time goddess of the amorphous and nugatory, and of the mechanical and fragmentary. She clouds things, but also minces them to bits. Blake's Urizen can perhaps help us to recognise this as two aspects of a single tyranny. A figure of abstraction involved in the labyrinth of his Tree of Mystery, Urizen is also the god of the material world who divides and measures, offering only the grim alternatives of mystery and fragmentation – clouding and mincing to bits.

VII

Pat Rogers has said that, 'For the Augustans, the primal fear was not that things would fall apart, but that everything would somehow merge'.[37] This should perhaps be amended to say of Pope, as of Blake, that both the merging *and* falling apart of things are equally negative ideas, since each involves a denial of relationship. Blake's commitment to form and outline and his disdain for the Burkean sublime of obscurity and indefiniteness[38] is paralleled in Pope's abhorrence of 'Metaphysic smokes', amphibious 'middle' natures and the absorptions of Dulness.[39] But the Whistonian nightmare of dissolution and dissipation is also a falling-to-pieces,[40] and in a similar way mere fragmentation, for Pope as for Blake, is part of the same destructive tendency: it is a gloomy self-contemplating isolation, in which the pieces pursue their individual existence with no sense of being part of any greater system. They are also (as *The Dunciad* shows) in danger of being whirled around passively in a vortex that draws them into a single tyrannical system which works by denying all alternatives or opposing viewpoints. The true 'wholeness' for both Pope and Blake is a dynamic and living system in which each item exerts itself and tests itself against its opposite while being part of a larger whole, never organically becoming one, but living equally in all its parts which continuously express the tension between them. To recall the words of Heraclitus: 'Out of all things one thing, and out of one thing all things'.

At the climactic close of *Jerusalem*,[41] Blake offers a powerful image of this in the moment when the four Zoas of Body, Emotions, Imagination and Reason (the four compass-points) reassemble in Albion's bosom. No sooner have they come together than the reconstructed Albion stretches his bow-grasping hand into infinity. In doing so he reaches out as if at the centre of a hall of mirrors, simultaneously to the south, the east, the west, the north. The triumphant unification is not a fusion, a compromise or a conquest: unified vision is a fourfold vision: the single bow is a bow of gold, of silver, of brass, of iron. Opposition is not resolved, but is reconstituted into terms which define a singleness/totality where 'One thought fills immensity'. As Pope says at the climactic moment of book I of *An Essay on Man*:

> To him no high, no low, no great, no small;
> He fills, he bounds, connects, and equals all.

> (i, 279–80)

'Pope and Blake', Mark Schorer has said, 'agree on the central issue, that a divine principle of order exists in the universe'.[42] If we feel uneasy as we read that remark, it signals a lingering conviction that a 'divine principle of order' *must* mean something very different in Pope criticism from its use when talking about Blake – after all, Blake is the poet of 'energy', not the static, hierarchical 'order' of Augustan thought. In attempting a concurrent reading of Heraclitus, Blake and Pope, I have tried to suggest that literary criticism should free itself from that sterile opposition and recognise a dynamic concept of order in which 'opposition' expresses an interdependence of principle. Perhaps the traditional opposition of Pope and Blake should be reconsidered in that light.

Notes

1. Pope's 'Newton' and Blake's 'Newton' are, of course, not the same concept: see Peter Fisher, *The Valley of Vision* (Toronto, Buffalo and London, 1971 edn), p. 109. Alexander Koyré has given a clear account of later Newtonianism in his *Newton Studies* (London, 1965), pp. 16–24. However, Donald D. Ault, in *Visionary Physics. Blake's Response to Newton* (Chicago and London, 1974), has argued convincingly for the interconnectedness of Blake's and Newton's systems in terms of an 'inverse homology', with Blake paralleling and exorcising Newton. Pope's relationship to Newton awaits a similar reassessment to show how Newton's dynamic system, rather than separating them, is a vital link between Pope and Blake.
2. Hazard Adams, *Blake and Yeats. The Contrary Vision* (New York, 1968 edn) Cornell Studies in English, vol. 40, p. 39; Robert F. Gleckner, *Blake and Spenser* (Baltimore and London, 1985), pp. 32, 40.
3. Northrop Frye, *Fearful Symmetry* (Princeton, 1969 edn), pp. 161–8.
4. *The Marriage of Heaven and Hell*, plate 20. Quotations from Blake are taken from *The Poems of William Blake*, edited by W. H. Stevenson and David V. Erdman (London, 1971).

David Fairer

5. I reject the term 'dialectic' in order to avoid the *logical* implication in the original senses of the term, and also its more specific philosophical use by Kant, Hegel, etc; 'dualistic' is not a dynamic concept; 'dialogic' is closer, but does not recognise the element of *contradiction* as essential; 'polar', on the other hand, is overspecific (though it should be subsumed under my larger term). 'Oppositional' (in the dictionary senses) also draws usefully together the notions of both astronomical and political opposition.
6. John Whale's essay in this volume discusses some of the organic assumptions behind Romantic criticisms of Pope. See especially pp. 158, 162–3. In *Pope's Imagination* (Manchester, 1984) I attempt to extricate Pope from a Coleridgean discourse of organic imagination (see pp. 2–7).
7. See Christine Gallant, *Blake and the Assimilation of Chaos* (Princeton, 1978), p. 46.
8. Blake's fullest exposition of the concept of contraries and negations is *Jerusalem,* 17:33ff; see also 10:7–16, and *Milton,* 40:32–6.
9. *Milton,* 30:1–3.
10. Martin Price, *To the Palace of Wisdom. Studies in Order and Energy from Dryden to Blake* (Carbondale and Edwardsville, 1970 edn), pp. 133, 413.
11. Wallace Jackson, *Vision and Re-vision in Alexander Pope* (Detroit, 1983), p. 13.
12. Wallace Jackson, 'The genius of Pope's genius: criticism and the text(s)', in *The Enduring Legacy,* pp. 171–84 (p. 179).
13. Ronald Paulson, 'Satire, and poetry, and Pope', in *English Satire: Papers Read at a Clark Library Seminar* (California, 1972), p. 80. Quoted in the above, p. 174.
14. Ralph Cohen, 'Pope's meanings and the strategies of interrelation', in *English Literature in the Age of Disguise,* edited by Maximillian E. Novak (Berkeley, Los Angeles and London, 1977), pp. 101–30.
15. Morton D. Paley, *Energy and Imagination. A Study of the Development of Blake's Thought* (Oxford, 1970), p. 13.
16. Leopold Damrosch, Jr, *Symbol and Truth in Blake's Myth* (Princeton, 1980), p. 176. Damrosch remarks that Blake's contraries are 'really no advance at all over the complacent Augustan notion of *concordia discors*' which he equates with 'order in variety' ('So much for *concordia discors* and lights and shades', p. 177). In his more recent book, *The Imaginative World of Alexander Pope* (Berkeley, Los Angeles and London, 1987), Damrosch argues that Pope was driven by 'a desire to affirm stability' (pp. 13–14). My essay argues the opposite case.
17. *TE,* III i, pp. liv–lv.
18. See Horace, *Epistle I 12,* 19, and Ovid, *Metamorphoses,* I, 433. Both make implicit reference to Heraclitean conflict. The fullest account of the term *concordia discors* remains that in Earl Wasserman's *The Subtler Language* (Baltimore, 1959), Chapters III and IV.
19. Alan Watts, *The Two Hands of God. The Myths of Polarity* (New York, 1963), p. 49.
20. Andrew Benjamin, 'Time and interpretation in Heraclitus', in *Post-structuralist Classics,* edited by Andrew Benjamin (London and New York, 1988), pp. 106–31 (p. 128).
21. Aristotle, *Categories,* ch. 10, 11b–12a. See G. R. Lloyd, *Polarity and*

Pope, Blake, Heraclitus

Analogy. Two Types of Argumentation in Early Greek Thought (Cambridge, 1966), pp. 161–9. See also his discussion of the Pythagoreans and Heraclitus, pp. 94–102. Aristotle separates out four kinds of opposite terms: *correlatives* (e.g. 'double' and 'half' – these remain in a static relationship with each other); *positive* and *privative* ('sight' and 'blindness' – having or lacking some power or quality); *affirmation* and *negation* ('he is sitting' and 'he is not sitting' – statements of which one must be true and the other false), and lastly *contraries*. Aristotle subdivides his category of contraries into mediated and unmediated. For him, paired concepts such as black and white, good and bad (*agathos/kakos*) may be mediated ('such contraries have intermediates. Between black and white, for example, are sallow and grey and so forth, while between good and bad we have that which is neither the one nor the other'), whereas 'health and disease, odd and even, have no intermediate between them'. Although Aristotle denies that his contraries are interdependent, his examples of unmediated opposites are of terms which define each other: e.g. the concept 'even' only makes sense in terms of the concept 'odd'.

22. A. D. Nuttall, *Pope's 'Essay on Man'* (London, 1984), p. 54: 'What is tolerated – or even welcomed – as an invigorating tension on a small scale is much harder to accept at the major level of the argument. It becomes, indeed, mere contradiction.'
23. John Barrell and Harriet Guest, 'On the uses of contradiction: economics and morality in the eighteenth-century long poem', in *The New Eighteenth Century*, pp. 121–43, especially pp. 123–6.
24. Leo Spitzer, *Classical and Christian Ideas of World Harmony* (Baltimore, 1963), p. 40.
25. I adopt the Diels-Krantz numbering of the fragments as given in *Heraclitus. Fragments*, edited by T. M. Robinson (Toronto, Buffalo and London, 1987), whose translations are also used here. Along with Robinson's, the best modern commentaries on Heraclitus are: Philip Wheelwright, *Heraclitus* (Princeton, 1959) and Charles H. Kahn, *The Art and Thought of Heraclitus* (Cambridge, 1979).
26. Kathleen Raine points out that Blake had access to Heraclitus' thought in Robert Fludd's *Mosaicall Philosophy* (1659); see her *Blake and Tradition* (Princeton, Bollingen Series 35.11, 2 vols, 1968), i, 363, n.9. Pope quotes Heraclitean fragments in the notes to his *Iliad* (see *TE*, viii, 347, 349), and Maynard Mack suggests the source for *Essay on Man*, ii, 31–4, may lie in Heraclitus' fragment 83: 'In the matter of wisdom, beauty, and every other thing, in contrast with God the wisest of mankind will appear an ape' (Robinson, p. 51). There are accounts of Heraclitus' thought in Thomas Stanley's *History of Philosophy* (3rd edn, 1701), and in Ralph Cudworth's *The True Intellectual System of the Universe* (1678). Pope owned both books. It should be pointed out that the fragments of Heraclitus have come down to us through being quoted in many familiar classical texts, e.g. Plato, Aristotle, Plutarch, Marcus Aurelius, etc.
27. For a discussion of this *crux*, see Robinson, pp. 115–16, and Kahn, pp. 195–200.
28. Spitzer, p. 9.
29. A. D. Nuttall, for example, comments on this line: 'the Heraclitean

187

universe of glorious strife [is] now firmly brought to order' (p. 76).

30. Wheelwright, p. 105.

31. Robinson, p. 185.

32. Price, p. 137.

33. On Cartesian vortices in relation to Blake, see Ault, pp. 147–50; in relation to Pope, see J. Philip Brockbank, 'The Book of Genesis and the genesis of books: the creation of Pope's *Dunciad*', in *The Art of Alexander Pope,* edited by Howard Erskine-Hill and Anne Smith (London, 1979), pp. 192–211, especially pp. 205–8.

34. Ian Donaldson, 'Concealing and revealing: Pope's *Epistle to Dr. Arbuthnot*', in *Yearbook of English Studies,* 18 (1988), 181–99, has detected a similar lack of oppositional energy in the scribblers of Pope's *Epistle*: 'These writers, like the poet himself, are certainly driven by passion, but they experience no struggle, no countervailing sense of reality or decorum . . . Pope's adversaries are depicted as fixed in one state or another: as forever emotionally unresponsive, or forever emotionally out of control.' (pp. 189–90)

35. See Koyré, *Newton Studies,* p. 99.

36. Wheelwright, p. 65.

37. Pat Rogers, *An Introduction to Pope* (London, 1975), p. 128.

38. 'The great and golden rule of art, as well as life, is this: That the more distinct, sharp, and wirey the bounding line, the more perfect the work of art' (*A Descriptive Catalogue.* See *William Blake's Writings,* edited by G. E. Bentley, Jr, 2 vols (Oxford, 1978), p. 861).

39. See, for example, Scriblerus's note to *The Dunciad,* iv, 248 ('And Metaphysic smokes involve the Pole').

40. 'All this beautiful *System* would fall to pieces, and dissolve into Atoms' (William Whiston, *Astronomical Principles of Religion* (London, 1717), p. 111).

41. *Jerusalem,* plates 96–7.

42. Mark Schorer, *William Blake: The Politics of Vision* (Gloucester, Mass., 1975), p. 145. See also Fisher, *The Valley of Vision,* p. 101.

11

Pope, politics and Wordsworth's Prelude

Nicholas Roe

The great cause of the present deplorable state of English poetry is to be attributed to that absurd and systematic depreciation of Pope, in which, for the last few years, there has been a kind of epidemical concurrence.

So wrote Byron in March 1820, and he fastened upon 'the Lakers' – Southey, Coleridge and Wordsworth – as responsible for contemporary prejudice against Pope. For his Lordship, 'the best sign of amendment' in English poetry was 'repentance, and new and frequent editions of Pope and Dryden'.[1] Byron's admiration for Pope is very well known; but his relative hostility to Wordsworth has contributed to the assumption that Wordsworth himself extensively 'depreciated' Pope's achievement. Certainly, in the second of his *Essays on Epitaphs* Wordsworth questions whether Pope's 'metrical Wit' is appropriate to the 'instinctive truths' of epitaph, but he also acknowledges Pope as 'this distinguished Writer'. Late in his life Wordsworth recalled: 'I have been charged by some with disparaging Pope and Dryden. This is not so', and he added: 'I have committed much of both [poets] to memory'.[2] More than this, he made creative use of what he had memorised, such that Pope assumes a fertile command over some passages of Wordsworth's greatest poetry – a status more frequently attributed to Milton.

Pope and Wordsworth's early verse

Wordsworth read Pope while at Hawkshead Grammar School, and he was reading Pope while in London during the spring and early summer of 1791. This explains the variety of echoes from Pope in *An Evening Walk* and *Descriptive Sketches,* published in January 1793; these have been well-listed by Wordsworth's French biographer Emile Legouis, and more recently by the editors of these poems in the Cornell Wordsworth series, James Averill and Eric Birdsall. Wordsworth was again reading Pope in London during Spring 1795, this time as a preparation for writing the 'Imitation' of Juvenal's eighth satire with his friend Francis Wrangham. It is from this moment that Wordsworth's reading in, and creative response to, Pope begins to intersect with his political life.[3]

The heroic-couplet 'Imitation' of Juvenal (never published in Wordsworth's lifetime) is a bitter response to contemporary political affairs, the war against France, and corruption in the British government and court. Writing to his university friend William Mathews from the isolation of Racedown Lodge in Dorset on 21 March 1796, Wordsworth confesses that to avoid forgetting 'the world' he 'season[s] [his] recollection of some of its objects with a little ill-nature'. 'I attempt to write satires!' he says, 'and in all satires whatever the authors may say there will be found a spice of malignity. Neither Juvenal or Horace were without it, and what shall we say of Boileau and Pope'.[4] Wordsworth takes his bearings as a satirical poet from the Latin classics and the Augustans; but his identification of satire with 'ill-nature' and 'malignity' derives equally from his own position in 1796 as a republican in opposition, if not in retreat. In the context of the two restrictive 'gagging acts', which became law on 18 December the previous year, Wordsworth's 'Imitation' reads as an effort to purge a vicious aristocracy and substitute a democratic 'people's choice': 'Plebeian hands the [   ] mace have wrenched/From sovereigns deep in pedigree intrenched' (147–8). But his invocation of earlier revolutionary ideals and achievements must have offered scant encouragement in a year that saw Napoleon's successful Italian campaign, and intensified repression in Britain.[5]

At this moment of 'dereliction and dismay' Wordsworth's satire lacks an alternative vision; its rhetorical questions work to suggest the impossibility of political dialogue, progress, and change. Wordsworth claims that his 'theme is fruitful' (57), but what follows defines an intractable state of affairs – corruption allied to oppression, against which any opposition proves ineffectual:

> My Lord can muster (all but honour spent)
> From his wife's Faro-bank a decent rent,

190

The glittering rabble, housed to cheat and swear,
Swindle and rob, is no informer there.
Or is the painted staff's avenging host
By sixpenny sedition-shops engrossed,
Or rather skulking for the common weal
Round fire-side treason-parties en famille?

(59–66)

The lord mortgaged to a 'Faro-bank', or gambling house, is a figure of the corrupt aristocracy whom Wordsworth, like other reformists, identified as the source of political corruption and social injustice. But Wordsworth's satire also cuts in another direction to suggest his own disenchantment with the cause of reform as a hopeless contest between 'sixpenny sedition-shops', 'fire-side treason-parties', and a network of spies and government informers.

The 'Imitation' of Juvenal is fragmentary, and Wordsworth had virtually given up work on it after April 1796. It presents an exhausted, negative response to political crisis, and in itself is a dead end. But Wordsworth abandoned the 'Imitation' to work on his play, *The Borderers,* which developed as a comparatively vital engagement with his own revolutionary experience over the previous years. In *The Borderers* the character Rivers is a good man betrayed into crime against his own nature, and it is possible to see how Rivers's personal history might represent the recent course of the revolution, from benevolent idealism to the Terror of 1794.[6] In 1796, therefore, Wordsworth's satire is a reactive commentary upon political deadlock, and it stands in apposition to the dramatic translation of revolution in *The Borderers.* Wordsworth's turning from satirical 'ill-nature' to an imaginative synthesis of experience might stand as an emblem for the larger development towards a Romantic consciousness in the course of the eighteenth century. More immediately, it also bears upon an unusual spot of time in *The Prelude*: the childish game at cards which originally appeared in the Two-part *Prelude.* And this spot of time in turn depends upon Wordsworth's reading of *The Rape of the Lock.*

For Wordsworth, Pope's example made itself·felt less through his abortive exercise in satiric 'ill-nature' than in his subsequent development as poet of *The Prelude* in 1798-9. In *The Rape of the Lock, 'Ill-nature'* is a forbidding 'wrinkled Form' who inhabits the Cave of Spleen (iv, 27–30), a repressive figure that is at odds with the generous spirit of Pope's satire in the poem as a whole. In discovering the truly genial character of Pope's imagination, Wordsworth found that the satiric voice could open out beyond 'ill-nature' into wider

191

areas of experience, enabling him to treat his own recent past within the larger context of his development as a poet. A fuller comprehension of Pope consequently led Wordsworth to a deeper understanding of himself.

'With what echoes'!: Two games at cards

'I would record with no reluctant voice/Our home amusements by the warm peat fire', Wordsworth writes in the Two-part *Prelude*:

> At evening, when with pencil and with slate,
> In square divisions parcelled out, and all
> With crosses and with cyphers scribbled o'er,
> We schemed and puzzled, head opposed to head,
> In strife too humble to be named in verse;
> Or round the naked table, snow-white deal,
> Cherry, or maple, sate in close array,
> And to the combat – lu or whist – led on
> A thick-ribbed army, not as in the world
> Discarded and ungratefully thrown by
> Even for the very service they had wrought,
> But husbanded through many a long campaign.
> Oh, with what echoes on the board they fell –
> Ironic diamonds, hearts of sable hue,
> Queens gleaming through their splendour's last decay,
> Knaves wrapt in one assimilating gloom,
> And kings indignant at the shame incurred
> By royal visages.
>
> (Two-part *Prelude*, i, 206–25)[7]

The passage is striking because it is one of the few moments in the early *Prelude* that gives voice to recent history: the soldiers and sailors 'discarded and ungratefully thrown by' into poverty after serving the British government. This was a major theme of contemporary opposition to the French war, for instance in Wordsworth's early protest poem *Salisbury Plain,* and it feeds into his imaginative perception of 'discarded' humanity in 'The Discharged Soldier'.[8] And that pun, 'discarded', alerts one to Wordsworth's playful reconciliation of an 'ungrateful world' and the kind familiarity of the child's 'home amusements by the warm peat fire'. By drawing that harsher world within the horizons of childhood memory, Wordsworth discovers a mock-heroic idiom which recalls Pope's social comedy in *The Rape of the Lock,* and Belinda's game at ombre in canto III in particular:

> The skilful Nymph reviews her Force with Care;
> *Let Spades be Trumps!* she said, and Trumps they were.
>   Now move to War her Sable *Matadores,*
> In Show like Leaders of the swarthy *Moors.*
> *Spadillio* first, unconquerable Lord!
> Led off two captive Trumps, and swept the Board.
> As many more *Manillio* forc'd to yield,
> And march'd a Victor from the verdant Field.
> Him *Basto* follow'd, but his Fate more hard
> Gain'd but one Trump and one *Plebeian* Card.
> With his broad Sabre next, a Chief in Years,
> The hoary Majesty of *Spades* appears;
> Puts forth one manly Leg, to sight reveal'd;
> The rest his many-colour'd Robe conceal'd.
> The Rebel-*Knave,* who dares his Prince engage,
> Proves the just Victim of his Royal Rage.
> Ev'n mighty *Pam* that Kings and Queens o'erthrew,
> And mow'd down Armies in the Fights of *Lu,*
> Sad Chance of War! now, destitute of Aid,
> Falls undistinguish'd by the Victor *Spade!*
>
> (iii, 45–64)

W. K. Wimsatt shows that the card game in *The Rape of the Lock* emblematically represents the whole poem, and that it is a technically correct account of ombre such that the various hands of the game can be reconstructed from the details given in the poem.[9] Pope's game also belongs in a tradition of poems on affairs of state in which cards were used for political satire.[10] Given this literary context, Howard Erskine-Hill offers an interpretation of Pope's game at ombre and the subsequent rape as a comment upon the revolution of 1688. The Jacobites opposed William's accession as the 'rape' of their kingdom, and he suggests that the poem may indicate Pope's awareness of Jacobite opinion – although he is careful to stress that Pope's attitude to the Jacobite cause was complex and never overtly expressed.[11] But in view of this political and literary background to *The Rape of the Lock,* Erskine-Hill compares Pope's game with Wordsworth's card game in the Two-part *Prelude,* and he suggests that Wordsworth's game – like Pope's – may allude to recent political events:

> with what echoes on the board they fell –
> Ironic diamonds, hearts of sable hue,
> Queens gleaming through their splendour's last decay,

> Knaves wrapt in one assimilating gloom,
> And kings indignant at the shame incurred
> By royal visages.
>
> (Two-part *Prelude*, i, 220–5)

The court cards dealt 'on the board' are fetched out of Wordsworth's early childhood. But their associated 'echoes' include courtly heads felled at the guillotine in France and, ironically, Burke's lament for Marie-Antoinette in his *Reflections on the Revolution in France*.[12] This 'shameful' depreciation of royalty in republican France was one cause for the 'indignant' coalition of European monarchs against the revolution. And for Wordsworth, Coleridge and other French sympathisers this, in turn, was a further 'shame incurred/By royal visages'. As Wordsworth's Juvenalian satire gave place to *The Borderers* in 1796, the card game in *The Prelude* represents a similar intersection between the 'public' voice of satirical protest and Wordsworth's internalisation of revolutionary history as part of his personal mythology. That creative appropriation of history was part of Wordsworth's self-discovery as a poet. Whereas Milton presided over Wordsworth's identity as visionary and prophet, it was Pope who enabled an early accommodation of revolution within the history of his own imagination. And this in turn suggests that, for Wordsworth, Pope's imaginative response to the revolution in 1688, and the alienation of the Jacobites, had in some way appealed to his own experience of political dislocation and personal crisis in the 1790s.

Erskine-Hill says that Pope's satire in *The Rape of the Lock* is written with the knowledge that the status of royalty (if not the person of the monarch) is unquestioned by his society.[13] At the close of the eighteenth century, however, the execution of Louis XVI demonstrated the vulnerability of royal government in an age of republican revolutions, and for a short time in 1793 Wordsworth believed that an ideal republic might be achieved in France. An example of that idealism in action was noted by *The Gentleman's Magazine* in April 1794, in a report from the National Convention that Wordsworth may well have read:

> *Oct. 22* [1793] A Member demanded the proscription and prohibition of the Kings of Hearts, Diamonds, Clubs, and Spades, of their Queens, and their whole pack: requesting that there might be substituted for them, figures emblematical of the reign of Liberty.[14]

The republican card pack was adopted by the Convention in a decree 'which proscribed all Feudal and Royal Signs' – as Wordsworth perhaps knew, for the previous issue of *The Gentleman's Magazine* (March 1794) had carried a favourable review of *An Evening Walk* that would not have escaped his notice.[15] Wordsworth's card game in the Two-part *Prelude* is republican to the extent that it mocks courtly pretension. But at the time Wordsworth was writing his poem, the republican revolution had been successively betrayed by the Terror and by France's imperial aggression. It was this dislocation of idealism that encouraged Wordsworth and his contemporaries to find personal alternatives to revolutionary politics, and which also, I think, encouraged Wordsworth's response to *The Rape of the Lock* as a poem which explores the personal consequences of loss, disappointment and alienation.

Pope and the genesis of Wordsworth's *Prelude*, 1798–9

Pope's game has a specific time, place and political milieu: an afternoon at Hampton Court during the reign of 'great ANNA!' His poem is socially engaged, and it is demonstrably in touch with contemporary and historical events. Wordsworth's poem treats childish experience and the growth of the poet's mind: its process is memorial and internal. One mediator between these different territories was William Cowper, whose *Task* (1785) had adapted the satirical card game to the homely pastimes of 'The Winter Evening' – albeit as a sombre *memento mori,*

> With spots quadrangular of diamond form,
> Ensanguined hearts, clubs typical of strife,
> And spades, the emblem of untimely graves.
>
> (iv, 217–19)[16]

Besides offering a model for Wordsworth's domestication of Pope's satire, it was Cowper – and more immediately Coleridge in *Frost at Midnight* – who also provided Wordsworth with a pattern for his blank verse in *Tintern Abbey* and *The Prelude*. Refracted through Cowper and Coleridge, Pope's card game is transformed in *The Prelude* as a recollection of childhood that also foreshadows political events which occurred years after the primary memory.

The coincidence of personal and revolutionary history in this single passage – or 'spot of time' – encapsulates the drawn-out process in which Wordsworth transforms the promise of political revolution into the 'fructifying' power of imagination, its radical source being located in his own childhood. But this sublimation also meant that, for Wordsworth, imaginative power was associated with the demise of the revolutionary cause in which he had himself participated. Self-implication in revolutionary failure disturbs many seemingly unrelated memories throughout *The Prelude*, for example in his formative experiences of childish guilt in the bird-snaring and boat-stealing episodes. Unlike these guilty 'spots', however, Wordsworth's card game follows *The Rape of the Lock* in reducing politics to 'play', the latent violence of which reflects the 'impassioned game' of revolution – whether in 1688 or 1789. Pope's immediate comment on Belinda's game urges wisdom upon 'thoughtless mortals', but Wordsworth concludes his game with an ominous interruption which serves, perhaps, as a reminder that the peaceful process of the early revolution gave place to sustained terrorism in later years.

'Meanwhile abroad', Wordsworth writes,

> The heavy rain was falling, or the frost
> Raged bitterly with keen and silent tooth,
> And, interrupting the impassioned game,
> Oft from the neighbouring lake the splitting ice,
> While it sank down towards the water, sent
> Among the meadows and the hills its long
> And frequent yellings, imitative some
> Of wolves that howl along the Bothnic main.
>
> (Two-part *Prelude*, i, 225–33)

If one reads this passage as a personal memory, 'the splitting ice' resounds from Esthwaite Lake to Ann Tyson's cottage in which Wordsworth boarded while a schoolboy at Hawkshead and where, no doubt, winter evenings were passed in playing cards. But the 'long/And frequent yellings' of the ice also derive from a literary context, which returns us once again to the political aspects of Pope's and Wordsworth's card games. In the distance may be a couplet from Pope's *Imitation of Horace, Epistle II i (To Augustus)*,

> Loud as the Wolves on Orcas' stormy steep,
> Howl to the roarings of the Northern deep.
>
> (328–9)

And perhaps also the 'wintry *Baltick*' and 'raging Troops' of wolves in James Thomson's 'Winter' (169, 395).[17] But the immediate echo is from *The Rime of the Ancient Mariner*:

196

> The Ice was here, the Ice was there,
> The Ice was all around:
> It crack'd and growl'd, and roar'd and howl'd –
> Like noises of a swound.
>
> (57–60)[18]

Wordsworth's ice-scape in *The Prelude* is a reminder of the 'dismal' scene of Coleridge's poem, and of the mariner's voyage, crime and penance. Furthermore, the violent disruption of play in both *The Ancient Mariner* and *The Prelude* is also the essential pattern of *The Rape of the Lock* and the game at ombre in particular. It is of course the card game and the succeeding ritual of coffee-making which form the dramatic context for the Baron's 'fatal' severance of Belinda's lock of hair. Erskine-Hill argues that by placing the game before the rape, Pope deliberately puts 'affairs of state' into his readers' minds to make the assault 'hint at political meanings relevant to 1688', and specifically the crisis of the Jacobite cause.[19] By a similar strategy, the wolfish 'yellings' of the 'splitting ice' that interrupt Wordsworth's game insinuate the viciousness of human nature – as revealed by Coleridge's mariner, and also by the violence of the French Terror in 1793–4.

Wordsworth's recourse to *The Rape of the Lock* in this context of revolutionary betrayal suggests that he may have discovered in it political and imaginative parallels to his own sense of alienation late in the 1790s. Pope's game is soon followed by a severing 'for ever and for ever!' (iii, 154). This decisive act leads to the disruption of Belinda's society ('To Arms, to Arms!' v, 37) and to Belinda's own inner revolution, when the sylphs are displaced by the 'melancholy' Gnome Umbriel and her genial humour is transformed to 'Rage, Resentment, and Despair' (iv, 9). Belinda's loss may well be Pope's oblique comment upon the Jacobite cause in his own time. But, at the end of the eighteenth century, could these passages of Pope's poem have reminded Wordsworth of his own revolution: of heads severed in Paris and, beyond this immediate horror, the lasting emotional significance of revolutionary terror?

As I have already suggested, *The Borderers* can be read as a stylised version of revolution, in which Wordsworth traces (in the character of Rivers) a comparable link between fatal action and self-betrayal. It was evidently a theme that preoccupied him during the mid-1790s, for he returned to it again in his *Lines Left upon a Seat in a Yew-Tree* (1797) in which the solitary responds to disappointment by rejecting society with 'rash disdain'. Both *The Borderers* and the *Lines* resemble *The Rape of the Lock* by relating an 'external' disruption to inward,

197

psychic crisis. Belinda's anguish in canto IV is wittily described by
Pope as a loss of faith in her own cosmetic image:

> Was it for this you took such constant Care
> The *Bodkin, Comb,* and *Essence* to prepare;
> For this your Locks in Paper-Durance bound,
> For this with Tort'ring Irons wreath'd around?
>
> (iv, 97-100)

Her questions find an important echo in Wordsworth's self-interrog-
ation at the start of the Two-part *Prelude*:

> Was it for this
> That one, the fairest of all rivers, loved
> To blend his murmurs with my nurse's song,
> And from his alder shades and rocky falls,
> And from his fords and shallows, sent a voice
> That flowed along my dreams? For this didst thou,
> O Derwent, travelling over the green plains
> Near my 'sweet birth place', didst thou, beauteous stream,
> Make ceaseless music through the night and day,
> Which with its steady cadence tempering
> Our human waywardness, composed my thoughts
> To more than infant softness, giving me
> Among the fretful dwellings of mankind
> A knowledge, a dim earnest, of the calm
> Which Nature breathes among the fields and groves?
> Beloved Derwent, fairest of all streams,
> Was it for this . . .?
>
> (Two-part *Prelude*, i, 1-17)

Wordsworth's questions are answered by a 'dim earnest' of the
natural restoration which is the philosophical justification of *The
Prelude* as a whole. Yet his acknowledgements of 'human waywardness' and 'the fretful dwellings of mankind' intimate a less happy
context for the poem in his personal experience of dislocation and
dejection. This human vulnerability emerges through an echo of 'the
fretful stir/Unprofitable' in *Tintern Abbey*, which Wordsworth had
written the previous July. But the initiating questions of the Two-
part *Prelude* are ultimately a recollection of Belinda's self-enquiry in
The Rape of the Lock: 'Was it for this you took such constant Care?' In
each poem, critical self-consciousness derives from an external and
ultimately political source.

In the Two-part *Prelude,* then, it is possible to see how in 1798-9
Wordsworth might read (or recall) *The Rape of the Lock* as a pattern

of his own recent history. More particularly, in the opening paragraph and in the childish card game one can see how Wordsworth might recognise Pope's poem as foreshadowing the fatal action, displacement and alienation which together formed the experience of his own generation in the revolutionary decade. Beyond this, however, Pope had offered Wordsworth a way out of political deadlock in turning revolutionary failure to creative gain.

'A sudden Star': Pope, Wordsworth and sublimated loss

Pope's juxtaposition of classical epic and the intrigues of Belinda's drawing-room is of course the essential strategy of mock-heroic. But the Baron's 'fatal' severance of Belinda's lock of hair 'for ever, and for ever' also recalls Satan's seduction of Eve in *Paradise Lost* book IX. Pope's mock-heroic verse accommodates the separation of mankind and God in *Paradise Lost* to the social milieu of his satire and Belinda's inward, personal crisis. This appropriation may be seen as a precedent for the Romantics' subsequent internalisation of *Paradise Lost* as personal myth. Pope turns Milton's tragedy of alienated humanity to a comic study of human vanity and emotional alienation. For Wordsworth, *Paradise Lost* supplies the controlling myth for the history of his own imagination in *The Prelude*, one crisis of which was the promise and the failure of the French Revolution. Like *The Rape of the Lock*, *The Prelude* confronts historical and personal dislocation in which 1688 finds a later parallel in 1789. Moreover, the defeat of that historical cause (whether Jacobitism or republicanism) is reflected in both poems by the process of loss enacted when comfort and security are disrupted to admit the grotesque terrors of Pope's 'Cave of Spleen' and of Wordsworth's fallen, predatory nature, where the 'yellings' of the ice re-echo as the 'howling' of wolves. Pope and Wordsworth may each have had in mind the 'groans' of nature that accompany the fall of man in *Paradise Lost* (ix, 782-3, 1001), and the conclusion of Milton's poem where Adam and Eve forsake their first home in paradise to wander through the world.

In the Two-part *Prelude* Wordsworth's card game is a complex intersection of personal memory and recent history, in which Milton, Cowper and Coleridge meet and enable a childish incident to give voice to the lost cause of Wordsworth's generation. But it was Pope who provided Wordsworth with his source for the card game and, specifically, the card game as a vehicle for political commentary and the possible internalisation of crisis. In this early version of *The*

Nicholas Roe

Prelude the game is limited to the court or colour cards in the pack, and it clearly works as a reference to the downfall of the French monarchy. By 1805, however, when Wordsworth completed *The Prelude* in thirteen books he had revised and extended the passage into a gloss upon the whole course of the revolution up to the terror of 1793–4. Once again it was Pope who enabled him to do so.

Wordsworth's principal revision to the early text of the card game was to eliminate his pun by substituting 'neglected' for 'discarded'. He also expanded its political reference in five additional lines which directly echo the 'one *Plebeian* Card' gained by Belinda in *The Rape of the Lock*:

> Uncouth assemblage was it, where no few
> Had changed their functions – some, plebean cards
> Which fate beyond the promise of their birth
> Had glorified, and called to represent
> The persons of departed potentates.
>
> (1805 *Prelude*, i, 548–52)

Erskine-Hill suggests that those 'plebean cards' stand for the Corsican peasant Napoleon and his followers, 'Glorified beyond the promise of their birth'. But if this is the case, then the remainder of the passage becomes somewhat obscure:

> Oh, with what echoes on the board they fell!
> Ironic diamonds – clubs, hearts, diamonds, spades,
> A congregation piteously akin . . . precipitated down
> With scoffs and taunts like Vulcan out of heaven.
>
> (1805 *Prelude*, i, 553–8)

It may well be that Wordsworth's 1805 'plebean cards' forecast the French emperor's defeat (then some ten years in the future). On the other hand, one may plausibly read Wordsworth's 'uncouth assemblage' as a reference to the motley composition of the revolutionary government at Paris between Louis' execution in January 1793 and the death of Robespierre in July the following year. And if one wants a more specific allusion in this version of Wordsworth's card game, then one could argue that it is to Robespierre and his Committee of Public Safety, who replaced the 'departed potentates' Louis XVI and his queen, and were subsequently 'precipitated down' by the very means they had used to enforce their authority. The identity of Wordsworth's 'piteous congregation' with Robespierre and his followers is further substantiated in 1805 *Prelude*, book X,

200

where the terrorists are likened to the 'foul tribe of Moloch', 'o'erthrown' like Vulcan during the battle in Heaven (x, 468).

Like the 1799 passage, the card game in the 1805 *Prelude* concludes with rain, frost and the sound of splitting ice heard in the cottage parlour. In the earlier version the sound of the ice was a reminder of the self-destructive end of the revolutionary game in France. In the 1805 poem the echo of *The Ancient Mariner* works as a more general comment upon the failure of revolution in which Jacobins and aristocrats are 'piteously akin' because of the flawed human nature they share with Coleridge's mariner, and ultimately with Pope's Belinda.

Twice in *The Rape of the Lock* Pope likens Belinda's 'dire Disaster' (ii, 103) to the shattering of delicate china:

> Whether the Nymph shall break *Diana*'s Law,
> Or some frail *China* Jar receive a Flaw
>
> (ii, 105–6)

And, after the rape,

> Not louder Shrieks to pitying Heav'n are cast,
> . . . when rich *China* Vessels, fal'n from high,
> In glittring Dust and painted Fragments lie!
>
> (iii, 157, 159–60)

This image of Belinda's loss 'fal'n from high,/In glittring Dust' has an equally brilliant, celestial counterpart in Pope's final vision of the lock as:

> A sudden Star, [that] shot thro' liquid Air,
> And drew behind a radiant *Trail of Hair*.
>
> (v, 127–8)

Poised above all revolutions (whether cosmic or cosmetic, historical or personal) the star's 'propitious Ray' (v, 134) shines as the ultimate triumph of imagination – 'Tho' mark'd by none but quick Poetic Eyes' (v, 124).[20] In turning human loss to imaginative gain *The Rape of the Lock* looks forward to the powerful sublimation worked by the Romantic imagination as a response to the failure of revolutionary idealism in France. More particularly, it forecasts Wordsworth's conclusion to book XIII of *The Prelude* where, like Pope, he asserts the 'lasting inspiration' of the imagination,

Which, 'mid all revolutions in the hopes
And fears of men, doth still remain unchanged . . .
(1805 Prelude, xiii, 449-50)

This constant satisfaction was to be the subject of Wordsworth's philosophic poem *The Recluse,* and when Wordsworth contemplated that greater work in his 1814 'Preface' to *The Excursion* he invoked the 'star-like virtue' of imagination as an image of security from 'those mutations that extend their sway/Throughout the nether sphere' (89, 92-3). In one respect those 'mutations' recall the vicissitudes of revolution, and the crisis of 'human waywardness' that Wordsworth (like Milton) had turned to poetic creativity. But in another direction Wordsworth's 'mutations' had been anticipated by the 'fantastick' extremities of emotion represented in Pope's Cave of Spleen, just as Wordsworth's claim for the divine constancy of the imagination was prefigured in the heavenly consecration with which *The Rape of the Lock* concludes.

Afterword

The card game in *The Prelude* suggests that Wordsworth was aware of the range and subtlety of political and emotional reference in Pope's poetry, and specifically so in *The Rape of the Lock.* Pope's assurance as a poet and his shrewdness as a political commentator attracted Wordsworth at a moment when he lacked an effective voice for his own political experience during the 1790s. But it was the inward register of crisis in Pope's poem that proved most relevant to Wordsworth's dilemma as a poet. In transforming Belinda's game at cards so as to articulate the recent history of the French Revolution, Wordsworth brought Pope within his own imaginative territory of personal memory and childhood. By so doing he modulated Pope's satire with the recognition that the sources of his own power as a poet lay not in public affairs and politics, but in his own earliest years and the inward life of the imagination. So Pope's presence in *The Prelude* is not simply a means to comment upon contemporary affairs after the defeat and isolation of Wordsworth's republican cause. It serves to register Wordsworth's gradual realignment from revolutionary partisan to the poet whose own greatest subject was himself. Rather surprisingly, perhaps, Pope and Milton preside together in Wordsworth's self-discovery as poet of *The Prelude.*

Notes

1. 'Some observations upon an article in Blackwood's Magazine', *The Works of Lord Byron,* 17 vols (London, 1832–3), xv, 55–98, 79, 88.
2. See *The Prose Works of William Wordsworth,* edited by W. J. B. Owen and J. W. Smyser, 3 vols (Oxford, 1974), ii, 76–8, and Christopher Wordsworth, *Memoirs of William Wordsworth,* 2 vols (London, 1851), ii, 470.
3. Duncan Wu, 'Wordsworth's reading 1779–1799' (unpublished). See also Émile Legouis' discussion of Wordsworth's 'early poems' in *The Early Life of William Wordsworth 1770–1798* (London, 1921, 1988), pp. 120–60.
4. *The Letters of William and Dorothy Wordsworth,* edited by E. De Selincourt, *The Early Years 1787–1805,* revised by C. L. Shaver (Oxford, 1967), p. 169.
5. 'Imitation of Juvenal – Satire VIII', in *The Poetical Works of William Wordsworth,* edited by E. De Selincourt and H. Darbishire, 5 vols (Oxford, 1940–9), i, 302–6. All quotations from Wordsworth's poems (except *The Prelude*) are from this edition.
6. See 'The date of Juvenal', in Mark Reed, *Wordsworth. The Chronology of the Early Years 1770–1799* (Cambridge, Mass., 1969), pp. 340–1.
7. Quotations from the 1799 and 1805 *Prelude* are from the texts in William Wordsworth, *The Prelude 1799, 1805, 1850,* edited by J. Wordsworth, M. H. Abrams and S. Gill (London and New York, 1979).
8. See, for example, my discussion of protest and poetry in *Wordsworth and Coleridge. The Radical Years* (Oxford, 1988), pp. 118–44.
9. W. K. Wimsatt, 'Belinda Ludens: strife and play in *The Rape of the Lock*', in *Pope: Recent Essays by Several Hands,* edited by M. Mack and J. A. Winn (Brighton, 1980), pp. 201–23.
10. For cards and political satire see Howard H. Schless's introduction to 'A game at cards', in *POAS,* iii, 225–8. See also Howard Erskine-Hill, 'The satirical game at cards in Pope and Wordsworth', in *English Satire and the Satiric Tradition,* edited by Claude Rawson (Oxford, 1984), pp. 183–95, especially pp. 183–91.
11. For the Jacobite associations of 'rape' see *POAS,* v, 59, and Howard Erskine-Hill, 'Literature and the Jacobite cause: was there a rhetoric of Jacobitism?', in *Ideology and Conspiracy: Aspects of Jacobitism, 1689–1759,* edited by E. Cruickshanks (Edinburgh, 1982), pp. 49–69, especially pp. 49–50. For Pope and Jacobitism more specifically see Maynard Mack, *Alexander Pope: A Life* (New Haven and London, 1985), pp. 258–66.
12. Edmund Burke, *Reflections on the Revolution in France,* edited by C. C. O'Brien (Harmondsworth, 1969), pp. 169–70.
13. Erskine-Hill, 'The satirical game', p. 193.
14. 'Minutes of the Proceedings of the National Convention of France', in *The Gentleman's Magazine,* 64 (1794), 367, I am grateful to Carolyn Williams for this reference.
15. See *The Gentleman's Magazine,* 64 (1794), 252–3.

16. William Cowper, *The Task,* in *Works,* edited by Robert Southey, 8 vols (London, 1853–5), vi, 81.
17. James Thomson, *The Seasons,* edited by James Sambrook (Oxford, 1981).
18. *Lyrical Ballads,* edited by R. L. Brett and A. R. Jones (Cambridge, 1963). In the verse immediately following the albatross appears and is welcomed with 'food or play' until the mariner shoots it (61–4).
19. Erskine-Hill, 'Literature and the Jacobite cause', p. 54.
20. See David Fairer, *Pope's Imagination* (Manchester, 1984), pp. 79–80.

12

An Essay on Man
and the polite reader

Stephen Copley and David Fairer

I

In his prefatory remarks on 'The Design' of *An Essay on Man*, Pope appears to announce a programme in tune with the educative project of polite literature: the poem which follows, he says, will provide transparent, accessible, non-specialised and comprehensible explanations of the universal design, and will set out an ethical system in a familiar and easy manner – even at the risk of violating poetic decorum. The science of human nature, like all other sciences, can be reduced to '*a few clear points*' ('There are not *many certain truths* in this world'), and 'in passing over terms utterly unintelligible', Pope presents a work which will form 'a *temperate* yet not *inconsistent*, and a *short* yet not *imperfect* system of Ethics'.

He contrasts his *Essay* with the promised epistles of his projected *Opus Magnum*,[1] which 'will be less dry, and more susceptible of poetical ornament', characterising it as systematic and schematic in design. In particular he presents its structure as argumentative and akin to prose (its substance is 'mixt with *Argument*, which of its Nature approacheth to Prose'). In this vein he claims that the heroic-couplet form has been chosen for the sake of its conciseness and memorability, adding: 'I was unable to treat this part of my subject more in detail, without becoming dry and tedious; or more *poetically*, without sacrificing perspicuity to ornament, without wandring from the precision, or breaking the chain of reasoning'. The 'Argument' to each epistle reinforces these claims by providing the framework of a logical structure for this 'reasoning', while Pope's incidental references to the poem elsewhere repeatedly restate his insistence on

205

the importance of clarity of exposition within it. In a letter to Warburton, for instance, Pope praises the latter's prose notes to the poem in extravagant terms:

> You have made my System as clear as I ought to have done & could not . . . I know I meant just what you explain, but I did not explain my own meaning so well as you: You understand me as well as I do myself, but you express me better than I could express myself
>
> (11 April 1739. Sherburn, iv, 171–2)

In the light of this presentation, the *Essay* has been treated by many historians of ideas since A. O. Lovejoy as though it were simply an expository didactic treatise, the 'arguments' of which can be endorsed, criticised for their logical inconsistencies and inadequacies, or refuted without regard for the problems of the poem's textuality. This reading remains current in some intellectual and 'background' histories of the eighteenth century. James Sambrook,[2] for instance, has recently presented the *Essay* as 'a systematic treatise on . . . natural religion', the thesis of which can be adequately encapsulated by a selection of key quotations. At most, readings of the poem in this school have paid grudging attention to the form of its verse, which is considered something of a distraction from its substantive arguments. C. H. Vereker,[3] for example, writes of the *Essay*'s relationship to the prose philosophical work of Bolingbroke: 'The *Essay on Man* was more complacent, less sensitive and less sceptical than its prose model', largely because 'the eighteenth-century heroic couplet was not a satisfactory poetic shorthand for expressing philosophical ideas'. 'In consequence', Vereker suggests, 'Pope mirrored imperfectly his master's influence.'

Of course, the sustained critical effort since the last war to reclaim the *Essay* as a literary work has produced a series of far more sophisticated accounts of its poetic form than Vereker has to offer. At the most general level, the literary models for the poem have been discussed at some length. Brean Hammond[4] has written: 'In so far as any systematic attempt has been made to define the genre within which the *Essay on Man* is working, the front runners are the Horatian epistle and the Lucretian philosophical epic', and he suggests that 'the difficulty' in discussing the relation between these forms 'is one of tone'. A related difficulty lies in tracing the consequences of both these implied models of coherence for the poem as a whole. As A. D. Nuttall[5] has written, a tension between readings which present the

Essay 'as a system' and 'as a miscellany' has frequently been expressed 'in terms of the relative importance of Lucretius (the great didactic poet) and Horace (the urbane aphorist) as models'.

In relation to the first, the *De Rerum Natura* has been taken – notably by Miriam Leranbaum and Bernard Fabian – as the model for an explanatory, didactic structure in the *Essay*. Fabian, for instance, suggests that Pope constructs a Lucretian didactic poem, but substitutes 'Newton's world view for Lucretius's'.[6] Hammond's rejection of this view raises two important problems.[7] First he quotes Bolingbroke's suggestion to Pope that if the poet were to 'pursue a long process of reasoning in the didactic style, he would be sure to tire his reader on the whole, like Lucretius', and he suggests that this reflects a widespread contemporary sense of the need to find appropriately familiar forms of address for works directed at a general readership, which, he claims, would render the Lucretian epic a most unlikely model for the poem. Second, he repeats a point made by a number of other commentators: that the *Essay* appears to satirise the human presumption involved in celebrating the capacity to expound Newtonian scientific principles as much as it expounds those principles themselves – a feature which is particularly evident in the description of the 'superior beings' who 'shew'd a NEWTON as we shew an Ape' (ii, 31–4). As J. M. Cameron[8] writes, 'who but Pope has drawn attention to the bankruptcy of Newtonian physics, not indeed as *descriptive,* but as *explanatory?*'

Aware of such criticisms of the poem, some have proposed the Horatian epistle as a model both for its loose organisation and for its tone of familiar address, and more generally, the model of satire has been seen as providing it with its general structure. Recently, for example, Douglas H. White and Thomas P. Tierney[9] have placed the *Essay* in a tradition of 'satires on mankind', within which it operates to demolish conventional facile views rather than construct a coherent philosophical system of its own. In this context they suggest that the poem's construction is paradoxical rather than expository, and that in large part it 'is what it is and does what it does through the agency of wit rather than dialectic'.

Pope's own professed negotiation between the *Essay*'s poetical and argumentative designs seems to have set the terms for much twentieth-century criticism. The commentaries of many literary critics, from M. Kallich, R. L. Brett and Douglas White to A. D. Nuttall, who are sensitive to the status of the *Essay* as poetry and to some of the problems this raises, hold nonetheless a residual allegiance to the view of the poem as a versified treatise, and ultimately tend to fall back on maintaining unhelpful distinctions between analysis of the technical adroitness of its versification, and discussion or refutation of an abstracted core of its 'Argument' – a critical division familiar from Dr Johnson's discussion of the poem onwards.[10]

In part, this tendency stems from a general commitment to the task of celebrating the value of coherence in literary texts, and a reluctance to tackle the contradictions within them as an interesting – and in this case we would argue, strategic – feature of their utterance. A deconstructive analysis of the poem, which sets out to challenge earlier readings of it as securely expository and didactic might seem to counter this problem. Murray Krieger,[11] for example (reversing the arguments of J. M. Cameron), argues that the first epistle, 'which seeks utterly to reduce our confusing reality to the clarity of a perfect, if unresponsive, art world ('All Nature is but Art, unknown to thee')' is modified by the later epistles, to the extent that 'the confident projection of Epistle One can no longer stand so confidently. Indeed . . . very little confidence in human knowledge can be left standing'. And G. Douglas Atkins[12] argues more radically that, 'the entire poem may be seen . . . as "an agent of disillusionment", with clear de-mythological and even deconstructive elements'. Such emphasis on the unsettling, disruptive, subversive potential of the poem is welcome. However, the problem we are left with is the ahistorical nature of Atkins's account. Rather disconcertingly, Pope is congratulated for proto-deconstructive insights which really he could not have had without the benefit of a twentieth-century academic education.

It is our intention here to stress the disruptive potential of the poem, but view its strategies of disruption as a historically located phenomenon. In this context, we want to adopt in part the vocabulary employed by John Barrell and Harriet Guest in their analysis of the role of contradiction in the eighteenth-century long poem,[13] but to argue to rather different ends in relation to the *Essay*. Adopting the emphasis placed by Jon Klancher upon the need to historicise the rhetorically constructed 'reader' of literary texts,[14] we want to suggest that the *Essay on Man*, with its contradictions and tantalising incoherences, can usefully be read in the light of its address to the eighteenth-century 'polite' reader of printed literature, and in particular in relation to the cultural project of the prose essay, defined by Addison in *The Spectator* as the creation of a community of readers schooled in the niceties of polite exchange, and so qualified for inclusion in the familiar and 'democratically' accessible discussions conducted in the periodical – a process outlined by Michael G.

Ketcham[15] when he writes that, '*The Spectator*'s whole program embraces an expanding readership while it creates the illusion of an intimate community'.

The demands of writing for a polite readership, with expectations formed largely by the periodicals of the early century, clearly play a large part in shaping the construction of a wide range of eighteenth-century literary and philosophical texts. Hume's progressive recasting of his early philosophical works for the polite general reader is only the most graphic example of the power of these demands.[16] As has frequently been pointed out, Pope's relation to the discourses of the polite is characteristically ambivalent. Thomas Woodman[17] has suggested that throughout his career, Pope's poetry can be seen 'in dialogue' with contemporary polite literature, the poet's early verse showing every sign of being positively influenced by the polite mode, and the later becoming increasingly hostile to it. In its manner of address to its readers the *Essay* seems to reveal every sign of this ambivalence. We propose, therefore, a way of reading the poem as a text that imitates and parodies the strategies of prose argument, and will argue that in doing so the *Essay* ultimately disrupts the ends to which those strategies are deployed in the contemporary polite prose essay.

II

In this context, it is worth examining the consequences of the form and familiar address of the polite prose essay itself. It is important to correct at the outset the misleading impression, encouraged by some critical accounts discussed earlier, that the 'essay' is a rigorously-argued form. Eighteenth-century definitions noticeably dwell on its looseness of construction. Dr Johnson defines the essay as 'A loose sally of the mind; an irregular, indigested piece; not a regular and orderly composition', and one of his illustrative quotations defined the term by juxtaposing the aesthetic completeness of a 'finish'd poem' against the formal looseness of the essay:

> Yet modestly he does his work survey,
> And calls his finish'd poem an essay. [18]

In this light, the polite essay is usually seen as providing an unpretentious vehicle for the presentation of unformulated thoughts, couched in terms of a familiar, accessible and democratic address. This does not mean that the essay is regarded as an inappropriate medium for the discussion of serious issues. In *Spectator* 435, for instance, Addison writes of his own 'Serious Essays and Discourses', written on 'Subjects that never vary, but are for ever fixt and immutable';[19] and in no. 571 he contrasts his 'Essays Moral and Divine' with his 'Papers of Humour and Learning'. In no. 249 he argues that the looseness of the essay form makes it ideally suited to treat subjects for which there is no literary precedent:

> When I make Choice of a Subject that has not been treated of by others, I throw together my Reflections on it without any Order or Method, so that they may appear rather in the Looseness and Freedom of an Essay, than in the Regularity of a Set Discourse.

Elsewhere, Addison's account of the form is contradictory. In no. 476, for instance, he suggests that the composition of essays involves him in an almost wilful refusal to provide the reader with a sense of organic development and rhetorical order in the writing:

> Among my Daily-Papers, which I bestow on the Publick, there are some which are written with Regularity and Method, and others that run out into the Wildness of those Compositions, which go by the Name of *Essays*. As for the first, I have the whole Scheme of the Discourse in my Mind, before I set Pen to Paper. In the other kind of Writing, it is sufficient that I have several Thoughts on a Subject, without troubling my self to range them in such order, that they may seem to grow out of one another, and be disposed under the proper Heads.

In his subsequent account of the effect upon the reader of this mode of writing, Addison employs a topographical metaphor which is interestingly similar to the one introduced at the opening of *An Essay on Man*:

> When I read an Author of Genius, who writes without Method, I fancy my self in a Wood that abounds with a great many noble Objects, rising among one another in the greatest Confusion and Disorder. When I read a Methodical Discourse, I am in a regular Plantation, and can place my self in its several Centers, so as to take a view of all the Lines and Walks that are struck from them. You may ramble in the one a whole Day together, and every Moment discover something or other that is new to you, but when you have done you will have but a confused imperfect Notion of the Place; in the other,

your Eye commands the whole Prospect, and gives you such an Idea of it, as is not easily worn out of the Memory.

Pope's choice of landscape, however, is problematic from the outset. Lines 6–8 of epistle I provide apparent metaphorical amplifications of the 'scene' of man, over which Pope and his addressee Bolingbroke intend to 'expatiate'. That scene, however, at once turns out to have radically different implications for its interpretation (or interpretability):

> A mighty maze! but not without a plan;
> A Wild, where weeds and flow'rs promiscuous shoot,
> Or Garden, tempting with forbidden fruit.

Pope's emendation of the first edition's wording is revealing. The original line 6 ('A mighty maze of walks without a plan') had insisted unequivocally on the unknowability of the universal design. In the later version the existence of a plan is asserted but not necessarily offered to be explained. Instead, the 'scene' is at first announced as a maze with a plan, then it is immediately presented as an undesigned 'wild' *or* as a designed 'garden' readable in terms of the landscape of Eden. Pope therefore juxtaposes the perspectives on the 'scene' offered by an authoritative explicator *and* a participating observer, and the interpretative possibilities of the lines remain open. The provision of such amplifying or alternative readings linked by 'or' is a characteristic device of the poem, and qualifies or undermines the authority of many of its apparently prescriptive statements.

Addison's further comments in *Spectator* 476 suggest that the gesture of casualness involved in the adoption of the 'Wildness' of the essay form may, in dramatising the assurance of a putative 'Genius', imply a less than 'polite' relationship with the reader:

> Irregularity and want of Method are only supportable in Men of great Learning or Genius, who are often too full to be exact, and therefore chuse to throw down their Pearls in Heaps before the Reader, rather than be at the Pains of stringing them.

Beyond the obvious tensions implicit in Addison's distinctions, the connotations of his scarcely suppressed biblical reference[20] suggest how the essay form might be adopted as the vehicle of a positive strategy for the disablement of the reader. For Addison, at moments like this the prose essay stands as the uneasy mediating form which must accommodate both the demands for expressive freedom of the

211

'Genius' author and the social demands of its readership for 'Regularity and Method'. Furthermore, it raises problems for the reader in locating any secure viewpoint in the various landscapes (s)he is presented with.

III

The notion of politeness as the 'mutual Complaisance and Intercourse of Civilities' (*Spectator* 119), although occasionally pushed into humorous excess, is the characteristic tone of Addison's *Spectator* papers. His cultural project was less to address an already-established readership than to create a polite readership for the reception of his work. If his successors in the form were able to direct their essays to a 'polite' audience, it was partly because *The Spectator* had polished its readers, smoothed them out to reflect perfectly the author's poise and urbanity ('Polite Bodies, as Looking-Glasses' is Ralph Cudworth's 1678 phrase[21]). In *Spectator* 135 Addison opposes 'polite' to 'rough' ('the Roughness of the *High Dutch*' as against 'a Politer Tongue'), and Lord Shaftesbury develops the logic of the image:

> All politeness is owing to liberty. We polish one another, and rub off
> our corners and rough sides by a sort of amicable collision . . .[22]

Towards the end of the seventeenth century there is a developing concept of 'polite' as combining the sense of 'smoothed out, polished' (Latin *politus*) with a suggestion of *comprehension,* as in Katherine Philips's 'Polite and comprehensive Mind', 1664.[23] From this it is a short step to see Pope's *Essay on Man* as regularly challenging, even frustrating, such a mind, by offering possibilities for comprehension (at moments of pointed elegance where difficulties are smoothed away) only to reinstate difficulty just when the reader is partaking in the polite mutuality of it all – the speaking voice turning in exclamation on the reader's presumption.

Advising on how to cultivate true taste (*Spectator* 409), Addison proposes 'Conversation with Men of a Polite Genius', during which the individual takes part in a communal smoothing and polishing – the assumption being that politeness is not a single or solitary possession, but a cultural currency whose worth is enhanced through circulation:

An Essay on Man *and the polite reader*

> Every Man, besides those general Observations which are to be made
> upon an Author, forms several Reflections that are peculiar to his own
> manner of Thinking; so that Conversation will naturally furnish us
> with Hints which we did not attend to, and make us enjoy other Mens
> Parts and Reflections as well as our own. This is the best Reason I can
> give for the Observation which several have made, that Men of great
> Genius in the same way of Writing seldom rise up singly, but at certain
> Periods of Time appear together, and in a Body; as they did at *Rome* in
> the Reign of *Augustus*, and in *Greece* about the Age of *Socrates*. I cannot
> think that *Corneille, Racine, Moliere, Boileau, la Fontaine, Bruyere, Bossu,*
> or the *Daciers,* would have written so well as they have done, had they
> not been Friends and Contemporaries.

There is an interplay of 'reflections' within the polite circle, and even
genius is in these terms something of a societal cultivation. Similar
images occur when *Spectator* 160 comments on 'all the Turn and
Polishing of what the *French* call a *Bel Esprit*, by which they would
express a Genius refined by Conversation, Reflection, and the
Reading of the most polite Authors'.[24]

In his final *Spectator* paper, no. 600, Addison indulges in a
metaphorical retrospection of his enterprise. His ostensible subject is
the experiences the human soul will have in the life to come; but it can
be seen as the sublime apotheosis of Addisonian 'politeness', in the
sense of smoothing out difficulties or contradictions. Finding his
instance in the beliefs of 'the Inhabitants of the more Western Parts of
Africk', Addison sublimates the urbane variety of the *Spectator* papers
into the blissful variety of Heaven, where the earthly author–reader
relationship is transfigured to that between the 'Great Author' and
the human soul:

> The Supreme Being, therefore, in Compliance with this Taste of
> Happiness which he has planted in the Soul of Man, will raise up from
> time to time . . . every Gratification which it is in the Humour to be
> pleased with. If we wish to be in Groves or Bowers, among running
> Streams or Falls of Water, we shall immediately find our selves in the
> midst of such a Scene as we desire. If we would be entertained with
> Musick, and the Melody of Sounds, the Consort rises upon our Wish,
> and the whole Region about us is filled with Harmony. In short, every
> Desire will be followed by Fruition, and whatever a Man's Inclination
> directs him to, will be present with him.

Such elision of wish into fulfilment involves no transposition, but is a
perfect reflection which cancels out tensions (even distinctions)
between reason and desire, self and society, imagination and reality:

Nor is it material whether the Supreme Power creates in Conformity to our Wishes, or whether he only produces such a Change in our Imagination, as makes us believe ourselves conversant among those Scenes which delight us. Our Happiness will be the same, whether it proceed from external Objects, or from the Impressions of the Deity upon our own private Fancies.

This is the bliss of the Addisonian 'polite reader', educated in the pleasures of the imagination and finding every variety of his cultivated Taste gratified. The assumptions behind, and conduct of, this passage could hardly be more different from the procedure of *An Essay on Man*. The latter's 'Go, wiser thou!', after an equivalent passage on the poor Indian's beliefs about the afterlife, immediately forces apart all those things that Addison draws together:

> Go, wiser thou! and in thy scale of sense
> Weigh thy Opinion against Providence;
> Call Imperfection what thou fancy'st such,
> Say, here he gives too little, there too much;
> Destroy all creatures for thy sport . . .
>
> (i, 113–17)

Reason and desire, self and society, imagination and reality are reinstated as inherent elements of contradiction. The 'poor Indian's, and our, expectations of continuity and fulfilment are disrupted: we are not made merely to shift the scale, but are subjected to an imperative which it is equally foolish to accept or decline. Where a polite discourse might deliver an invitation or allow a concession – even issue a warning – Pope's exhortation manoeuvres us awkwardly through the thought, begging the question of our wisdom and ability to 'weigh' opinions.

IV

To be a reader of *The Spectator*, however casual, was to enrol oneself as one of Mr Spectator's 'Disciples', and this privilege entailed a responsibility:

I may reckon about Three-score thousand Disciples in *London* and *Westminster*, who I hope will take care to distinguish themselves from the thoughtless Herd of their ignorant and unattentive Brethren.
(*Spectator* 10)

Behind Addison's educative project is the assumption that each disciple has the capacity to be the *ideal* discerning reader, the 'Man of Taste' who can

> 'discern . . . not only the general Beauties and Imperfections of an Author, but discover the several Ways of thinking and expressing himself, which diversify him from all other Authors, with the several Foreign Infusions of Thought and Language, and the particular Authors from whom they were borrowed.'
>
> *(Spectator* 409)

In *An Essay on Man* Pope's approach to the reader, by seeming less exclusive, is more covert in operation. In his prefatory remarks, his misleading information about its authorship is amplified by a disingenuous denial that it is an 'imitation': 'As he *imitates* no Man, so he would be thought to vye with no Man in these Epistles'. The poem ostensibly offers the unprecedented, unmediated, transparent directness of an original essay. However, as his own references to it elsewhere suggest, Pope's assumption is always that a discerning reader will recognise the imitations of Lucretius, Horace and others on which it is grounded, and read it mediated through those models.

Thus, from the start, Pope's poem makes the characteristic gesture of his satiric verse, surreptitiously defining competent and incompetent, privileged and excluded readers. Moreover, as with the satiric poems, the *Essay* not only never identifies a secure position for a privileged reader to occupy, it also problematises the relationship between the privileged and the 'ideal' reader, to the extent that we might say that the poem's address depends upon the structured absence of that ideal reader. (S)he is apparently offered an immediately apprehensible exposition of the promised pattern of universal order within which mankind is placed:

> What is now published, is only to be considered as a *general Map* of MAN, marking out no more than the *greater parts,* their *extent,* their *limits,* and their *connection* . . .
>
> ('The Design')

At the same time, the authoritativeness of the exposition is implicitly undermined by the sense that there is an occluded version of that order, available to and apprehensible by a notional ideal reader, from which they are excluded – the tantalising and disabling possibility that there *may* be aesthetic coherence at some uncomprehended level beyond the poem's apparent contradictions.

This frustration has implications for the act of reading itself. In the

terms of Barrell and Guest, the poem is written with an intense
awareness of the inevitable distinctions between a 'synchronic'
medium and a 'diachronic' one such as poetry.[25] However, instead of
attempting to annex the advantages of a synchronic medium, as they
suggest that descriptive poetry of the period does, we would argue
that the *Essay*'s construction depends on its demonstration of the
impossibility of synchrony in reading.

Earlier in his career Pope had sketched a model of the ideal critical
comprehension which *An Essay on Man* assumes. In the relevant
passage of *An Essay on Criticism* Pope seizes on a metaphor of
synchronic visual comprehension:

> A perfect Judge will *read* each work of *Wit*
> With the same Spirit that its Author *writ*,
> Survey the *Whole* . . .
> Thus when we view some well-proportioned Dome,
> (The *World*'s just Wonder, and ev'n *thine* O *Rome*)
> No single Parts unequally surprize;
> All comes *united* to th'admiring Eyes.

(233–50)

An Essay on Man rests on a postulated God who sees and knows the
order which binds the multifarious, and whose existence is repeatedly
insisted on but repeatedly said to be unknowable to man, as though
the ideal reader were a Miltonic God-the-Father who beholds
simultaneously 'past, present, future' (*Paradise Lost,* iii, 78). This
comprehension requires an act of aesthetic faith: in the above passage
the activity of a human mind striving to comprehend is in tension
with a passive wonderment; to shift Pope's emphasis: 'All *comes
united to* th'admiring Eyes'.

The dilemma is inevitably at its most intense at the meeting-point
of human and divine. Where Milton and Addison typically negotiate
such moments with care – even manifesting them in terms of a polite
human renunciation – Pope involves the reader in a disruptive
experience. In Milton's Eden, for example, Adam is securely guided
by Raphael through the problematic issue of mankind's comprehension of the divine: the angel's speech about planetary motions
(*PL*, viii, 66–178) is built up rhetorically around a repeated 'What if'
('What if the sun/Be centre to the world . . .', 'what if . . ./. . . the
planet earth. . .', 'What if that light . . .'), and Raphael's conclusive
'be lowly wise:/Think only what concerns thee and thy being' finds
a responsive echo in Adam's reply:

216

> Therefore from this high pitch let us descend
> A lower flight, and speak of things at hand
> Useful
>
> (*PL*, viii, 198–200)

Adam's humanity carefully modulates the angelic voice to the human level: he has been, he says, not merely 'taught', but (in words which will become highly charged in the remaining books) 'cleared', 'satisfied' and 'freed' by the angel's speech; relieved of 'perplexing thoughts', Adam can now focus on 'That which before us lies in daily life' (viii, 183, 193).

The equivalent passage in Pope's *Essay* (i, 267–84) is calculatedly disconcerting: a fervid evocation of the 'stupendous whole/Whose body, Nature is, and God the soul' accelerates to its climax, only to reach an impasse:

> Lives thro' all life, extends through all extent,
> Spreads undivided, operates unspent,
> Breathes in our soul, informs our mortal part,
> As full, as perfect, in a hair as heart;
> As full, as perfect, in vile Man that mourns,
> As the rapt Seraph that adores and burns;
> To him no high, no low, no great, no small;
> He fills, he bounds, connects, and equals all.
>   Cease then, nor ORDER Imperfection name:
> Our proper bliss depends on what we blame.
> Know thy own point: This kind, this due degree
> Of blindness, weakness, Heav'n bestows on thee.
> Submit . . .
>
> (i, 273–85)

After an imaginative journey through the plenum of creation, the reader is brought up short and allotted a single point. Instantaneously, human perfection ('in a hair as heart') becomes human limitation ('blindness, weakness'), but at the same moment human limitation becomes the guarantee of that perfect order from which we have been excluded. This represents a model of the reader's dilemma in the *Essay*. The passage in a sense contains, through the interdependence of 'bliss' and 'blame', its own temptation, fall and redemption, and the disruption at line 281 is a pivotal moment in a complex strategy of disablement. Pope does not smooth away the awkwardness, but signals its discomfort.

We can set against this an equivalent moment in *Spectator* 420, when Addison turns from speculating about the infinite scale of the universe to consider the incapacity of human imagination:

217

> Nay, we might yet carry it farther, and discover in the smallest Particle of this little World, a new inexhausted Fund of Matter, capable of being spun out into another Universe.
>
> I have dwelt the longer on this Subject, because I think it may shew us the proper Limits, as well as the Defectiveness, of our Imagination; how it is confined to a very small Quantity of Space, and immediately stopt in its Operations . . . Our Reason can pursue a particle of Matter through an infinite variety of Divisions, but the Fancy soon loses sight of it.

Addison's polite discourse sustains the tone from exploration to explanation; there is no instantaneous cessation or submission; 'proper Limits' and 'Defectiveness' are reassuringly differentiated, rather than troublingly equated (as in Pope's point that Heaven 'bestows' blindness and weakness upon us), and Addison's 'Reason' compensates for Fancy's failure. What is more, the strategy of the *Spectator* passage is to accompany the reader and establish an easy commerce between 'I' and 'we', whereas Pope's 'our . . . we' (282) is awkwardly placed between two imperatives within a second-person address. In various ways, therefore, Pope can be seen as offering an impolite version of the Addisonian essay, a calculated roughness and brusqueness at a point where a finely gauged transition might have seemed in order. It is not surprising to find A. D. Nuttall castigating Pope for misjudging the tone demanded by the moment:

> That 'whatever is' is really and ultimately 'right' might have been made to emerge gradually, as a difficult yet credible idea, requiring the utmost stretch of faith and imagination. But what the poet must not do – and what Pope has now done – is to bring it forward with an air of briskly complacent confidence. In a chairman of a committee it would be rank bad timing and would cost him the vote he sought.[26]

Pope's challenge to polite discourse can easily be seen as impolitic.

Instead of providing an unproblematic synthesis, *An Essay on Man* offers the reader a sequence of fragmentary encapsulations of its central theses, proposing and juxtaposing versions of universal order in different forms, modes and tones, and formulating and reformulating them throughout, while their status is questioned and qualified, but never finally resolved. These formulations are proposed as the potentially comprehensible parts of an aesthetic whole, which would require simultaneous rather than sequential apprehension to be understood.

The nearest thing to a model of that possible comprehension, from which the polite reader is always excluded, is the privileged interchange between Pope and Bolingbroke as they range free over the estate of man, making multiple essays at their subject, laughing where they must and being candid where they can – activities which may be illustrative of their exemplary modesty in the face of the impossibility of human comprehension of the universal design, or may demonstrate the arrogance of the Addisonian essayist-genius, secure in his breadth and comprehension, and content to cast his pearls before . . . his readers.

The dramatic exclusivity of the Pope–Bolingbroke interchanges complicates our expectations about the inclusive familiarity of a polite essayist's address. This address is often blandly read by critics. Recently, for instance, William Bowman Piper has seen the *Essay* as characterised throughout by 'its pointed presentation of politely shared experience and understanding', constituting 'a fabric of what Pope and his age, quite appropriately, called common sense'. For Piper, the Pope–Bolingbroke relationship in the poem is representative of its focus 'on nature as experienced by the human mind and as shareable between friends'.[27] In a similar vein Vicki Sapp Bailey[28] has suggested that as Pope moves across ' "The Great Chain of Being" ' in the poem, 'With him is his St John, another individual man, whom he calls into conversation, social activity, sharing of the experience. The reader is, naturally, also included in this experience and conversation'. We would argue, however, that the readers of the poem are anything but 'naturally . . . included' in the conversation of the two philosophical friends. The presence of Bolingbroke as dedicatee/ addressee regularly embarrasses the poet–polite reader relationship. The poem's alternation of satiric scorn, enthusiastic buttonholing and philosophical catechism is in itself difficult to accept in terms of a sustained rapport,[29] and it is destabilised even more by the ghostly presence of the 'ideal' reader/friend, who is at once the inspirer, co-author, editor, interlocutor and judge of the work-in-progress. Symptomatic is the awkward moment at the opening of epistle IV, when Pope evokes the elusiveness and contradictoriness of human happiness:

> Which still so near us, yet beyond us lies,
> O'er-look'd, seen double, by the fool, and wise . . .
> Where grows? – where grows it not? – If vain our toil,
> We ought to blame the culture, not the soil:
> Fix'd to no spot is Happiness sincere,
> 'Tis no where to be found, or ev'rywhere;
> 'Tis never to be bought, but always free,
> And fled from Monarchs, ST. JOHN! dwells with thee.
>
> (iv, 5–18)

With sudden certainty ('ST. JOHN! dwells with thee') Bolingbroke is

219

permitted a comprehension and inclusiveness that the reader is denied. At this moment the text evokes an ideal reader who is exempted from its discourse of contradiction.

V

An Essay on Man provides the promise and the apparatus of an argumentative structure. At the same time it exposes the whole process of constructing proofs of a divine design as evidence of arrogant anthropocentrism. It postulates a coherent totality but repeatedly announces its denial of access to that totality. Its expository formulations insist on the unknowability of the design it asserts. Its conclusive moments can be seen as pivotal, its answers turn into questions, its assurances into deceptions, and its many attempts at (and promptings of the reader towards) synthesis come to seem like precarious moments of poise, rather than achieved resting places. An example is the well-known prescriptive passage which concludes epistle I:

> All Nature is but Art, unknown to thee;
> All Chance, Direction, which thou canst not see;
> All Discord, Harmony, not understood;
> All partial Evil, universal Good:
> And, spite of Pride, in erring Reason's spite,
> One truth is clear, 'Whatever IS, is RIGHT.'
>
> (i, 289–94)

The lines are, in fact, pivotal rather than conclusive: they form the didactic climax of the first epistle, but are also the starting point for the explorations of the later ones, where they will be varied and their terms juxtaposed and opened to scrutiny. Each line insists on the disablement of the reader from knowing the order that is affirmed, and asserts the impossibility of constructing a model of it in rational terms. The first continues variations on an opposition that has run through the poem from the opening metaphors of the maze, wild and garden, and which will continue to be recast in the remaining epistles, just as the other formulations that appear here as prescriptive absolutes will recur in new contexts, or with crucial variations in phrasing.

This is particularly clear in epistle IV, where the climactic formulation of the first epistle is incorporated into dialogic exchange, and is set as a generalisation against specific examples which, at least potentially, offer the basis for a critical re-examination of the validity of the original generalisation; and they in turn lead to further questioning:

> 'Whatever IS, is RIGHT.' – This World, 'tis true,
> Was made for Caesar – but for Titus too:
> And which more blest? who chain'd his country, say,
> Or he whose Virtue sigh'd to lose a day?
>
> (iv, 145–8)

The original declamation 'One truth is clear' now becomes a conversational concession (' 'tis true . . . but') in which the phrase 'was made for' flirts with the irony of human pride and presumption, and leads on to some provocative questions. This opening out of prescriptive to at least partially interrogative formulations is characteristic of the last epistle as a whole. In a similar movement, other key phrases from the climax of epistle I are progressively reformulated to accommodate the possibility of multiple interpretations. 'All partial Evil, universal Good', for instance, emerges in the last epistle as:

> Or partial Ill is universal Good,
> Or Change admits, or Nature lets it fall,
> Short and but rare, 'till Man improv'd it all.
>
> (iv, 114–16)

where 'universal Good' is destabilised by a new emphasis on post-lapsarian change, in which the Good is itself refracted into evil and loss. Some of these developments can be traced through epistle III. It begins with a postulation, taken to be the conclusion to the argument of the previous epistle ('Here then we rest: "The Universal Cause/ Acts to one end, but acts by various laws." '), and it ends with a conclusive 'thus':

> Thus God and Nature link'd the gen'ral frame,
> And bade Self-love and Social be the same.
>
> (iii, 317–18)

In between, however, epistle III does not give the transparent argument that it seems to promise. Instead it offers an account of historical development in which primitivist and progressive political programmes, and idealising, normative and satirical explanatory strategies are overlaid to bewildering effect. It is striking that in this process divine harmony is characteristically represented by its absence. It is locatable historically in the pre-lapsarian or primitive past; in the present it is postulated as being mediated through, or created by, the 'patriot' or the 'poet'. The primitive originary ideal state involves a harmony perceptible by man:

> Nor think, in NATURE'S STATE they blindly trod;
> The state of Nature was the reign of God . . .
>
> (iii, 147–8)

> . . . Ere Wit oblique had broke that steddy light,
> Man, like his Maker, saw that all was right.
>
> (iii, 231–2)

The alteration of man from that state involves the refraction of a previously unmediated vision (231) which is both a fall and a development: we are exhorted (in another variation on an opposition that has been extended throughout) to 'See him from Nature rising slow to Art!' (iii, 169).

The dislocating, rather than reassuring, effect of the *Essay on Man*'s repetition of certain phrases is suggested by Addison's *Spectator* paper on 'Method' (no. 476). Here he characterises an unmethodical discourse as one which lacks proper order and connection:

> There is always an Obscurity in Confusion, and the same Sentence that wou'd have enlightened the Reader in one Part of a Discourse, perplexes him in another.

This is the perplexity that Pope risks in the *Essay*. Addison's 'Methodical Discourse' works in the reverse way:

> For the same Reason likewise every Thought in a Methodical Discourse shews its self in its greatest Beauty, as the several Figures in a piece of Painting receive new Grace from their disposition in the picture.

Addison's aesthetic language here reminds us that for him religion and aesthetics were not discontinuous. The 'disposition' of things was the work of a God for whom the imagination's delight in a scene or picture was preparatory for (indeed educative towards) the soul's contemplation of the divine (a 'new Grace' indeed). Addison's discourse of the polite, here taking its image from both divine and aesthetic 'disposition', once more achieves a cumulative effect: each individual figure smooths out and reflects another, creating a community that is greater than the sum of its parts – Augustan Rome again, or the France of Louis XIV. The discourse of the polite as

Addison presents it, can join the 'Man of a Polite Imagination' (*Spectator* 411) to his God, and make the mutually-reflective society of polite authors and readers into an image of perfect communion. In resisting this discourse, Pope is making not just a social and aesthetic point, but is distancing himself from Addisonian theology.

In his review of Pope's *Essay on Criticism* (*Spectator* 253), Addison's one adverse judgement was that the young poet had allowed himself, through the essay's satiric elements, to betray the mutuality of polite authorship. He took his example again from Augustan Rome:

> As there are none more ambitious of Fame, than those who are conversant in Poetry, it is very natural for such as have not succeeded in it to deprecate the Works of those who have. For since they cannot raise themselves to the Reputation of their Fellow-Writers, they must endeavour to sink it to their own Pitch . . .
> The greatest Wits that ever were produced in one Age, lived together in so good an Understanding, and celebrated one another with so much Generosity, that each of them receives an additional Lustre from his Contemporaries . . . I need not tell my Reader, that I here point at the Reign of *Augustus*, and I believe he will be of my Opinion, that neither *Virgil* nor *Horace* would have gained so great a Reputation in the World, had they not been the Friends and Admirers of each other.

'I believe he will be of my Opinion', says Addison with the confidence of someone who knows, even feels he has created, his readership. It was against the spirit of this community that Pope had offended. The reader of *An Essay on Man* remains tantalisingly aware of the possibility, but excluded from the actuality, of this postulated but permanently deferred ideal readership.

Notes

1. See Miriam Leranbaum, *Alexander Pope's 'Opus Magnum'. 1729–1744* (Oxford, 1977).
2. James Sambrook, *The Eighteenth Century. The Intellectual and Cultural Context of English Literature, 1700–1789* (London, 1986), pp. 34–5.
3. C. H. Vereker, *Eighteenth-Century Optimism* (Liverpool, 1967), pp. 118–19.
4. Brean S. Hammond, *Pope and Bolingbroke: A Study of Friendship and Influence* (Columbia, 1984), p. 79.
5. A. D. Nuttall, *Pope's 'Essay on Man'* (London, 1984), p. 185.
6. Hammond's summary, p. 83. See Bernard Fabian, 'Pope and Lucretius: observations on *An Essay on Man*', MLR, 74 (1979), 524–37; and Leranbaum, p. 39.

7. Hammond, pp. 80–3.
8. J. M. Cameron, 'Doctrinal to an age: notes towards a revaluation of Pope's *Essay on Man*', in *Essential Articles for the Study of Alexander Pope*, edited by Maynard Mack (Hamden, Conn., 1964, 1968), pp. 353–69 (p. 362).
9. Douglas H. White and Thomas P. Tierney, '*An Essay on Man* and the tradition of satires on mankind,' *MP* 85 (1987), 27–41 (p. 28).
10. See Martin Kallich, *Heav'n's First Law: Rhetoric and Order in Pope's 'Essay on Man'* (De Kalb, Ill., 1967); R. L. Brett, *Reason and Imagination* (Oxford, 1960); D. H. White, *Pope and the Context of Controversy* (Chicago, 1970); and Nuttall. See also Samuel Johnson, 'Life of Pope', in *Lives of the Poets*, edited by George Birkbeck Hill, 3 vols (Oxford, 1905), iii, pp. 161–71, 242–5.
11. Murray Krieger, ' "Trying Experiments upon Our Sensibility": the art of dogma and doubt in eighteenth-century literature', in *Poetic Presence and Illusion: Essays in Critical History and Theory* (Baltimore, 1980), p. 80.
12. G. Douglas Atkins, *Quests of Difference: Reading Pope's Poems* (Lexington, Kentucky, 1986), p. 44.
13. John Barrell and Harriet Guest, 'On the use of contradiction: economics and morality in the eighteenth-century long poem', in *The New Eighteenth Century*, pp. 121–43.
14. Jon P. Klancher, *The Making of English Reading Audiences, 1790–1832* (Madison, Wisc., 1987).
15. Michael G. Ketcham, *Transparent Designs: Reading, Performance, and Form in the 'Spectator' Papers* (Athens, Ga., 1985), p. 156.
16. For an account of the significance of this process, see Jerome Christiansen, *Practicing Enlightenment: Hume and the Formation of a Literary Career* (Madison, Wisc., 1987).
17. Thomas Woodman, 'Pope and the polite', *EC* 28 (1978), 19–37 (p. 26).
18. Samuel Johnson, *A Dictionary of the English Language* (London, 1755), s.n. 'Essay' 2: 'Poem to Roscommon'.
19. Quotations from *The Spectator* are taken from the edition of Donald F. Bond, 5 vols (Oxford 1965).
20. Matthew 7:6.
21. Ralph Cudworth, *The True Intellectual System of the Universe* (1678), I v, 731 (*OED* s.n. 'polite' 1a).
22. Shaftesbury, *Essay on the Freedom of Wit and Humour*, Part I, section 2.
23. Katherine Philips, *Poems* (1667) (*OED* s.n. 'polite' 2b).
24. Addison is here contrasting a 'great natural Genius' with a *Bel Esprit*.
25. *The New Eighteenth Century*, pp. 121–2.
26. Nuttall, p. 77.
27. William Bowman Piper, 'Pope's vindication', *PQ*, 67 (1988), 303–21 (pp. 312–13).
28. Vicki Sapp Bailey, 'Pope and antithesis: "Law and War With Words" ', *SEL* 27 (1987), 437–54 (pp. 443–4).
29. This feature of the poem is interestingly discussed by Simon Varey, 'Rhetoric and *An Essay of Man*', in *The Art of Alexander Pope*, edited by Howard Erskine-Hill and Anne Smith (London, 1979), pp. 132–43.

13

'Guard the sure barrier'
Pope and the partitioning of culture

Brean S. Hammond

I

I begin by calling attention to an interesting eighteenth-century experiment in the utilisation of public space – Richard Steele's so-called Censorium. Sometime in 1712, Steele rented a house in York Buildings, a few doors from the lower end of Villiers Street off the Strand.[1] One room of the house was magnificently decorated and set aside as a cultural performance centre. George Berkeley described it as follows:

> [Steele] is likewise proposing a noble entertainment for persons of a refined taste. It is chiefly to consist of the finest pieces of eloquence translated from the Greek and Latin authors. They will be accompanied with the best music suited to raise those passions that are proper to the occasion. Pieces of poetry will be there recited. . . . I have seen the place designed for these performances: it is in York Buildings, and he has been at no small expence to embellish with all imaginable decorations. It is by much the finest chamber I have seen, and will contain seats for a select company of 200 persons of the best quality and taste, who are to be subscribers.[2]

Steele's own description of the venue is given in *Town-Talk*, the informal weekly paper devoted to theatrical matters that he started in 1715. An elegant environment (allegorical paintings of Truth and Eloquence on the walls, skilful lighting, architectural designs) and subscription funding indicate the aristocratic pretensions of the venue. Clearly, Steele saw the Censorium as another arm of the campaign he was waging as Patentee of Drury Lane Theatre to raise the level of public taste – if this plan for a learned tableau vivant was typical of programming policy:

> Diversions proposed in this Undertaking, are to consist of the Representation of some great Incidents in Antiquity, in the Manner in which they were Transacted, according to the best Information to be obtained from Men the most conversant in Medals, Paintings, History and Philosophy.[3]

Although the Censorium is to be dedicated to the pleasurable promotion of knowledge, ladies will still be admitted because their presence raises the level of politeness in the audience; and the Censorium's sponsor is confident that the product will be cheaper than opera, and much superior both to it, and to the theatre.

The name 'Censorium' is best explained by one of Addison's *Spectator* essays, no. 565 of 9 July 1714, in which Addison, following Newton, had represented the immensity of space as a giant '*Sensorium* of the Godhead', a sort of storage space for the Deity's sense data, but with overtones also of a cosmic performance centre where God can witness the marvellous spectacle of the sunset and the luminous appearance of the stars.[4] Steele planned to present to his audience of two hundred opinion leaders in 'politeness, taste and learning' a programme not just based on the arts and classic eloquence, but also on 'the Sciences, as well as mechanick Arts'. In November 1719 scientific lectures were given by such noted virtuosi as Dr Desaguliers. Given that Steele wished to establish the Censorium as an academy with government support, he probably saw it as an up-market alternative to the Royal Society, as a place where ladies and gentlemen could go to keep abreast of the latest developments in the laboratories without the disadvantages of the smell.[5] The Royal Society itself had moved to new premises in Crane Court in November 1710, so contemporaries may have had a sense of rival establishments separated by a short walk up the Strand.

A measure of cultural adjudication is perhaps implied in the punning spelling 'Censorium': a place presided over by a Censor, yet also a place where sensory pleasure was to be afforded.[6] The Censorium was an attempt to enshrine élite culture and hedge it in with the protection of status, to provide it with a suitably fashionable architectural space, free from the hurlyburly of the theatre. Yet that coin has a reverse side. The Censorium was also an attempt to market that culture, and Steele's role as entrepreneur is entirely consistent with his function as the impresario of middling culture in other spheres. The figure of Richard Steele in fact straddles the cultural tiers. His work on the periodicals is aimed at the cultivation of middle-brow taste, while the patent that he was granted for the licensing of Drury Lane Theatre specifically charged him with the responsibility of raising theatre's moral standards. Culture and cash are firmly connected in Steele's letter of March 1716 to Spencer Compton, in which he requests Compton's intercession with the Lord Treasurer for the payment of his pension. The money is needed, Steele explains, to defray the expenses of refurbishing York Buildings 'for select Audiences, where there will, I doubt not, be performances in Eloquence and Musick transcending . . . what has ever appeared before in any Age or any Nation. This matter has already cost me a thousand pounds, and made me very bare of money'.[7]

Steele's Censorium is one example of a process that was gathering ground in the Augustan era, labelled by J.H. Plumb the 'commercialisation of leisure'. By the end of the seventeenth century England had become a major paper-producing nation, the newspapers had emerged as a distinct form, the novel was on the point of being created out of a typographical 'primal soup', and anxiety over the control of print, finely balanced against a new permissiveness, is obvious from contemporary legislation. As Plumb stresses:

> Printing combined with our alphabet system made self-education possible, making therefore . . . for a steady cultural seepage: ideas adumbrated in narrow élitist groups might, and often did, permeate society. No knowledge was necessarily the arcane possession of a limited class once printing and publishing had got into their stride and – most important of all, once the lower classes were in a position to purchase cheap books.[8]

Evidence, if not exactly of 'cultural seepage' then certainly of transgressive mingling of different social tiers in leisure-time activity and in custom-designed architectural spaces, is provided by Terry Castle in her brilliant account of the eighteenth-century masquerade. Castle calls attention to the masquerade's aspiration to be exclusive and to maintain the *bon ton,* and to the commercial interests that sabotaged this:

> Contemporary descriptions of the public masquerade universally call attention to the inclusiveness of the occasion, and the fact that the 'Lower Orders' invariably did penetrate the inner sanctum. And herein

227

lies a basic paradox of masquerade sociology: though on one level the masquerade advertised itself as a gathering of the upper classes, on another it was popularly recognized as the event, virtually unique among modern civil institutions, that did in fact 'promiscuously' mingle the classes, bringing together men and women from all social ranks. Despite its superficial aura of fashionable exclusivity – the invention of the entrepreneurs – the masquerade actually drew upon a suggestively varied clientele. Up to a point, like the protean City itself (with which it was metaphorically connected), it was indeed a 'strange Medley' of persons – a rough mix of high and low.[9]

II

Pope's *Dunciad* is also readable as an intervention against various forms of cultural seepage and transgressive mingling of social strata. It is an example of the way in which an instantiation of dominant cultural production – the classical epic – is locked in conflict with the culture of the populace and of the marketplace. Culture popularised and culture commercialised are, for Pope, scarcely distinct aspects of the same ideological formation. Although *The Dunciad* tries to fight a rearguard action for the separation of 'low' art forms and popular writing from 'high' art forms and writing informed by the classic tradition, the poem is clearly nurtured by the demotic forms it ostensibly despises. In their book *The Politics and Poetics of Transgression,* Peter Stallybrass and Allon White have analysed the mediation between the 'grotesque' and the 'classical' in Pope's period, showing that public spaces are the site for the struggle of the competing discourses of the time, especially for those struggling for the possession of the term 'art'.[10] They show how new forms of corporate assembly, particularly the coffee-house as a hygienic and well-regulated public space, created new patterns of discourse.[11] Attention drawn to the prioritising and sanitising of public space in the period throws light on *The Dunciad*. Banishing the rowdy, the carnal and the grotesque from bourgeois meeting places, the Augustans reinscribe these elements in discourse as a locus of imaginative energy. *The Dunciad* anxiously depicts popular culture militant, the 'Smithfield muses' on the march, transgressing the territory of Court culture, contaminating the high by the low:

> Thro' Lud's fam'd gates, along the well-known Fleet
> Rolls the black troop, and overshades the street,
> 'Till show'rs of Sermons, Characters, Essays,
> In circling fleeces whiten all the ways

(ii, 359–62)

From the poem's outset in the Argument to book I it dramatises a process that reverses the sanitising of public space. 'The College of the Goddess in the City, with her private Academy for Poets in particular' is the opening setting, an alternative Gresham's College, though that 'private Academy' is a protean space further figured as a troglodyte publishing house, 'the Cave of Poverty and Poetry'. Very soon it is transformed into an allegorical throne-room. From her throne the Queen of Dulness gazes on a court that, with astonishing metaphorical energy, becomes a dormitory, a tadpole-infested pond, a lying-in chamber, a factory for literary production, a promenading space, a hall in which an assembly or rout or masquerade is taking place, and finally the entire spectacle is viewed by the queen as a kind of changeable scenery, special effects engineered for her as if by a scenographer like Lambert or Devoto. When Cibber is introduced, the interior decor of his cell is notated in terms of the familiar Scriblerian icon, the hack in his garret. Unlike the Hogarthian representation, however, Cibber's garret also houses a substantial library. But this salient feature of a house with social pretentions is here a polluted space, a 'Gothic Library', giving space only to 'The Classics of an Age that heard of none'.

Impressively, then, *The Dunciad* renders the struggle between the mediators of popular, low-brow and irrational culture like Cibber and Settle and those who would prevent their infiltration into respectable cultural vicinities, as a struggle over territory, over *lebensraum*. This is a prime example of what Stephen Greenblatt, in his recent *Shakespearean Negotiations,* would term 'symbolic acquisition', where a set of social practices or 'modes of social energy' is transferred to the domain of literature by means of metaphorical and metonymic representation.[12] Conflicts over proprietorship of space being fought out in the theatre stalls, in display spaces, galleries and elsewhere are in 'dynamic exchange' with literary representation of these conflicts in the poem. *The Dunciad,* therefore, takes its place alongside various other attempts in the late seventeenth and early eighteenth century to police cultural frontiers, attempts which result in disparate phenomena. A distinction between popular prints and élite publication is created, according to Peter Holland, by Congreve's issuing of his *Works* in octavo in 1710.[13] Whereas the quarto versions are performance-texts, aspiring towards a kind of short-hand notation that tries to render plays in performance, the revised *Works* is a reading text, a bid for gentlemanly status, an attempt to confer prestige upon play-texts as objects worthy of leisured perusal. Similarly, we might read the various attempts to create, on the French model, an Academy for refining and fixing the English language as an élite response to the threat of proliferating print. In the early 1680s the Earl of Roscommon recruited Dryden, Dorset and Halifax for this endeavour and later, of course, Swift advocated his 'Proposal for Correcting the English Tongue' as a response to the stylistic butchery of hacks like John Dunton:

> How then shall any Man, who hath a Genius for History, equal to the best of the Antients, be able to undertake such a Work with Spirit and Chearfulness, when he considers, that he will be read with Pleasure but a very few Years, and in an Age or two shall hardly be understood without an Interpreter?[14]

Yet I allude here to Greenblatt's new-historicist insights, and earlier to those of Stallybrass and White, because they draw attention to the extent to which *The Dunciad*'s ideology is rooted in the value system that it ostensibly opposes. By implication the poem draws various distinctions between good and bad writers, between valuable and worthless art forms, between rational and irrational printed works, between lasting art and commercial, evanescent entertainment; and it tries to hold the line between élite or 'classic' and merely 'popular' cultural forms: 'Or, if to Wit a coxcomb make pretence,/Guard the sure barrier between that and Sense' (i, 177–8). *The Dunciad* puts its mock-heroic processes to work in holding the line against mindless and debased art that appealed both to aristocratic and popular sections of the public. (Its class basis is not simple, as is evident in the attack on opera, which was attended and patronised exclusively by the well-heeled.) This poem, and Scriblerian satire generally, constructs as target a new type of writer that I will designate 'Homo mechanicus', whose relations with the public are those of the market and whose art is merely a species of production quite on the level with any other: art as trade.[15] Scriblerian satire thus contributes to a way of thinking about popular written and theatrical culture that, as Raymond Williams has pointed out, equates it with 'mass culture' where the masses are constructed as a threat to culture.[16] It also helps to shape a lasting prejudice against any kind of commercial motive operating in the production of what is called 'art'. These positions have contributed to the formation of the literary canon, influencing the system of exclusions upon which the nineteenth-century sense of an unbroken literary tradition was based.

But as my brief discussion suggests, demotic and high cultural forms, low-brow and high-brow art, are mutually dependent even in Pope's own writings and even though there are intellectual forces at work making for their separation. Stuart Hall, in his essay 'Notes on deconstructing "The Popular" ', insists that 'there is a continuous and necessarily uneven and unequal struggle by the dominant culture, constantly to disorganise and reorganise popular culture; to enclose and confine its definitions and forms within a more inclusive range of dominant forms.[17]' As historians point out, eighteenth-century Britain was a society that permitted an unrivalled degree of social mobility. Cultural forms travelling up and down the social escalator is exactly what we would expect from such a society, and it does occur. Not only is it the case that the social circumstances of the dunces included in Pope's poem are considerably varied (so that one of the poem's achievements is to create of this diversity the impression of a swarm-culture that effectively mythologises social mobility) but their literary abilities are equally diverse. Lewis Theobald figures as the hero of the early *Dunciad* not because he was in any way incompetent, as modern verdicts on his edition of Shakespeare would confirm, but because as a contriver of mindless pantomimes, he was for Pope a profoundly ambiguous cultural token.[18] He was locked in a struggle with Pope for possession of the most prestigious literary property available – Shakespeare himself.

It is therefore too simple to say, as Pat Rogers does in *Hacks and Dunces,* that 'the gap between, say, Pope and Leonard Welsted [has been] underestimated rather than overstated in the received wisdom about the subject'. [19] Leopold Damrosch, in his excellent book *The Imaginative World of Alexander Pope,* quotes this remark with approbation, but it transpires that Damrosch, like many of us, has his favourite dunce, vying for promotion into the category of serious writer. He makes an eloquent case for James Ralph, arguing that Pope's dismissive couplet:

> Silence, ye Wolves! while Ralph to Cynthia howls,
> And makes Night hideous – Answer him, ye Owls!
>
> (iii, 165–6)

which renders him an early comic prototype of Wordsworth's Winander Boy, is unfair. Ralph, it turns out, was really quite a good writer.[20] And if Damrosch had glanced a few lines before this reference to Ralph in *Dunciad* III he would have found other redeemables: Ned Ward, author of *The London Spy,* and John Dennis, surely a highly influential figure in the history of criticism . . .? And so the garment of duncehood unravels.

231

III

The contradictoriness of *The Dunciad*'s ideological position on popular forms and on the spread of print is really only a tiny crack amidst a vast continental drift: the gradual shift from the patronage system to the commercial alienation of literary production to print. A dramatic illustration of the difficulties endured by authors caught in this evolutionary change is afforded by the case of John Dryden.[21]

Dryden's rejection of the Puritan faith in which he was brought up is explicable, according to James A. Winn's biography, in terms of his need to benefit from the refuelled patronage system after the Restoration. Professional playwriting, as Dryden admitted many times, was only a way of making a living, really the only way open to him of supplementing his irregularly paid state pensions: 'For I confess my chief endeavours are to delight the Age in which I live. If the humour of this, be for low Comedy, small Accidents, and Raillery, I will force my Genius to obey it, though with more reputation I could write in Verse.'[22] Of his own *Amboyna*, Dryden remarked that it 'will scarcely bear a serious perusal, it being contriv'd and written in a Moneth, the Subject barren, the Persons low, and the Writing not heightened with many labored Scenes'.[23] Dryden's greatest desire was to achieve a quality of patronage much higher than the £200 per year he obtained from his posts as laureate and Historiographer Royal, so that he could buy time to compose an epic on the Stuarts. Poetry, as the pittance Milton had received for *Paradise Lost* had shown, was not commercially viable. In the 1670s, however, Dryden was forced into the position of fiercely defending professional writers against aristocratic amateurs like Rochester and Sir Robert Howard who threatened to take the bread from his mouth. Winn argues that Rochester's feud with Dryden was motivated by the former's dislike of Dryden's literary success and his aping of aristocratic manners. By way of response, Dryden formulated a spirited defence of the career professional, suggesting that gentleman-amateurs should stick to what they are good at, which is not writing. The preface to *All for Love* (1677) contains a fine attack on those who impose their taste and talents on the public by means of rank rather than ability, as well as an ambivalent defence of writing for money:

> Men of pleasant Conversation, (at least esteem'd so) and indu'd with a triffling kind of Fancy, perhaps help'd out with some smattering of

Latine, are ambitious to distinguish themselves from the Herd of Gentlemen, by their Poetry;

Rarus enim ferme sensus communis in illa Fortuna [Juvenal, *Satires* 8, 73–4: 'For common sense is rare in that station of life']

And is not this a wretched affectation, not to be contented with what Fortune has done for them, and sit down quietly with their Estates, but they must call their Wits in question, and needlesly expose their nakedness to publick view? Not considering that they are not to expect the same approbation from sober men, which they have found from their flatterers after the third Bottle? If a little glittering in discourse has pass'd them on us for witty men, where was the necessity of undeceiving the World? would a man who has an ill Title to an Estate, but yet is in possession of it, would he bring it of his own accord, to be try'd at *Westminster?* We who write, if we want the Talent, yet have the excuse that we do it for a poor subsistence; but what can be urg'd in their defence, who not having the Vocation of Poverty to scribble, out of meer wantonness take pains to make themselves ridiculous?[24]

Winn's biography reminds us of how far, for much of his life, Dryden was from the poet idealised by Pope in the *Epistle to Dr. Arbuthnot.* Only in the 1690s, when Dryden had been forced by his conversion to relinquish all state support and was producing his noble translation of Virgil supported by subscription, did he at all conform to Pope's image of the independent man of letters. As a professional concerned with new writing for the theatre, Dryden was a 'modern' rather than an 'ancient' and knew from experience the compromises forced on him by the marketplace and by patrons in an intensely partisan period.

Unlike Dryden, Pope never spoke in the voice of the professional author, however reluctantly. For him, as for the other Scriblerians, great literature was the result of independent endeavour, born after a long gestation period of leisured study. This being so, the professional writer, with his 'time is money' attitude, was not likely to produce a great work. Yet although Pope overtly embraced the academic poetic tradition of Milton, he also helped to form its opposite, the conception of the spontaneous genius who neither needs the assistance of learning nor has mimesis as his ultimate goal, but owes allegiance to the independent world of the imagination. While this aesthetic was not fully articulated until the late 1750s, Pope's preface to his 1717 *Works* clearly shows the old and new views in competition:

> I writ because it amused me; I corrected because it was as pleasant to
> me to correct as to write; and I publish'd because I was told I might
> please such as it was a credit to please . . . the Ancients . . . had as much
> Genius as we; and . . . to take more pains, and employ more time,
> cannot fail to produce more complete pieces. . . . All that is left us is to
> recommend our productions by the imitation of the Ancients: and it
> will be found true, that in every age, the highest character for sense and
> learning has been obtain'd by those who have been most indebted to
> them.[25]

Pope's account of his own writing activity makes it sound effortless,
the result of natural genius; but his sponsorship of the ancients and his
revision-fetish ('the Last and Greatest Art, the Art to Blot') suggests
otherwise.

We can ground this contradictory account of artistic creation more
firmly in a brief account of Pope's own poetic career. Even a very
rapid inspection of the material basis for Pope's success as a poet
should warn us against taking his cultural adjudications at face value.
Pope's emergence as a cultural mandarin was accomplished in three
stages. First, he made himself fabulously wealthy by translating
Homer, but doing so by means of subscription publishing. This
system exposed the author to his readership in heavily mediated
ways, effectively mystifying the relationship between writing and
profit. While raising native cultural standards and making a fan club
out of large sections of influential society, Pope achieved the
independence that his *Epistle to Dr. Arbuthnot* was later to mytho-
logise. In that poem Pope represented himself as a man of genius who
is not subject to the market forces that bring lesser writers into
existence. In the course of the poem, Pope appears to cut himself off
from all models of literary production then available. 'Independence'
becomes a creative immaculate conception or levitation act, since
Pope claims to have no visible means of support. Yet there is no hint
of a suggestion that Pope is self-made, nothing of the Josiah
Bounderbyish vulgarity that attaches to, for example, Charles
Churchill, the self-appointed genius of the 1760s. Looking down
from an eminence, from the position of untainted purity, and as the
mediator to the reading public of Homer and Shakespeare, Pope
accomplished the third stage of his cultural hegemony. His revised
Dunciad reinvigorated his earlier construction of 'duncehood', creating a category of badly educated, merely popular writers who shared
the fact that they wrote for money and drew on demotic forms. Their
literary endeavours were a gross form of materialism. For the popular
writer, *The Dunciad* insinuates, writing is not a vocation but a trade –

and scarcely even a lawful one. It results in a set of physical marks not worth the paper they are printed on. Less than fifteen years after Pope's death, however, the erstwhile dunce James Ralph would publish his *The Case of Authors by Profession or Trade* (1758), in which he would eloquently plead the hack's right to earn a living, comparing the garreteer to a slave in the mines:

> Both must drudge *and* starve; and neither can hope for deliverance. The compiler must compile; the composer must compose on; sick or well; in spirit or out; whether furnished with matter or not; till, by the joint pressure of labour, penury, and sorrow, he has worn out his parts, his constitution, and all the little stock of reputation he had acquired among the *Trade*; who were all, perhaps, that ever heard of his name.[26]

Three years earlier, Johnson's *Dictionary* had already elevated drudgery to monumental status, heralding the coming of the professional writer as hero of a new age of print.[27]

Pope's hatred of professional writers is an aspect of his wider suspicion of 'the moneyed interest', which in turn is put in a dialectical perspective by Michael McKeon when he shows that those like Swift and Pope who wished to oppose the progressive prescriptions of 'the moneyed interest' were drawn by their conservative stance into an uneasy alliance with aristocratic positions they could not wholeheartedly share. In his words:

> To Swift and those who shared his views, the solidity of the landed estate and the personal relations it sustained seemed to offer the best model to counterpose to the unreality of exchange value and the limitless indulgence of human appetite. One problem with this stance, however, was that it was very difficult to separate the idea of land as exclusively value-creating from other, genealogical, elements of aristocratic ideology to which it had been welded by force of long habit. Moreover, by 1700 the attempt to isolate a pristine enclave of noncapitalist land use – 'the landed interest' – from the omnivorous economics of the marketplace was not without a certain quixotic futility. In fact, the dilemma of incorporation by the enemy entirely suffused the experience of the Tory radicals, and it was essential to the dangerous quality of paranoid volatility, which gave to the best of their writings a distinctive brilliance. It may be most accurate to see the conservative ideology of the early eighteenth century not as the negation of capitalist ideology but as the expression of a wish to halt the implacable juggernaut of capitalist reform at a stage that preserved, at least for property owners of a certain political and social persuasion, the best of both worlds.[28]

That 'paranoid volatility' is nowhere more evident than in Pope's brilliant construction, in his poems, of heroes and villains. There is no shortage of testimony to the effect that Colley Cibber was a coxcomb. To some, his very appearance was a kind of ungentlemanly conduct, an affront to civilised values. Aaron Hill wrote a mock-obituary of him in *The Prompter*:

> His Features were *narrowly Earnest,* and *attentively Insignificant*; – There was a *peeping Pertness* in his Eye, which wou'd have been *Spirit,* had his Heart been warm'd with Humanity, or his Brain been stor'd with *Ideas.* In his Face, was a contracted Kind of *passive,* yet *protruded,* Sharpness, like a Pig, half roasted:- And a *Voice,* not unlike *his own,* might have been borrow'd from the same suffering Animal, while in a Condition, a little less desperate. . . . His very Extravagancies were colour'd with *Propriety,* and Affectation sat so easy about Him, that It was in danger of appearing Amiable.[29]

Many contemporary attacks on him witness to his lack of education and to his loitering without intent in the purlieux of high culture. To Pope, however, Cibber was an especially potent symbol of marketed (that is, degraded) culture, because as playwright, actor, theatre impresario and laureate he was a public monument to art's relationship with capital, symbolic of the prostitution of genius to popularity. Theatre was the art-form that had the most direct relationship with the marketplace, subject to the vagaries of public taste long before other literary forms were so exposed. Singing, dancing, variety shows and low-brow popular entertainment – the gradual move towards what, in the eighteenth century, became the 'whole show' – suggests a changing audience composition and a broadening of the social base. The 1728 *Dunciad* arises directly out of theatre's search in the 1720s for a programming formula that would tap wider sections of its potential market, and to Pope this was socially transgressive, diluting the purity of art forms and lowering the social standing of art's patrons.[30] John Gay was Cibber's antitype in Pope's scheme of things, an antithesis nicely pointed by the fact that it was Cibber who had the distinction of turning down *The Beggar's Opera.* Elsewhere I have argued that Gay is best seen as a thoroughly professional writer who could not settle comfortably into such a sense of himself because Pope was determined to figure him as a neglected genius, the great poet who was allowed to starve at a time when such as Cibber could prosper.[31] Encouraged by Pope to despise the literary prostitution of the marketplace, he failed to achieve the lucrative position at court that would have freed him from it. In fact, however, there is more similarity between Gay and Cibber than there is difference.

IV

If this account of *The Dunciad*'s cultural location carries any conviction, and if Pope's role as perceiver and creator of the emergent print-culture is recognised, a reappraisal of his importance to literary history is required. Looking back at the end of the eighteenth century on the events of the Walpole period, Edmund Burke was less than impressed by their historical importance:

> The events of that era seemed then of magnitude, which the revolutions of our time have reduced to parochial importance; and the debates which then shook the nation now appear of no higher moment than a discussion in a vestry.[32]

There is, one has to admit, a clear sense in which, compared with Milton's era, or Dryden's or Burke's, the events of Pope's lifetime are uninspiring. As Carole Fabricant has put it, the fate of Jenkins's pickled ear does not stand comparison with that of the British monarchy itself.[33] Yet if Pope's outbursts in the 1730s lack a historical 'objective correlative', if he was a rebel without much of a cause, it is still wrong to dismiss his struggle as unimportant or disingenuous. Its true importance was cultural rather than political in the narrow sense. In and through the *Imitations of Horace,* Pope won a victory over Walpole that extended far beyond the skirmishes over the Excise Bill crisis and the war with Spain. Pope captured the cultural high ground by bestowing on the events of his own life and writing career an exemplary status, and using this highly fictionalised autobiography to underwrite his satiric practice. Pope, as Fabricant says, encoded ideological issues exclusively in moral terms and made his own style of living the crucial litmus test of that ideology's truth. His success in establishing the legitimacy of these terms is manifest in the fact that no subsequent biographer, Maynard Mack included, has been able to operate outside the moral domain that Pope's own discourse established. Biographers accept that their central task is to *evaluate* their subject's life, to apply to it a calculus that will establish whether he was more sinned against than sinning. A Pope biography, even one as admirable as Maynard Mack's, can come to seem a mere footnote to the *Epistle to Dr. Arbuthnot.* As Mack puts it, in Shakespearian cadence:

> Without concealing his warts, I have consciously avoided magnifying them or dwelling on them to the exclusion of all else; and where there

237

are extenuating circumstances to be considered, as for most discreditable actions there are, few of us being dyed-in-the-wool villains, I have thought it proper to consider them.[34]

Thus Pope has enlisted his biographer as an ally in his own cultural project.

Let me conclude by returning to where I began – to the Censorium. It is no surprise to find that Pope was involved in the early stages. There is speculation that his 'Ode for Musick on St. Cecilia's Day' was written for performance there; and among the curiosities found at his home in Twickenham when it went up for auction in 1802 was a medal bearing a picture of the sun, surrounded by the inscription 'Sensorium. Anno Primo. Georgii. 1715' which may have an admission ticket.[35] By 1715 Pope had only just worked his ticket. Soon he would feel that this was the cultural environment to which he belonged. Yet as we have observed, Steele's aristocratic venture was also an example of bourgeois economic activity; and so, for all its horror of literary commodification, was Pope's *Dunciad*.

Notes

1. *London County Council Survey of London, vol. 18: The Strand,* edited by Sir George Gater and Walter H. Godfrey (London, 1937), p. 62.
2. *The Correspondence of George Berkeley and Sir John Percival,* edited by Benjamin Rand (Cambridge, 1914), p. 110.
3. *Richard Steele's Periodical Journalism, 1714–1716,* edited by Rae Blanchard (Oxford, 1959), p. 209.
4. *The Spectator,* edited by Donald F. Bond, 5 vols (Oxford, 1965), iv, 532.
5. The best account of the Censorium is given in John Loftis, *Steele at Drury Lane* (Berkeley and Los Angeles, 1952), part 2, ch. 4. Loftis thinks that the Censorium was modelled on the Continental academies. I think the inspiration was nearer home. See also George A. Aitken, *The Life of Richard Steele,* 2 vols (London, 1889), i, 361–2; ii, 59–63.
6. Steele himself explains the term in *Town-Talk* no. 4 (6 January 1716): 'The *censorium,* every Body knows, is the Organ of Sense, as the Eye is of Sight; and, it seems more proper to use a Word, which implies the *Sensio tantum,* the bare Conception of what is presented to the Spectator, rather than any Name which, in a Didactick Manner, pronounces what ought to be received or rejected.' (Blanchard, *Steele's Periodical Journalism,* pp. 209–10.) This is clearly ironic in view of the overtones of 'censorship' in the name. (I owe some suggestions in this paragraph to discussion with Professor Thomas Kaminski of Loyola University, Chicago.)

7. *The Correspondence of Sir Richard Steele,* edited by Rae Blanchard, (London, 1941, 1968), pp. 113, 114n.
8. J. H. Plumb, 'the commercialization of leisure', in *The Birth of a Consumer Society,* edited by Neil McKendrick, John Brewer and J. H. Plumb (Bloomington, In., 1982), pp. 265–85 (p. 267).
9. Terry Castle, *Masquerade and Civilization: The Carnivalesque in Eighteenth-century English Culture and Fiction* (London, 1986), p. 28.
10. Peter Stallybrass and Allon White, *The Politics and Poetics of Transgression* (London, 1986), ch. 2 *passim.*
11. I think the empirical facts are even more subtly nuanced than Stallybrass and White suggest. If Thomas Southerne's play *The Maid's Last Prayer* is accepted in evidence, the coffee-house in the 1690s is still regarded as an unsuitable milieu for the fashionable. Lord Malapert's foppish friend Sir Faeminine Fanville will visit the 'Play-House, Chocolate-House, or Drawing-Room' in search of gossip, but he leaves the Coffee-Houses to 'such as can endure the stink of Tabacco'. (*The Works of Thomas Southerne,* edited by Robert Jordan and Harold Love (Oxford, 1988), i, 378.)
12. Stephen Greenblatt, *Shakespearean Negotiations: the Circulation of Social Energy in Renaissance England* (Oxford, 1988), pp. 10–11.
13. Peter Holland, *The Ornament of Action: Text and Performance in Restoration Comedy* (Cambridge, 1979), pp. 125–37.
14. Swift, *Prose,* iv, 18.
15. Robert Adams Day, in an interesting article entitled 'Richard Bentley and John Dunton: brothers under the skin', *Studies in Eighteenth-century Culture* 16, edited by O. M. Brack, Jr (Madison, Wisc., 1986), pp. 125–38, invents the term 'Homo typographicus' for the dunces (p. 126). This coinage may conceal the extent to which *The Dunciad* is itself a typographical triumph. Few writers were more interested in the capabilities of print and in every aspect of literary marketing than Pope.
16. Raymond Williams, *Culture and Society 1780–1950* (Harmondsworth, 1985), p. 288ff.
17. Stuart Hall, 'Notes on deconstructing "The Popular" ', in *People's History and Socialist Theory,* edited by Raphael Samuel (London, Boston and Henley, 1981), pp. 227–40 (p. 233).
18. The editors of the recent *Oxford Shakespeare* deliver this verdict: '[Lewis Theobald's] *Shakespeare Restored* was the first book entirely devoted to the textual problems of the Shakespeare canon – but also . . . a successful bid to nominate himself as the man best equipped to replace Pope's edition. . . . Theobald was the better scholar, and indeed remains one of the finest editors of the last three centuries. His collection of early quartos was larger than Pope's, his knowledge of Shakespeare's period wider, his enthusiasm for the task greater, his aesthetic preconceptions less obviously anachronistic.' (Stanley Wells and Gary Taylor, with John Jowett and William Montgomery, *William Shakespeare: A Textual Companion* (Oxford, 1987), p. 54.)
19. Pat Rogers, *Hacks and Dunces: Pope, Swift and Grub Street* (1972, reprinted London, 1980), p. 15.
20. Leopold Damrosch, Jr, *The Imaginative World of Alexander Pope* (Berkeley, Los Angeles and London, 1987), pp. 123–5.

Brean S. Hammond

21. James Anderson Winn, *John Dryden and His World* (New Haven and London, 1987).
22. *The Works of John Dryden*, edited by H. T. Swedenborg *et al.* (Berkeley and Los Angeles, 1956–), ix, 7–8.
23. Winn, p. 239.
24. *The Works*, xiii, 14.
25. *The Prose Works of Alexander Pope*, edited by Norman Ault (Oxford, 1936), i, 292–3.
26. James Ralph, *The Case of Authors by Profession or Trade* (London, 1758), p. 22.
27. Alvin Kernan, in his *Printing Technology, Letters and Samuel Johnson* (Princeton, 1987), presents Johnson and Pope as antithetical symbols of the print culture and its opposition.
28. Michael McKeon, *The Origins of the English Novel 1600–1740* (Baltimore, 1987), p. 209.
29. *The Prompter*, 19 November 1734.
30. Colley Cibber held, for Henry Fielding, a somewhat similar cultural significance. He is satirised in *The Author's Farce* and in later plays, while an amusing sideswipe at him in *The Champion* effectively captures his cultural pretension and the fustian of his performances as laureate: 'I know it may be objected that the English Apollo, the prince of poets, the great laureate abounds with such a redundancy of Greek and Latin that, not contented with the vulgar affectation of a motto to a play, he hath prefixed a Latin motto to every act of his *Caesar in Egypt.* . . . Nay, his learning is thought to extend to the Oriental tongues, and I myself heard a gentleman reading one of his odes cry out, "Why, this is all Hebrew!"' (Quoted in Philip H. Highfill, Jr, Kalman A. Burnim and Edward A. Langhans, *A Biographical Dictionary of Actors* (Carbondale and Edwardsville, 1973–), iii, 231.)
31. Brean S. Hammond, ' "A Poet, and a Patron, and ten Pound": John Gay and patronage', in *John Gay and the Scriblerians*, edited by Peter Lewis and Nigel Wood (London, 1988), pp. 23–43.
32. Edmund Burke, *Letters on a Regicide Peace* (1797), letter 1 in *Works* (8th edition, London, 1899), v, 289.
33. Carole Fabricant, 'Pope's moral, political, and cultural combat'. Lecture given at the William Andrews Clark Memorial Library, Los Angeles, May 1988. I am grateful to her for allowing me to see a copy of the typescript.
34. Maynard Mack, *Alexander Pope: A Life* (New Haven and London, 1985), p. viii.
35. See *The Correspondence of Richard Steele*, pp. 63, 65–6.

Notes on the contributors

STEPHEN BYGRAVE is Lecturer in English at King's College, University of London, having taught previously at the universities of Cambridge, Leeds and East Anglia. Publications include *Coleridge and the Self* (1986) and essays on Thomas Gray and on eighteenth-century fiction. He is working on a study of Kenneth Burke, *Kenneth Burke: Rhetoric and Politics*.

STEVE CLARK is currently a British Academy Research Fellow at Queen Mary and Westfield College, University of London. Recent projects include *Blake, Locke and the Poetry of Sensibility*, and *Paul Ricoeur;* he has edited a volume of selections from Akenside, Macpherson and Young, and is at present working on a study of misogyny in English poetry, *'Sordid Images': a Study of the Poetry of Masculine Desire*.

STEPHEN COPLEY is Lecturer in English at University College of Wales, Cardiff. He has edited *Literature and the Social Order in Eighteenth-century England* and has published articles on polite culture and economic writing in eighteenth-century England and Scotland. With John Whale he is currently editing a volume of essays, *Out of Romantic Isolation: Renegotiating Texts and Contexts, 1780–1830*.

J. A. DOWNIE is Senior Lecturer in English at Goldsmiths' College, University of London, having taught previously at the University of Wales (Bangor) and Leeds. He is co-editor of *The Scriblerian*, and is author of *Robert Harley and the Press: Propaganda and Public Opinion in the Age of Swift and Defoe* (1979) and *Jonathan Swift, Political Writer* (1984), as well as of many essays on eighteenth-century literature and politics.

DAVID FAIRER is Senior Lecturer in English at the University of Leeds. He is author of *Pope's Imagination* (1984) and *The Poetry of Alexander Pope* (1989) and has published many articles and reviews on the eighteenth century. His edition of *The Correspondence of Thomas Warton, 1728–90* is to be published by the University of Georgia Press.

REBECCA FERGUSON is Lecturer in English at St David's University College, Lampeter (University of Wales). She is author of *The Unbalanc'd Mind: Pope and the Rule of Passion* (1986), and of a study guide on Pope in the Akadimias Educational Software series. She also has interests in modern drama and Afro-American writing, and is currently pursuing work on the novelist Toni Morrison.

CHRISTINE GERRARD is a Fellow of Lady Margaret Hall, Oxford. Formerly Thouron Fellow at the University of Pennsylvania and Research Fellow at Exeter College, Oxford, she has published on political poetry in the eighteenth century and on American literature. *Patriots and Poets*, a study of the dissident Whig opposition to Walpole, is shortly to be published by Oxford University Press. She is currently writing a literary biography of Aaron Hill.

BREAN HAMMOND is Rendel Professor of English Literature at the University of Wales, Aberystwyth. As well as numerous articles on seventeenth and eighteenth-century poetry, prose and drama, he is author of *Pope and Bolingbroke: A Study of Friendship and Influence* (1984), *Pope* (Harvester New Readings, 1986), and *Gulliver's Travels* (Open Study Guides, 1988). He is general editor of the *British Journal for Eighteenth-century Studies*.

SUSAN MATTHEWS is Lecturer in English at Roehampton Institute of Higher Education, having taught previously at the University of Leeds. She has completed a book on *Blake and the Epic Revival* and is now working on a study of Pope and the discourse of femininity.

NICHOLAS ROE is Lecturer in English at the University of St Andrews. He is author of *Wordsworth and Coleridge: The Radical Years* (1988) and has edited *Coleridge's Imagination* (1985) and introduced a new edition of Emile Legouis' *The Early Years of William Wordsworth* (1988). His book *Jacobins and Poets: A Study of History and the Imagination* will appear shortly, and he is currently working on a study of the politics of allusion in Wordsworth.

JOHN WHALE is Lecturer in English at the University of Leeds. He is author of *Thomas De Quincey's Reluctant Autobiography* (1984) and essays on Burke, Hazlitt and Wollstonecraft. He is currently working on *Imagination Under Pressure*, a study of the relationship between aesthetics and politics in Romantic prose, and with Stephen Copley is editing a volume of essays, *Out of Romantic Isolation: Renegotiating Texts and Contexts, 1780–1830*.

CAROLYN D. WILLIAMS is Lecturer in English at the University of Reading. Having completed a thesis on Dr Arbuthnot and the Scriblerus Club, she has published on Shakespeare, Swift, Pope, Gay, Richardson, Fielding and the presentation of sexual infidelity in *The Gentleman's Magazine*. Her main interest is in definitions of sexuality, 1600–1800, and her present projects include a book on sexuality in Pope's *Homer* and a study of sexual liminality.

THOMAS WOODMAN is Lecturer in English at the University of Reading. He is the author of *Thomas Parnell* (Twayne Series, 1985) and *Politeness and Poetry in the Age of Pope* (1989). He is now working on a study of British Catholic fiction.

Index

245

Index

Index

Index

249

Index

Index

William III, King, 9, 15–19 *passim*, 23, 25, 32, 38, 39, 55, 193
Williams, Carolyn D., 203
Williams, Raymond, 230, 239
Williamson, Judith, 105, 106, 120
Wilson, Dr, of Dublin, 37
Wilson, Penelope, 76, 79, 99
Wimsatt, W. K., 193, 203
Winn, James A., 99, 232, 233, 240
Wollstonecraft, Mary, 103, 107–9, 110, 113, 115, 116, 120

Woodman, Thomas, 209, 224
Wordsworth, William, 6, 153–61 *passim*, 164, 166–8, 170, 189–204, 231
Wrangham, Francis, 190
Wu, Duncan, 203
Wycherley, William, 15, 16
Wyndham, Sir William, 34, 36

Young, Edward, 83, 84, 97

Zimmermann, Hans-Joachim, 77